The Holocaust Denial

Antisemitism, Racism & the New Right

GILL SEIDEL

[BEY]OND THE PALE COLLECTIVE

First published in 1986 by:
Beyond the Pale Collective,
Box No 6, 59 Cookridge St., Leeds LS2 3AW, England

ISBN 0 9509636 1 5

BRITISH LIBRARY CATALOGUING IN PUBLICATION DATA
Seidel, Gill
The Holocaust Denial: antisemitism, racism and the new right.
1. Holocaust, Jewish (1939-1945)
2. Antisemitism-history-20th century
1. Title
940.53' 15' 03924 D810.J4

Distributed by:
Turnaround Distribution
27 Horsell Rd., London N5 1XL
01-609 7836

Printed by:
The Russell Press Ltd.,
Gamble Street, Nottingham NG7 4ET

Contents

Acknowledgments
I should like to thank the Anne Frank Foundation (Amsterdam), the Board of Deputies (London), the Institute of Jewish Affairs (London), *Searchlight* (London), and Martin Gilbert and Abba Eban for permission to reproduce their Holocaust maps.

I am also grateful to friends and colleagues, too numerous to mention, who have helped, directly and indirectly, with texts, comments, hospitality and support.

This has not been an easy book to write. My revulsion for the subject matter is such that there have been days when I have been unable to either write or speak. And, given the chequered history of this book, this albatross has been with me since 1980.

Any study of neo-Nazism or racism published in England is subject to the very restrictive libel laws. It is these constraints which may account for the apparent lack of definition of certain political categories and affiliations.

Paris, London and Bradford 1986

Note on book and author

Throughout the world neo-Nazis are attempting to deny that the Holocaust ever took place. Their aim is to rehabilitate Nazism and Hitler. Seidel's hypothesis is that the Holocaust denial myths constitute a new version of the *Protocols*. Whereas the *Protocols* served as a warrant for genocide, the Holocaust denial is a further symbolic genocide: it is an attempt to destroy history.

The Holocaust Denial, which also addresses readers unfamiliar with the facts of genocide, is a painstaking investigation into the different international versions of the myth. This is the first time this material has been made available in a single volume. In a rigorous and stimulating presentation, it also analyses the racist and frequently sexist arguments that are gaining ascendency on the New Right, their intermeshing, together with the general upsurge of anti-egalitarian discourse. Documented examples are discussed from Britain, France, West Germany and the States.

Seidel also takes issue with the 'anti-Zionist' debate at both ends of the political spectrum, and its effect on the women's movement in Britain. In this important and critical study, the conceptualisation of antisemitism and racism is taken much further, while emphasising the specificity of each. In the conclusion, Seidel discusses some of the implications of a feminist voice and ethic in anti-racist struggles; and reflects on what it means to be 'British' for Jewish and black communities in Britain today.

Gill Seidel is a Lecturer in French and Discourse Studies at Bradford University, England. She enjoys an international reputation as a political discourse analyst. In 1981 she set up a Paris-based international team (CNRS) to investigate the vocabulary and discourse of the contemporary Right.

Dr Seidel has contributed to *Langage et Société* and *MOTS* (Paris); and in Britain to *New Society* and *Searchlight*. Her recent publications include 'Political Discourse Analysis' in T. van Dijk, ed., *Handbook of Discourse Analysis*, vol 4 *(New York: Academic Press, 1985)*, 'The concept of culture, "race" and nation' in R. Levitas, ed., *The Ideology of the New Right (Oxford: Polity Press: Blackwell, 1986)*, and an edited collection of feminist papers on racism and sexism, *The Nature of the Right: a feminist analysis of order patterns (Amsterdam: Benjamins, 1987)*. She is currently writing a book on right-wing language.

The book includes an introduction by *Michael Billig*, author of *Fascists: a social-psychological view of the National Front (New York: Academic Press, 1978)*; *L'internationale raciste (Paris: Maspero, 1981)*; and *Ideology and Social Psychology (Oxford: Blackwell, 1982)*. Michael Billig is Professor of Social Sciences at the University of Loughborough, England.

Publisher's Preface: The Holocaust in history

The rise of Nazi Germany resulted in the near-annihilation of European Jews. Recent attempts to deny the very existence of this Holocaust might appear bizarre and unbelievable — the ultimate Big Lie. How can it be asserted that the death camps did not exist, and that some six million Jews were not murdered? Fascist mythology has long held that the war of 1939-45 was the responsibility of a Jewish conspiracy. Now it is being argued that Jewry emerged unharmed! *Beyond the Pale Collective* is publishing this book because the denial of the Holocaust cannot simply be dismissed as phantasy or perversity, or the product of a few individuals' warped imaginations. The Holocaust denial propaganda is all of these, but it is also part of the re-emergence of organised antisemitism and the development of the New Right. It is both profoundly political and profoundly dangerous. As such it has to be resisted along with all other forms of racism.

Gill Seidel analyses those forces which, on an international level, claim that the genocide of Jews simply did not happen. Our aim in this Preface is to situate this antisemitic claim in the context of other distorted attitudes towards the Holocaust, attitudes which are not merely confined to the political right. We wish to challenge several popular misconceptions about the Holocaust which have obtained the general status of 'common sense' in most historical interpretations.

We need to challenge such interpretations, for they constitute a reactionary attempt to re-write fact and hence to destroy history. This re-writing denies Jewish resistance to the Holocaust and underestimates the historical tradition of antisemitism throughout Europe. It also exonerates the Allies from any responsibility for the genocide of Jewry. In referring to the Allies, we concentrate throughout on the specific role of the western democracies of the UK and USA. This is not because the other Allied power, the USSR, was not (and is not) also complicit in antisemitism, especially during the Soviet-German pact, but because a particular hypocrisy emanates from the Western powers concerning their role in the war.

As Seidel points out in chapter one, the fortieth anniversary of the end of the war was celebrated in the West in such a way as to exclude the USSR altogether. The Soviet Union was seen as having had no part, let alone a decisive one, in the defeat of Germany. We now look in some detail at popular historical distortions of the Holocaust, which, whilst falling short of actual denial, may be seen to contribute to the antisemitic context in which Holocaust denial propaganda circulates and is nourished.

'Jews did not resist'

The question is often asked 'Why did Jews go like lambs to the slaughter, why didn't they resist?' A political consequence of looking at the Holocaust from this perspective is that the Jews are seen as responsible for their own deaths, thereby absolving their murderers from responsibility. It also reflects and perpetuates an antisemitic imagery of Jews as weak and passive.

In fact, there was a massive and heroic resistance by Jews within the limited possibilities of such resistance. The most famous example is the Warsaw Ghetto uprising of April 1943 which was timed to coincide with the Jewish Passover.[1] This was the first civilian uprising of the war within Nazi occupied territory. Historical accounts have virtually suppressed the fact that Warsaw was only one of many ghettos where Jews organised uprisings against the Nazis.

Most incredible of all were the uprisings in the death camps themselves. In August 1943 several hundred prisoners rose up at Treblinka, in October six hundred Jews escaped from the extermination camp of Sobibor, and even in Auschwitz there was an armed uprising in November 1944 in which no one escaped.[2] In

October 1944 prisoners killed several SS men and set fire to the building of the crematorium number three. Although the revolt was suppressed, one of the four Birkenau crematoria was destroyed and never put into operation again.[3] As Kulka points out, it is significant that:

> the only success in the struggle against mass extermination in Auschwitz was indeed the action carried out by the Auschwitz prisoners themselves. Their escape broke the barrier of the 'secret matter of state', revealed its fraudulent nature, and gave the world the possibility of effective action. The uprising of the Auschwitz 'special detachments' was the only purposeful action; it destroyed a fourth of the capacity of the extermination camps while the death factory was going on at full blast by planned operation. At this time the approaching Soviet army was still far from Auschwitz.[4]

The real question — the political question — is surely not 'why didn't Jews resist?' but 'why were they left to fight unaided?' What can this tell us about antisemitism? For instance, the Jewish Fighting Organisation in Warsaw made desperate pleas to both the Polish underground movement and to the Allies for arms and supplies, but these went virtually unheeded. Szmul Zygielbojm was a member of the Bund (the Jewish non-Zionist workers' party within Poland formed at the end of the nineteenth century) who was exiled in the UK. He committed suicide after the failure of the Warsaw Ghetto uprising. In a note written before his death he declared that:

> The responsibility for this crime — the assassination of the Jewish population in Poland — rests directly on the murderers themselves, but falls indirectly upon the whole human race, on the Allies and their governments, who have so far taken no firm steps to put a stop to these crimes... Let my death be an energetic cry of protest against the indifference of the world which witnesses the extermination of the Jewish people without taking any steps to stop it.[5]

Indeed, we must remember that not only was help refused to Jews, but they were sometimes murdered by those from whom they sought help. Some Jews who managed to escape through the Warsaw sewers hoping to continue fighting outside the Ghetto were murdered by antisemites within the Polish underground.

> Those Jews who managed to flee into the Polish forests to join with underground forces fighting the Germans not only had to elude the implacable Germans forever hunting them, but were also compelled to do battle with the vicious anti-Semitism of the Polish partisans. Shortly after General Ladeusz Komorovski (Bor-Komorovski) took over as commander in chief of the Polish Home Army in the summer of 1943, he issued an order to his commanders to kill — his word was "liquidate"... "robber gangs" which he claimed were marauding the countryside. The order explicitly referred to Jews: "Men and women — in particular Jewish women — participate in these attacks." No doubt this order gave a cloak of legality to the murder of Jews by the Polish Home Army. Besides, the right-wing military groups in Poland that had refused to recognise the Home Army's authority and were organised separately in the Nardowe Sily/brojne — NSZ (National Armed Forces) — accumulated an impressive record of murdering Jews who had escaped into the woods. No one will ever know precisely how many hundreds of Jews were murdered by Polish partisans in the Polish forests and marshes.[6]

Recently in France, the television network screened the documentary "Des Terroristes à la Retraite", which showed how the Manouchian partisans (mainly Jewish members of the French resistance) were deliberately denied help by their comrades in the French Communist Party.[7]

The antisemitism of the Allies

There is a common misconception that the Allies were free of antisemitism and that Jew-hatred was the sole prerogative of the "enemy" — Nazi Germany; in fact, antisemitism flourished at both popular and state level throughout the war. In this section, we draw on examples of popular antisemitism from the UK. Similary examples, however, are available elsewhere. The UK is not unique.

Throughout the war years antisemitism figured very prominently in the Home Intelligence Weekly Report prepared by the British Ministry of Information. Towards the end of 1942, the HIWR reported that:

> antisemitism appears actually to have been revived by the authoritative disclosures of the Nazi's systematic massacres of the European Jews.[8]

In January 1942 the Home Intelligence Unit of the Ministry of Information drew up a report on antisemitism in this country.[9] It reported that antisemitism was "latent in most districts" and that there was a "continuous simmering of anti-Jewish feeling" in Leeds and Sheffield; that there was a general belief that the "black market" was being run by Jews, that Jews were being accused of evasion of military service and Civil Defence duties, and that there was a feeling that Jews were being evacuated to the safest areas.

In her recent study of German-Jewish immigrants who came to Britain in the 1930s, Berghahn's interviewees recalled how anti-German feeling mingled with antisemitism:

> Their neighbours called them "dirty Jews", whereas their neighbours' children called shouted "Nazis" after them. The situation became so unpleasant that the respondents had to move house. Mrs. G. remembered having been appalled by the anti-German and anti-Jewish talk she overhead in the officers' mess when she worked as an interpreter for the British Army in Germany. 'It was bad enough to be German; even worse to be Jewish; but worst of all to be German-Jewish.'[10]

In 1942, the Communist Party activist, J. Rennap, publicly exposed some of these manifestations of antisemitism. He used contemporary reports to show that there was resentment against Jews using public air-raid shelters.

He also linked his investigation of attitudes towards Jewish evacuees with *Jewish Chronicle* reports of "disgruntled mutterings about a Jewish invasion" and "grumblings about Jews and foreigners".[11]

In the latter years of the war, allegations of Jewish "black market" activity increased to such an extent that in 1942 the matter was eventually raised in the House of Commons. A perverse illumination of the depth of this antisemitism can be gauged by the following:

> A frontal attack on black markets was made in the House of Commons. No bones are made about the fact that Jews were chiefly implicated in profiteering in the food market. Heading

> the procession were the Jewish immigrants who went from Germany to Holland.[12]

This source is Dr Goebbels, Nazi Minister of Propaganda, in his private diary. These comments are worthy of note not because Nazi accounts of events are of any intrinsic merit, but significant in that Goebbels was able to recognise a continuity between the political expression of popular antisemitism in the UK and his own cruder strategies.

Conventional wisdom holds that the 1939-45 war was a "good" war in that it was waged against the linked evils of fascism and antisemitism. It was undoubtedly the case that the masses of people who fought and died for the Allies did so with an anti-fascist consciousness, although it is significant that on a popular level within the UK "the connection between Nazism-Fascism and anti-semitism was not widely grasped."[13]

Attitudes to Jewish refugees

The popular antisemitism in the UK also has to be seen against the post 1938 background of widespread press hostility towards the admission of Jewish refugees. The *Daily Mail* warned against "misguided sentimentalism" and argued that:

> Once it was known that Britain offered sanctuary to all who cared to come , the floodgates would be opened and we should be inundated by thousands seeking a home.

It is interesting that the only acknowledgement of popular antisemitism by the British state was used to exclude Jews, many of whom were left to perish at the hands of the Nazis. The UK justified non-admission in terms of fears of stirring up popular antisemitism, or else the drain on British resources in the war effort, or argued that

> these particular refugees; pitiable as is their plight, are hardly war refugees in the sense that they are in danger because they have fought against the Germans, but simply racial refugees.[14]

The British press need not have worried. The UK government — like the USA — adopted a distinctly negative attitude towards the admission of refugees. A Foreign Office official has been documented as saying:

> In my opinion a disproportionate amount of time of this office is wasted in dealing with these wailing Jews.[15]

It is not necessary to believe that every official held these views — it was not a majority view — but it is, nevertheless, alarming that such views were held within the Foreign Office.

Some Jews did manage to enter the UK and the USA — particularly from 1933 until the declaration of war. During this period, the British Government was anxious to be seen to be admitting immigrants, whilst from the beginning it adopted a rigorously selective admissions policy. Even as early as 12 April 1933, it was decided at a Cabinet meeting to:

> try and secure for this country prominent Jews who were being expelled from Germany and who had achieved distinction whether in pure science, applied sciences, such as medicine or technical industry, music or art. This would not only obtain for this country the advantage of their knowledge and experience, but would also create a very favourable impression in the world, particularly if our hospitality were offered with warmth.[16]

Such aid as was given was provided by individual friends, relatives and, in some cases, professional contacts. Perhaps the most fortunate group were academics where some feeling of international solidarity led to the formation of the Academic Assistance Council (later called the Society for the Protection of Science and Learning).[17]

Apart from these 'special cases', admission was only granted on a temporary basis. The official British attitude was that the UK was a country 'of transit, not of settlement'.[18]

After 1938 the situation grew much worse, especially for German and Austrian nationals who were, paradoxically, identified as "enemy aliens". As Berghahn comments:

> The more strongly Jews felt the pressure to leave Germany, the more reluctant became the potential countries of refuge to accept them.[19] Even the so-called Children's Transports, a private initiative to rescue children under the age of seventeen, and founded after the Nazi pogrom in 1938, met with increasing restriction from British and US immigration policies.[19]

About fifty five thousand Jews entered the UK[20] and perhaps twice that number into the USA. This was the result of draconian immigration laws which excluded a far greater number of refugees. Any sincere policy of helping Jews and other victims of Nazism would, at the very least, have entailed a complete open door policy to refugees. However, the immigration laws were already there, having been introduced as a piece of state antisemitism in 1905 in Britain to exclude Jews fleeing from pogroms in Eastern Europe.[21] Subsequently, the Alien Restrictions Act of 1919 was used to keep out Jews fleeing from the Nazis. The only concession made by the British Government to immigration controls was its acceptance in 1933 of an undertaking by Jewish organisations that all Jewish refugees would be maintained... "by the Jewish community without ultimate charge to the state".[22] This had an unfortunate analogy with the collective financial levies imposed by Nazi Germany, in which the entire entire Jewish community was periodically forced to provide vast sums to the Nazi government.

The obstacles placed by the USA on Jews entering as refugees have been well documented.[23] US immigration laws contained prohibition on those '...likely to become a public charge'. In October 1934 the Third Reich limited each emigrant to taking only ten Reichmarks (about four dollars). This effectively trapped most Jews who therefore could not prove their financial independence to the US authorities. In addition, US immigration controls contained a 'contract labour' provision which made it impossible for workers to enter under employment contracts. Thus any prospective immigrant could not overcome that provision by arranging employment in advance. Jews trying to flee Nazism had also to contend with Section 7(c) of the US Immigration Act of 1924, which required an applicant to furnish a police certificate of good character for the previous five years, a record of military service, two certified copies of a birth certificate and '...two copies of all other available public records'. The idea of Jews dropping into the local Nazi police to obtain a certificate of good character would be surreal, if it were not grotesque. The August 1939 issue of the Nazi journal *Weltkampf* cynically commented:

> We are saying openly that we do not want Jews while the democracies keep on claiming that they are willing to receive them — and then leave the guests out in the cold! Aren't we savages

better men after all?[24]

This refusal to mount any rescue attempt of European Jewry continued after war was declared. In 1940 the Nazis stated they would be prepared to allow the two thousand Jews in Luxembourg to leave, but the UK refused to accept them into the British Commonwealth, and most subsequently perished in the camps.[25] In 1942 the possibility of admitting one thousand Jewish children from 'unoccupied' Vichy France was raised. Herbert Morrison, Home Secretary and prominent Labour Party figure, stated that allowing children to enter might:

> stir up an unpleasant degree of antisemitism (of which there is a fair amount just below the surface), and that would be bad for the country and for the Jewish community.[26]

No children were allowed entry. Their fate is unknown.

There is a final, poignant, illustration that helping Jews was hardly on the agenda as far as the UK and USA were concerned. In 1944 the Zionist Jewish Agency made repeated pleas to the British and US governments that they should bomb the railway lines leading to Auschwitz and the camp itself. Though this inevitably would have cost Jewish lives, it was calculated that it would slow down considerably the current deportations. This request was consistenly refused on two grounds. The first was that it was claimed to be technically impossible to pinpoint bomb targets such as Auschwitz. However, this was possible, as was demonstrated on 13 September 1944 when the US Fifteenth Airforce Command bombed the I.G. Farben industrial complex, actually adjacent to the camp. The second reason given by the US War Department was that the bombing could only be executed

> by the diversion of considerable air support essential to the success of our forces now engaged in decisive operations.[27]

In other words, there were more decisive military matters than an attempt to rescue European Jewry from extermination. The failure to take even this relatively simple strategic measure inevitably leads one to question the priorities of the democracies.

As already mentioned above, this Preface concentrates on documentating the role of the Allies. It must not be forgotten that the USSR was also in a position to bomb the death camps and failed to do so.

The Holocaust is not a uniquely German responsibility

It is a moral question whether responsibility for a crime such as the Holocaust can be laid on any group as a whole. We reject the whole concept of collective guilt, whether applied to Germans or any other group. Nothing that we have written denies that there were many courageous people within Nazi-occupied territories who helped Jews. Not all Germans were implicated — and those who were were not all implicated to the same extent. However, the post-Holocaust period has seen the rise of another myth, namely, that only Germans were responsible. This demonstrates a blatant political effort to deny and confine blame. As we have already seen, the governments of the UK, USA and USSR, were indirectly complicit in the genocide. However, the Jews suffered in many countries other than Germany, often with the active support of the local populations. Even where this support was not particularly active, any popular view of history which considers that 'Jews went like lambs to the slaughter' should at the very least ask why the local populations sat back like lambs watching the slaughter. In fact, 'only' a minority of Jews who perished (two hundred and fifty thousand) lived within the frontiers of the German state prior to 1939 — a fact made much of by Nazi apologists.

The activities of antisemites outside Germany have been well documented. Slovak border guards shot Jews trying to escape across the frontier to Hungary. In both the Ukraine and Croatia local antisemites joined in the massacre of Jews. In France, as Seidel has shown in chapter five, the Vichy regime also handed over Jews for deportation and death.[28] As one leading authority comments about the atrocities carried out by Roumania, Germany's ally in the war against the USSR:

> In the autumn of 1941, one hundred and eighty five thousand Roumanian Jews were deported to the camps in the Roumanian-occupied area of the USSR known as Transnistria. This area and the camps in it were under direct Roumanian (not German) control: by May 1947 two thirds of the Transnistrian Jews were dead. When Roumanian forces occupied Odessa in October 1941, one hundred and ninety thousand Jews were driven into the harbour area and concentrated in a square enclosed by a wooden fence. They were then shot by the Roumanians and their

> bodies burned. Another forty thousand Jews were transported outside the city and shot by the Roumanians in anti-tank ditches.[29]

The fact that antisemitism existed outside and autonomous of Germany is also seen clearly in relation to Poland, where the majority of European Jewry lived and perished. As the eastern outpost of Roman Catholicism and surrounded by the Greek Orthodox Church and Protestantism, Poland is historically an antisemitic country. Mass pogroms occurred there in 1917 during the first world war. In the 1930s Polish Jews were murdered by Endeks — local antisemites. During the war, as we have seen, some Polish anti-German partisans are known to have killed Jews. Polish soldiers stationed in the UK in the war frequently threatened and attacked their Jewish 'comrades'.[30] Most incredible and revealing of all is the fact that pogroms took place in Poland immediately after the war, notably in Kielce:

> Jews who returned to claim homes and property were greeted with terror, violence, even murder. After all, the experience of German occupation had demonstrated to the Poles that Jews could be murdered with impunity. The Poles did not want the Jews back, even if they amounted to one tenth of their pre-war numbers... From March 1945 to April 1946 more than 800 Jews were murdered in Poland, the ugliest pogrom occurring in Kielce on July, 4, 1946, when nearly 50 Jews were killed by a mob backed up by militia men.[31]

The Holocaust is not an aberration in European history

The Holocaust is often viewed as some form of 'aberration', an event so horrific and beyond belief as to be unique and inexplicable. But this is an emotional and political mechanism to minimise the strength of Jew-hatred by denying its history. The Holocaust could only occur because of the deep *historical* roots of antisemitism within Europe. Hitler was able, effectively, to channel and redirect older antisemitic sentiments by making it the focal point of Nazi politics.

Antisemitism can be seen as a product of Christianity.[32] It is an ideology, a world-view, which depicts the Jew as Christ-killer and, therefore, the Devil. It is based on demonic phantasies, myths and delusions. Central to these delusions is the notion of the Jewish conspiracy — a conspiracy of Jew plotting with fellow Jew to take over and destroy the world. Joshua Trachtenberg in his monumental work, *The Devil and the Jews,* has shown the form that these mythologies took. In his introduction he writes:

> Here, in this region of the mass sub-conscious we shall discover the source of many a weird notion — of horned Jew, of the Jewish thirst for Christian Blood, of the Jew who scatters poison and disease, of the secret parliament of world Jewry meeting periodically to scheme and plot, of a distinctive Jewish odor, of Jews practising black magic and blighting their surroundings with the evil eye — notions that still prevail amongst the people and that have been advanced by official Nazi publications for all the 'scientific' verbiage of current antisemitism.[33]

Moreover, central to this historical understanding of antisemitism is an appreciation of it as a distinctly *European* phenomenon: antisemitism as an ideology was consolidated during the time of the Crusades.[34] The latter are conventionally viewed as a war against the 'pagan' Muslims. In fact, the Crusades also represent the struggle within Europe for the ascendency of feudalism, and of its standard bearer, the Christian church. Within Europe, and in the name of Christianity, a war was waged against Jews. The massacre in 1189 of the entire Jewish community of York, assembled in the Minster, was fuelled by the same Christian antisemitic ideology — a barbaric act, and one of many such massacres, in the name of Christianity.[35]

So strong was antisemitism within Christianity that whenever there was a schism within the Church, the new heresy immediately denounced the Jews as Satan. For example, the Flagellent movement of 1349 played an important and active role in the great massacre of European Jewry that accompanied the Black Death — for which the Jews were held reponsible, and which virtually annihilated Jewry within Germany and the Low Countries.[36] Martin Luther, in founding the Protestant movement, invoked a virulent antisemitism. His pamphlet, *Of the Jews and Their Lives,* published in 1543 gave the following 'advice' which could have come from any fascist text, past or present:

> First, their synagogues or churches should be set on fire... And this ought to be done for the honour of God and of Christianity... Secondly, their homes should likewise be broken down and destroyed... Thirdly, they should be deprived of their prayer-books and Talmuds... Fourthly, their rabbis must be forbidden under threat of death to teach any more... Fifthly, passport and travelling privileges should be absolutely for forbidden to the Jews.[37]

In the nineteenth century all these myths took a secular form with the publication of *The Protocols of Zion,* a czarist forgery which claimed to be the secret deliberations of a Jewish world government. As Seidel has documented in chapter three, millions of copies of were distributed in Europe and Russia. Nazism simply reverted to the basic image of the Jew as equated with the Devil. Hitler wrote:

> It is the inexorable Jew who struggles for his domination... Two worlds face one another, the men of God and the men of Satan. The Jew is the anti-man, the creature of another God... set the Aryan and the Jew ever against each other.[38]

From this perspective, the Holocaust can be seen not as an aberration, but as an almost intrinsic part of European culture, which has existed in different forms for a millenium. It is Gill Seidel's hypothesis, which she develops throughout this book, that the Holocaust denial literature is the new version of the Protocols. Yet, as she emphasises, antisemitism is not an inevitability. It can be defeated politically.

Antisemitism did not end with World War II

The final irony is that for many years it has been assumed (by non-Jews) that the 1939-45 war ended antisemitism. The end of the war simply represented the military defeat of the Nazi state. And despite the protestations of 'guilt' and 'shock' at the Holocaust — guilt by those who were defeated and shock by those who were victorious — antisemitism has never been challenged as an ideology. Characterising it as an aberration, or a peculiarly German phenomenon, was a way of preventing such a challenge. Revulsion at the Holocaust merely led to a forty-year interlude where it was no longer 'respectable' to be a open Jew-hater, if only because of its Nazi and, therefore, unpatriotic associations.

Today we witness the end of the interlude. Today it is becoming possible for even government officials to be openly antisemitic. Only recently, Herman Feliner, a prominent CSU member of the German parliament, proclaimed:

> Jews are quick to show up when money tinkles in German cash registers.[39]

This was said in response to a demand by Jewish groups that compensation be paid to surviving Jews who had been employed as slave labourers during the war by the Flick industrial conglomerate, recently taken over by the Deutsche Bank. The Bank, like Flick before it, is resisting the claim on the grounds that the company had to pay concentration camps for 'hiring' Jewish labour. President Reagan visited SS graves at Bitburg on his visit to Germany in 1985. As an alliance of former enemies now united in a crusade against communism, the Western Allies are having to distance themselves from the reality of the Holocaust as a symbol of the second world war. At the same time, antisemitism has re-emerged on an *organised* basis throughout Europe. Once again Jews and their organisations are under physical attack. Just four decades after the end of the war — a war that 'eradicated antisemitism' — every Jewish community has to be constantly alert to the danger of assault on its members and institutions. This is not widely reported in the mainstream press but, as Seidel has emphasised, is part of the reality of being Jewish in Britain and western Europe today.

Linked to the view that Jew-hatred no longer exists, is the frequently articulated opinion that any attempt to understand or relate to the Holocaust itself is an 'obsession' — an obsession with a past which is unconnected with the present. The natural concern that Jewish people have about the Holocaust and its possible repetition is reduced to a psychiatric issue — a morbid concentration on nightmares. As Seidel shows, not only the neo-fascist press, but the establishment *Daily Telegraph* also circulated the 'morbid obsession' argument at the time of Bitburg. Of course the truth is that it is absolutely reasonable for Jews to be 'obsessed' by the attempt to liquidate them. Some few Jews did 'survive' the death camps. In another sense, all Jews of the wartime generation alive to-day are Holocaust survivors. The Final Solution was aimed at them personally.

The three of us who comprise the *Beyond the Pale Collective* are not Holocaust survivors. We were born after the war, but our consciousness has naturally been shaped by the Holocaust — both as a phenomenon in its own right and, also, as part of the continuing history of antisemitism. As far as we are concerned, a personal 'obsession' with the Holocaust is not only legitimate: it is a political necessity in order to gain the necessary insight to face up to contemporary racism. Antisemitism is the model of racism in Europe and plays a crucial part in the discourse and practice of racism today. Post-Holocaust Jews, especially Jewish women, are now beginning to write about this counsciousness.[40]

Anti-black racism and antisemitism are not the same. They have different historical origins, a different momentum and take different forms. However, we have a common experience, sometimes as immigrants, always as victims of racist oppression. We publish Gill Seidel's book to expose the reality of antisemitism as an integral part of racism, and to make a contribution to the struggle against racism and all other forms of discrimination.

Beyond the Pale Collective

Notes

1. L. Steinberg, *Not as a Lamb* (London: Saxon House: 1974).
2. Y. Suhln ed., *They fought back* (London: Macgibbon and Kee, 1968).
3. Ibid.
4. B. Wasserstein, *Britain and the Jews of Europe* (Oxford: Clarendon Press: 1979), 304.
5. A. Morse, *Why Six Million Died* (New York: Hart Publishing Company: 1967), 57.
6. L. Dawidowicz, *The Holocaust and the Historians* (Cambridge, Mass: Harvard University Press: 1981), 94.
7. *Observer,* 16 June 1985.
8. W. Laqueur, *The Terrible Secret* London (Weidenfeld and Nicolson: 1981), 92.
9. Wasserstein, op.cit., 120
10. M. Berghahn, *German Jewish refugees in England* (London: Macmillan: 1984), 92.
11. I. Rennap, *Antisemitism and the Jewish Question* (London: Lawrence and Wishart: 1942), 108-114.

12. Wasserstein, op.cit., 119.
13. Wasserstein, op.cit., 130.
14. Wasserstein, op.cit., 109.
15. Wasserstein, op.cit., 351.
16. Berghahn, op.cit., 76.
17. Berghahn, op.cit., 78.
18. Berghahn, op.cit., 77.
19. Berghahn, op.cit., 113.
20. Wasserstein, op.cit., 10.
21. S. Cohen, That's Funny: You Don't Look Antisemitic (Leeds: Beyond the Pale Collective, 1984).
22. Wasserstein, op.cit., 82.
23. Morse, op.cit., 130-148.
24. Morse, op.cit., 288.
25. Wasserstein, op.cit., 108-110.
26. Wasserstein, op.cit., 112.
27. Wasserstein, op.cit., 309-320.
28. Wasserstein, op.cit., 137.
29. Wasserstein, op.cit., 138
30. Wasserstein, op.cit., 120-130.
31. Dawidowicz, op.cit., 94-5.
32. N. Cohn, *The Pusuit of the Millenium* (Mercury Books: London, 1961).
33. J. Trachtenberg, *The Devil and the Jews* (Yale: Yale University Press, 1942), 6.
34. S. Eidelberg, ed., *The Jews and the Crusades* (Wisconsin: University of Wisconsin Press, 1977).
35. Ibid.
36. Cohn, op.cit., 138.
37. M. Gilbert, *Exile and Return* (London: Weidenfeld and Nicolson: 1978), 20.
38. Quoted in S. Cohen, op.cit., 13.
39. *Guardian,* 8 January 1986.
40. The Jewish Women's History Group, *You'd prefer me not to mention it* (London: 1983) (roneo).
41. E. Tornton Beck, ed., *Nice Jewish Girls: a Lesbian Anthology* (Watertown, Massachussetts: Persephone Press: 1982), chapter one.

Introduction

There are people with all manner of strange beliefs. Some people are convinced that flying saucers regularly circle the night skies. Others cling to the notion that they are the reincarnations of famous historical figures. No doubt it would be possible to find individuals who remain unshakeably certain that the earth is flat, or that just beneath its crust still survive lost civilisations. The belief that Dr Seidel documents, in her detailed and painstaking investigation, is the fantasy that the Nazi murder of six million Jews never took place.

At first sight, this denial of the Holocaust seems to be just as eccentric a belief as that which asserts the flatness of the world. Both beliefs fly in the face of obvious evidence, and their adherents must reject well documented facts, if they are to cling to their fixations. However, there are crucial differences between the two sorts of belief. The believers in the flatness of the earth, like those who claim to be regularly visited by extra-terrestial beings, can be dismissed as colourful oddities, whose obsessions are both harmless and amusing. The world is a brighter place thanks to quirky eccentrics. There is no such enjoyment to be gained from the believers in the non-existence of the Holocaust.

A number of years ago, Jean-Paul Sartre wrote in his *Portrait of the Anti-Semite,* that anti-semitic prejudice should not be considered merely as opinions, on a par with all sorts of other interesting opinions. The flatness of the earth, or the reality of flying saucers might be interesting opinions, but the denial of the Holocaust is not just another opinion to be placed in this collection of wonderful phantasies. Instead, it belongs to the long and violent history of antisemitism. As Dr Seidel shows, those who today are denying the reality of the Holocaust, are not harmless cranks, but are the contemporary heirs of a murderous tradition. They spring from the same sources as those who propagated older myths that, for instance, Jews ritually murder Gentile children, or poison the drinking-water of Christians, or conspire to dominate the world. These are the very myths which paved the way for murder, pogroms and, ultimately, the Holocaust.

Unlike the beliefs of individual eccentrics, the denial of the Holocaust possesses a social significance and a political danger. The belief has its own social milieu, as it circulates in the shadowy world of the professional antisemite. Dr Seidel introduces us to unfamiliar figures grouped around small political parties and tiny publishing outfits. The intellectual shabbiness of this strange world prompts the question whether it is worth devoting scholarly attention to its products. It might be argued that the denial of the Holocaust is so absurd that no sensible person, outside of the lunatic fringe, would entertain such a belief. As for the lunatic fringe, there will always be oddities on the edge of political life, and one should expect those on the lunatic fringe to hold lunatic beliefs. Thus, one might conclude that, so long as the lunatic fringe is clearly identified as the lunatic fringe, then it is better left well alone, and we should ignore those embittered individuals who persist in their antisemitic phantasies.

However reasonable this argument might seem at first glance, there are other considerations, which warn us against ignoring the lunacy of the political lunatics. In the first place, contemporary Nazis are not content to enact their fantasies in the privacy of their homes. Were neo-Nazism merely a matter of eccentrics posing secretly in their uniforms in front of their bedroom mirrors, then perhaps there would be little need for the sort of investigation, which Dr Seidel has undertaken. However, today's Nazis, like their forebears, mix their violent fantasies with political ambitions. They might be confined to the outer margins of political life, but they dream of a major political role. This combination of wild phantasy, hate-filled ideology and unfulfilled political ambitions is a dangerous mixture. The frustration, arising from the gap between political reality and political ambition, can so easily spill over into violence. In consequence, those, whose minds are filled with race-hatred, constitute, those, whose minds are filled with race-hatred, constitute a direct threat, and the violence, which a fascist group can unleash, can be out of all proportion to the group's political significance, as assessed by votes or membership figures. In this way, the mere existence of fascist ideas carries its own dangerous significance.

In addition, there is no necessary law of politics to stipulate that dangerous and absurd ideas must be confined to the margins of political life. The political successes of fascism in the inter-war years showed how easily the traditions of liberalism can be pushed aside in times of deep social unrest. Nor can we in the post-war years be confident that the lessons of history have been well learnt. At present, in Britain and in Germany, fascist parties may be of minor political significance. However, France has seen the sudden electoral emergence of Le Pen's *Front National.* No longer confined to the street gutter, over thirty FN members now sit in the dignified respectability of the French parliament. Perhaps the tone of their speeches will now reflect the dignity of their surroundings. However, one should not be misled by the tone of public pronouncements. Instead, it is always necessary to look at the ideological heritage of fascism. When fascists achieve some sort of political success, and when they moderate the tone of their messages, it is all the more necessary to uncover the links between the public display and the murky underworld of fascist politics.

This entails examining the traditions of antisemitism, even though, as in the case of Le Pen and the *Front National,* the antisemitic message may not be the dominant theme in the fascist's ideological armoury at present. The history of antisemitism shows how the accusations against the Jews have changed to reflect social conditions. Whatever the actual circumstances of Jews, antisemites have managed to manufacture complaints. Whether Jews have been successful or unsuccessful, rural or urban, modern or traditional, their mere existence has been sufficient to cause offence to the antisemite. Since the establishment of the State of Israel one old antisemitic theme has disappeared in its traditional garb, only to be replaced by another. Formerly antisemites viewed Jews' lack of a homeland with suspicion, with the image of the rootless, cosmopolitan Jews uppermost in prejudiced mythology. For example, this is the way Arnold Leese, the pre-war British antisemite, who advocated the mass gassing of the Jews, started his tract, which re-asserted the mediaeval myth that Jews ritually sacrifice Gentile children: "The Jews are a nation without a home", and in consequence they have "contaminated almost every country in the world" (*Jewish Ritual Murder,* 1938, 2). Now that the Jews have a homeland, the accusation has altered. Instead of being the nation without a home, Jews are accused of illegitimately possessing a homeland, and Israel is stigmatised as being the national state without a genuine nation.

The denial of the Holocaust fits into this new twist in the old antisemitic mythology. The antisemites assert that the Jewish state of Israel was only established in the wave of sympathy, which followed the Holocaust: take away the Holocaust, and you take away the moral basis for an independent Jewish state, they argue. Thus, ideologically, they proceed to take away the Holocaust. Not only is its existence denied, but the modern antisemite claims that the very idea of Nazi genocide was invented by Zionists, in order to win gullible sympathy for their cause. David McCalden, the ex-National Front member, in charge of the Institute for Historical Review, whose sole *raison d'être,* was to deny the Holocaust, said about the Nazi murder of six million Jews: "If we can show that it didn't happen as they said it did, Israelis won't have an excuse for depriving the Palestinians of their civil rights"[1]

This sort of remark has become increasingly familiar in fascist publications in recent years. The result has been a curious blend of pro-Palestinian rhetoric, combined with racist, and frequently anti-Islamic, bigotry directed at non-whites living in Western countries. For example, the National Front in Britain will invoke predictably crude stereotypes against Pakistanis, and these frequently involve derogatory remarks about mosques and Islamic dietary rules. Yet at the same time, these groups have been expressing a support for Palestinian nationalism against Zionism and even an admiration for Khomeini's Iran. For example, the National Front's magazine, *Nationalism Today,* has called for "National Revolutionaries" (i.e. fascists) to forge a "Euro-Arab alliance" for the "creation of a Third Way and anti-Zionist voice" (June 1985).

Of course, contradictions are to be expected in the fascist ideology of hatred. However, these particular contradictions are worth a moment's attention. By invoking pro-Palestinian and anti-Israeli rhetoric, the fascist groups are attempting to hitch their antisemitism, which is of limited appeal, to a much wider current of political opinion. The tactic is to come in from the cold of mediaeval antisemitism, in order to enter the more populated corridors of anti-Zionism. Of course, the distinction between anti-Zionism and antisemitism is blurred at the best of times. It is not antisemitic to show sympathy for the sufferings of Palestinians in their diaspora since the foundation of the State of Israel. However, as has been argued elsewhere, the anti-Zionist position of the far-left is often, but by no means always, based on antisemitic, or, more precisely, anti-Jewish, assumptions.[2] Jewish nationalism is singled out for special treatment, and castigated as an improper form of nationalism. On the left, little sympathy is shown to any form of Jewish identification. All too frequently Jews are defined as being no more than co-religionist, and, then, religion, and with it Jewish identification, is dismissed as reactionary dogma. As this position is articulated in some left-wing circles, new anti-Jewish myths have been propagated, such as the myth that the Zionists worked hand in glove with the Nazis during the Second World War. This myth serves to give concrete form to unthinking slogans, which equate Zionism and Nazism.[3]

Apart from a few very minor exceptions, which Dr Seidel documents, left-wing circles have not adopted the myth of denying the Holocaust. Yet, this does not mean that this particular myth has been confined to the outer edges of politics. In fact, there is evidence that Western antisemites have been able to establish certain points of contact with the Arab world. The Institute of Historical Review has invited sympathetic Palestinians to its conferences. The IHR, in advertising cassettes of its 1982 Conference proceedings, offers recordings of the speech given by "Mr. Hadawi, a Palestinian with a long and illustrious diplomatic career". The previous year the conference had been addressed by Mr Issah Nakhleh, who describes himself as "Legal Adviser to the World Muslim Conference". In 1982, when the Swedish Holocaust-denier, Ditlieb Felderer, was convicted of defaming the Jews, Nakhleh sent at telegram of protest to the Swedish District Attorney. In this, he described Felderer as "a man who is trying to publish what he believes is true and to defend the right of the Palestinian people".

On its own, the participation of Mr Nakhleh and Mr Hadawi in IHR activities would have little significance. Perhaps they are both eccentrics, who are as unrepresentative of public opinion as McCalden is unrepresentative of British attitudes. Certainly the official PLO does not participate in IHR activities. However, there is additional evidence, which lifts the relations between Arab anti-

Zionism and antisemitic denial of the Holocaust beyond the level of individual eccentricity. There is also the possibility the western antisemites have not only succeeded in making individual contacts in the Arab world, but also that they have succeeded in attracting funding for their activities.

As Dr Seidel has shown, they myths of the Holocaust-deniers have been circulating almost since Auschwitz was liberated. Until the mid-1970s the denial was confined to the sorts of grubby and ill-produced pamphlets, which are typical of small fascist publishing houses. However, in the last ten years there has been a growth of well-produced, glossy publications peddling the same lies. It is hard to resist the conclusion that now more money is available to the publishers of this material, or perhaps that more money is to be made from its publication. In one instance, at least, it has been possible to trace the source of funding, and the source does not lead to a wealthy eccentric but to a government agency. Dr Seidel quotes the report which show that the Saudi Arabian government has been promoting and distributing Holocaust-denial material. When a nation state, expecially one that is praised by Western governments for its political moderation, is involved in the production and distribution of such ideas, then we can be sure that we are far from the province of individual eccentricity: the ideas, which properly belong only to the furthest corners of the lunatic fringe, have been allowed to encroach dangerously on to a wider political context.

Dr Seidel alludes to the shock which the Holocaust-denial material has given to Jewish sensibilites, as if the mere existence of these beliefs were shockingly surprising in themselves. The history of antisemitism, as long as that of the Jews themselves, gives no reason for supposing that malevolent intentions had run their course in 1945. In a sense Jews are warned to expect such things. The Passover *Haggaddah,* recited each year in the family home, tells the story of the Children of Israel and their flight from Pharoah. At one point the *Haggaddah* states that there "was not one man only who stood against us to destroy us, but in every generation that there those who stand against us to destroy us". In our century the passage takes on particularly vivid meanings. There is not one Hitler who stood against the Jews, but in subsequent generations we see others exonerating the crimes of the past as they prepare for the crimes of the future.

Michael Billig

Notes

1. Quoted in S. Littwin, 'The new face of Anti-Semitism', *Los Angeles Times,* June 1981.
2. Examples and analysis of anti-Jewish themes in left-wing anti-Zionism are to be found in M. Billig, 'Anti-Jewish themes and the British far left — I, *Patterns of Prejudice,* 1984, 18(1), 3-17; M. Billig, 'Anti-Jewish themes and the British far left — II', *Patterns of Prejudice,* 1984, 18 (2), 28-34. These two articles are incorporated into a longer piece: M. Billig, 'Anti-semitic themes and the British far left: some social psychological observations on indirect aspects of the conspiracy tradition'. In *Changing Conceptions of Conspirary, C.F. Graumann and S. Moscovici, eds., (New York: Springer) (in press).*
3. On the far left there is a pronounced reluctance to discuss the issue of marxist antisemitism, including the well-documented antisemitism of Marx himself. An early version of this introduction, as well as Dr Seidel's manuscript, encounted this reluctance at first hand. Originally the left-wing publishers, Pluto Press, were to publish both.

1. The Holocaust: interpretations

Why is the Holocaust important? More than forty years on it is necessary to put the question so baldly. And why talk of a **holocaust** and not of **genocide? Holocaust** has religious connotations. It refers to a sacrifice partly or wholly consumed by fire.[1] Yet what is more profane than mass murder? The term seems glaringly inappropriate. It suggests a frozen, anachronistic image shut off from the force of Nazi ideology and practice, an act impenetrable to resistance. It may only serve to blunt our questioning of how the destruction of European Jewry by the Nazis was possible. It is not part of any reflective framework which could help us understand how, according to the National Socialist doctrine, 'the Jew' was the 'mortal enemy' of the German 'Aryans', or the role of the bureaucratic, technologically advanced state. **Genocide**,[2] by contrast contributes to a rational account. The term was coined in 1944 by Raphael Lemkin, a New York lawyer. It refers to the destruction of a people, and has greater explanatory power. Yet the **Holocaust** is the term widely used in both Jewish and non-Jewish sources to refer to the mass murder of European Jewry by the Nazis. For this reason alone it figures in the title of the book and in the text. However, as I have indicated, it is problematic; and I wish to record my critical distance from this convention. At the same time, it is perhaps an indication of the state of our reflection. The American historian, Lucy Dawidowicz, author of *The War Against the Jews*[3], once commented that 'we [the Jews] research the Holocaust, we write books about it, and we ourselves read these books'.[4] She could have added 'and publish them too', as issues relating to the genocide of

European Jewry are frequently confined to the annals of Jewish history.

The perception of the Holocaust as a discrete event has very particular implications for Jewish-Gentile relations and for the anti-racist and anti-fascist struggle. The question educationists need to ask themselves is not whether to teach about the Holocaust, but *how* to do it. The Holocaust is central to European culture. The destruction of European Jewry threatened the basis of European liberalism. It was also an indictment of European science and civilisation. Now there is an international movement seeking to destroy history, denying that the Holocaust ever took place. The aim is to rehabilitate National Socialism and Hitler. It is plain that radical antisemitism did not die in 1945.

The Holocaust denial movement has been addressed in separate articles and in televeision documentaries. However, it has not been the focus of a single, accessible volume. This is the updated version of a book of the same title originally contracted for Pluto Press in 1981 when it was a scarcely known phenomenon. It was scheduled for publication in spring 1983.[5] Its appearance, therefore, is well overdue.

Chapter one is in a sense both an introduction and a postscript It discusses the meanings of the Holocaust after President Reagan's controversial visit to the Bitburg War Cemetery in West Germany as part of the fortieth anniversary, and some fascist and anti-fascist responses. It address the 'Never Again' position exploring the paradox of the Jewish and universal focus. It summarises the position in which the universalisation of the phenomenon, an increasing trend in east and west reporting, contributes to the writing of Jews and their specific treatment out of history. Although this universalist interpretation derives from diverse political perspectives, it is seen to contribute to an antisemitic discourse.

Chapter two concerns the Holocaust itself. It sets out the facts for readers unfamiliar with the 'Final Solution'. It illustrates the centrality of antisemitism to Nazi ideology and practice. It shows how popular antisemitism was channelled and managed by an efficient, totalitarian state. It refers to the role of 'scientific racism' and the appeal to scientific authority, particularly to biology, psychology and anthropology, to justify racist and sexist practices. It summarises the role of institutional antisemitism and outlines the different stages in the destruction process.

Chapter three examines why the Holocaust denial is crucial to neo-Nazi propaganda and discusses the different international variants. Using largely **Searchlight*** sources, it identifies the international networks and their publishing links: principally, the World Anti-Communist League, the Northern League and the US Liberty Lobby; and, in Western Europe, the French and German old and new right; and the neo-Nazi publishing ventures and operations in Britain. It also identifies a more general upsurge in 'race-thinking' and attacks on egalitarianism. It is argued that these are not restricted to neo-Nazi parties or publications: they are a feature of the conservative authoritarian right.

Chapter four is concerned with the Institute for Historical Review in the States, the organising core, the contributors to their conventions and journal, and their backers. It also offers a detailed description and analysis of Arthur Butz's *The Hoax of the Twentieth Century,* the chief US exponent of the denial myth. This chapter also addresses a particular left-wing version of antisemitism as exemplified in Lenni Brenner's *Zionism in the Age of the Dictators* which alleges Nazi-Zionist collaboration. Although Brenner's writing does not contribute directly to the Holocaust denial, it serves to delegitimise Israel, a discourse common to both extremes of the political spectrum.

Chapter five focuses on the Faurisson affair in France: Robert Faurisson, the major French exponent, his socialist mentor, Paul Rassinier; the offensive interview with Darquier de Pellepoix, former Vichy minister for Jewish Affairs, published in the **Express;** Faurisson's trial; the anarchist involvement (La Vieille Taupe, publishing house, and Serge Thion), including the controversy provoked by Noam Chomsky's preface to Faurisson's book.

Chapter six is largely concerned with Britain and the British counterpart of the Institute for Historical Review, the Historical Review Press. It discusses versions of the denial by Michael McLaughlin, David McCalden and Richard Harwood. Neo-Nazi newsheets like 'Holocaust News' are part of this data. It also analyses a 'soft' variant: the insidious allegations of Hitler's innocence of the 'Final Solution' in David Irving's *Hitler's War,* the

---

* *Searchlight* is an anti-fascist monthly magazine incorporating CARF (Campaign against Racism and Fascism) which grew out of the confederation of London's anti-racist and anti-fascist groups.

arguments in Irving's other writings, and draws attention to his political activities and associations.

Chapter seven advances the general hypothesis that the Holocaust denial variants are a new version of the tsarist fabrication, *The Protocols of Zion,* a conspiracy for world domination. *The Protocols* served as a warrant for genocide. The Holocaust denial is a further symbolic genocide. The chapter goes on to comment on the reception of the Hollywood 'Holocaust' film in West Germany and France. Finally, it invites reflection on contemporary manifestations of anti-black racism and nationalism in Britain and Western Europe. It takes issue with the culturalist discourse of the British New Right, about what it means to be 'British' in Thatcher Britain today; and considers its implications for both Jewish and black communities.

40 years on: meanings of the Holocaust after Bitburg

The fortieth anniversary of VE day has come and gone. For many Jews it was less a cause for celebration than a poignant reminder.[6] With millions of war dead and most of European Jewry exterminated, the very idea of victory, or victory celebrations, is insensitive and jarring. In 1984 the international media attempted to focus public attention of the official celebrations of the D-day landings in Normandy. As Anthony Barnett commented in the *Guardian*[7], it was no doubt an attempt to wrest the legacy of victory from any association with the Soviet Union.

Yet there can be no doubt that victory over fascism could not have been won without the Soviet Union. Twenty million Soviet dead. Too massive a figure, perhaps, for the west to contemplate. Irrespective of the gulag, the nature of Soviet state bureaucracy and official Soviet antisemitism, the orchestration of anti-socialist voices must not be allowed to silence this basic fact. It was a division of the Red Army which liberated Auschwitz, not Allied bombing.[8]

In May 1985 we witnessed the fortieth anniversary of VE day as a media event. In Britain this was portrayed as a victory, reproducing Churchillian phrasing and symbols. The *Mail* saw in the commemoration

> 'a rededication of the national spirit'.[9]

The language was reminiscent of the tabloids' coverage of the

Malvinas/Falklands War.[10] The two wars became almost interchangeable in the media hype, with Galtieri as the new Hitler. A *Sun* cartoon exemplified this cynical manipulation. Both were 'good wars'.[11] Both serve to cue British nationalism where the Dunkirk and Falkland spirit were one body.

In France the emphasis was not on victory but on liberation and resistance. Very little has been written to date, and particularly by French scholars, on the anti-Jewish decrees enacted in France by Marshal Pétain's Vichy government.[12] Major films about the period are still denied national TV screening. In France, too, it was a largely media and state-managed event with both right and left-wing parties laying claim to the political capital of the resistance heritage.

The most controversial event of the fortieth anniversary celebrations was President Reagan's trip to the Bitburg war cemetery in West Germany. The invitation had been extended by West German Chancellor, Helmut Kohl, as an act of reconciliation. But the presidential aides apparently overlooked the presence of SS graves. Members of Hitler's elite troops, most of them very young, had been buried alongside their victims. This amounted to a diplomatic gaffe with very particular resonances. It was a momentous affront to the victims of Nazi oppression, and deeply offensive to Jewish sensibilities. In several cities, rallies to remember the Holocaust turned into protest against the symbolism of Bitburg. Reagan could have extricated himself. There was mounting pressure for him to do so. It was an 'agonising' decision. But he chose to go.[13] The decision was an act of 'moral blindness'[14] Reagan's 'historic mistake' in visiting the Bitburg war cemetery was 'to equate murderers with their victims'.[15]

The majority of the American Senate sent him a letter 'strongly urging' him to cancel the visit.[16] In Britain, too, a group of 93 MPs headed by Greville Janner (Labour, Leicester West) signed a parliamentary motion condemning the visit as 'offensive to the memories of Jews and so many other persecuted and murdered by the Nazis'. The visit was 'outrageous'.[17]

Immanuel Jacobovits, Chief Ashkenazi Rabbi in Britain, while not referring to Reagan by name, appealed for the avoidance of 'any gesture which could dishonour the memory of Holocaust victims, cause offence to the survivors and blunt the abhorrence of racist persecutions'[18].

Perhaps the most moving intercession was that of Elie Wiesel, author, child prisoner in Auschwitz, Chair of the US Holocaust Memorial Council. In an unscheduled public intervention he begged the President to 'find another way'.

> I have seen the SS at work. I have seen the victims... How can you compare soldiers and their fate with prisoners in concentration camps and their fate — people who went up in smoke, people who were victims of hunger and persecution. There is something wrong in such an equation.[19]

Some 700 Jewish students from all over Europe marched down the main street at Bitburg to protest against the visit. Perhaps the most encouraging aspect in terms of anti-racist alliances was the presence of some 50 Arabs from France. They took part in solidarity with Jews so that no-one will forget that Nazism is the most extreme form of racism.[20]

But it was *realpolitik* at work: the cementing of the western alliance at whatever cost must not be endangered. This sentiment was encapsulated by the *Express:*

> Reconciliation with West Germany — the West's ally for 40 years — is central to the VE ceremonies. The Bitburg Bungle should not be allowed to get in the way.[21]

Meanwhile, according to Agence France-Presse, neo-Nazis were thrilled at the prospect of a posthumous rehabilitation of war criminals; and SS veterans spruced up 50 or so tombstones in time for President Reagan's arrival. The *Telegraph*[22] reported that fresh flowers lay on the graves of SS men buried there; and the *Sunday Telegraph*[23] that wreaths in Nazi colours lay nearby carrying an inscription in Gothic lettering: 'Born Germans, lived as fighters, died as heroes'.

Former members of the Totenkopf (Death's Head) division, concentration camp guards, gathered for a reunion at Nesselwang, West Germany, are quoted by the *New York Times* as echoing Reagan's position:

> We were soldiers like all the other soldiers in the war, and I think that is what the President is trying to say. The pressures for him to cancel the visit are predictably "Zionist". The Zionists stop at nothing. But the President is an honest man. He made his decision and is sticking to it.[24]

Helmut Kohl referred to the uniqueness of the Holocaust in world history. The extreme right-wing paper, *Deutsche National Zeitung,* set the tone of the neo-Nazi response:

> the fact is the Jews are still around, aren't they?, not only suffering no persecution but actually in positions of power — in Israel, in the USA, and in West Germany where they are among the "over-privileged minorities" in contrast to the ordinary Germans who belong to the underprivileged.[25]

This constitutes a slightly oblique version of the denial. At the same time it is an update of the Nazi propaganda suggesting that Jews exercise extraordinary power over non-Jews, a paraphrase of the conspiracy theory, as set out in the infamous tsarist forgery, *The Protocols of the Elders of Zion,*[26] of which many different versions were put into circulation.

Meanwhile, the US Nazi journal, *Spotlight,* saw hysteria over Reagan's Bitburg visit orchestrated by the media.

> The message is clear — white Christians who oppose political Zionism are sadistic killers.[27]

Predictably, the strength of Jewish reactions to Reagan's Bitburg visit led to an upsurge in antisemitism in West Germany, according to a high West German official on a visit to the US. Jewish visibility tends to be seen as problematic in Christian countries. Britain is no exception: The *Telegraph* editorial of 7 May 1985, '40 years on', talked of the 'morbid sensitivity' of the Jews. An article in the *Times* by David Watt of 6 May 1985 called the row over Bitburg 'grotesque and absurd'. It was complicated by 'the Jewish factor', 'the most powerful and complicated element of all', and 'the extraordinary strength of the Jewish lobby in American politics'. It is as if 'Jewish power' were the agenda, not the trivialisation of genocide. It is insidious and frightening. Jewish visibility even causes embarrassment to many assimilated Jews who have internalised antisemitism and seek to distance themselves from any form of Jewish identity or solidarity.[28] It is scarcely surprising that the expression of Jewish outrage at the Bitburg affair was unacceptable to many older Germans.

Such a reaction illustrates the traditional antisemitic argument whereby Jews themselves are responsible for antisemitism, in much the same way as women are frequently seen as responsible for rape.

It is part of the same racist and sexist argument in which victims are cast in the role of oppressor; and thereafter become the focus of the enquiry in the place of the racists or male supremacists. It has the effect of fudging the real power dimentions. At the same time, in a broader framework, it fails to address the nature of the power relations at work in a white, Christian and heterosexist society.

The outcome of Bitburg, Reagan's equating of Nazi oppressors with their victims and his reduction of Nazism to mere autocratic rule, has a profound significance:

> The war against one man's totalitarian dictatorship was not like other wars. The evil world of Nazism turned all values upside down. Nevertheless, we can mourn the German war dead today as human beings crushed by a vicious ideology.[29]

Such sentiments voiced by the leader of a superpower shape the public perception of Nazism and its victims at a crucial point in history. Hitherto, this kind of discourse has been restricted to extreme right-wing sources. It has now been legitimated at a time when memories of the Holocaust are fading, and neo-Nazis in particular are attempting to deny that the Holocaust ever took place. Even at the height of the Bitburg row, an article by a leading Egyptian journalist referred to the Holocaust as 'an event whose occurrence has yet to be proved scientifically'.[30]

The Bitburg affair more than the anniversary itself causes us to reflect on the meaning of the Holocaust in our political culture, how that meaning is changing and being challenged, and what precisely is at stake. This is not exclusively a Jewish concern, though it necessarily cues Jewish sensibilities. It was Nazi and British Union of Fascists' propaganda that the Allies entered the war on behalf of the Jews. Lucy Dawidowicz's phrase, 'the war against the Jews', the title of one of her books, is far more apposite.

A little prior to Bitburg, a right-wing German historian, Bernard Willms, argued for the need to build 'a new revolutionary national consciousness' in Germany by unhooking the associations between nationalism, national socialism and Auschwitz. He argues that people have been conditioned to think in terms of 'the chain of associations — nation, nationalism, National Socialism, Hitlerism, Auschwitz'.[31] This programmatic statement is extremely significant. It summarises the radical enterprise in which to present-day neo-Nazis are engaged. It is an attempt to remake the way we construct our world, and language is central to this process. It is an attempt through language, through discourse, that is, through the social creation of meanings, to erase our struggles and our history; to erase the memory of our dead. This is the nature of the neo-Nazi enterprise of which the Holocaust denial is a central strategy.

The Holocaust: its specificity and universality

Yehuda Bauer, Professor of Holocaust Studies at the Hebrew University of Jerusalem, in an important article in the conservative American Journal, *Midstream,* addressed the problem of reconciling the uniqueness of the Holocaust with its universalist meaning. It is entitled 'Whose Holocaust?'[32] He argues that a growing recognition of the Holocaust Memorial Day has flattened its meaning to accord with American political reality, that it is becoming 'de-Judaized and Americanized'. Any injustice inflicted on any section of the population, including blacks in run-down urban areas, and women suffering inequality, tends to be dubbed a 'holocaust'. Its meaning, therefore, is becoming over-generalised. This contributes to the misunderstanding and trivialisation of the event. It is a familiar phenomenon. Vladimir Nabokov characterised it as *poshlost,* a Russian word that may be summarised as vulgar clichés or bogus profundities.[33]

In Bauer's view, the word genocide as coined by Lemkin has a limited meaning. He suggest that the term is appropriate when used to refer to the suffering of the Polish nation. The Poles sustained enormous losses. However, the murder of Poles was not a planned, total annihilation insofar as Poles were needed as a slave labour force for the subsequent rebuilding of Germany. With Jews, it was different. The Nazis operated a hierarchy even among those peoples they regarded as subhuman species. The Jews were a satanic power in the world and had to be destroyed like vermin. Economic and political arguments were no more than rationalisations. In Hitler's conception they were a parasitic anti-race who preyed on the bodies of healthy nations. Control by Jews led to decomposition, collapse and death.

> What makes the Holocaust unique is the existence of two elements: planned total annihilation of a national or ethnic group, and the quasi-religious, apocalyptic ideology that motivated the murder.

The fact that the Holocaust took place in Christian Europe

and that its antecedents are clearly connected with the development of Christianity, has been noted by Christian commentators who argue that the Holocaust is a tremendous credibility crisis for Christianity, and that it poses even more basic problems for non-Jews than it does for Jews.[34]

Bauer is therefore seeking to mark the distinctiveness of Jewish fate with a particular name — Holocaust — so that the presence of antisemitism cannot be lost, minimised, or disclaimed, and anti-Jewishness allowed to become 'normal' currency in Christian society.

The argument is persuasive. But at the same time he also accepts that there is a necessary blurring of the lines between **holocaust** and **genocide,** particularly when weapons of mass destruction are involved. The anthropologist, Leo Kuper, an authority on genocide, makes an apparently simple yet profound observation:

> One of the interesting things about genocide is that there is a difference of religion between murderers and victims... There are not many exceptions.[35]

In *The Holocaust and the Historians*, Lucy Dawidowicz has also examined the ways in which the Holocaust has been trivialised, exploited and erased by historians. There is a further paradox here. Internationalists would tend to put the case for universality of Jewish suffering and empathy. This is consonant with an egalitarian ethic as part of an anti-nationalist political project. But in so doing, the distinctiveness and understanding may be fudged. Dawidowicz argues that while the 'universalisers of Auschwitz do not necessarily deny the uniqueness of the mass murderers', they tend to deny the specificity of their victims:

> By subsuming the Jewish losses under a universal or ecumenical classification of human suffering, one can blur the distinctiveness of Jewish fate and consequently one can disclaim the presence of antisemitism ... Therefore one can feel free to reject political or moral responsibility for the consequences of antisemitism.[36]

The Jewish specificity of the Holocaust is not only being flattened in the US and the west. This has been the pattern in Eastern Europe in official publications for some time. A recent example is an official publication of East Germany *(Verlag Zeit Im*

Bild) in an English edition entitled *Upholding the Anti-Fascist Legacy*. It is quoted in the English section of the New York *Morning Freiheit:*

The toll of blood left behind by the German fascists totals 50 million lives, including those of 20 million Soviet people, over six million Poles, 1.7 million Yugoslavs, 600,000 French, 400,000 US citizens and 375,000 Britons. From the German people the fascist beast claimed over six million lives, among them men and women who had fought in the resistance movement and laid down their lives for the cause of freedom.

As the [East German] editorial points out, the word "Jew" is not entered into this account at all. It is argued that the Russian Jews are included in the Soviet figure, the Polish Jews in the Polish figure, and that it is not necessary to keep any separate Jewish account!

The problem with this chain of reasoning is that it conceals the fact that Jews were not subjected to exceptional laws under the Hitler regime and that there was nothing exceptional about the annihilation of the Jews.

Consequently, there were no death camps, there were no crematoriums, there was no race theory and no specific extermination policy directed against Jews which was based on racism and "Aryan" racial superiority. Thus there is no reason to detach and single out the Nazi murder of the Jewish people.

In the same way Jews are not specifically mentioned on the monument at Babi Yar[38] in Kiev or at the monument at Ponary outside Vilnius (Vilno).

DELIBERATE OMISSION

This East German document has therefore deliberately omitted — these things just don't happen! — the entire subject of the Nazi racial policies, the singling out of the Jewish people for complete extermination — only because they were born Jews.[37]

This is part of the conspiracy of silence about the destruction of the Jews.

Commemoration of the Holocaust tends to be subsumed under the slogan 'Never Again'. That, too, in common with any other symbolic capital, may be drawn upon or exploited in different ways as part of different political designs, or a particular set of lived experiences. 'Nunca mas' ('Never Again') is the title of a report by a

National Commission on Disappeared People in Argentina which described practices reminiscent of the horrors that occurred in the Second World War. Among 'the disappeared' were a disproportionate number of Jews; and those Jews detained were frequently singled out for particular humiliation.

Ronald Aronson in an existential study on the *Dialectics of Disaster (1982)*[39] articulates the tension and the dilemma, opening up the overtly political dimensions of the debate:

> Jewish ex-communist survivors on Israeli kibbutzim overlooked by the now-silent bunkers of the Golan heights speak of the death of internationalism at Auschwitz, of the need to protect "our own" even if against all humanity.

Given the experience of these survivors,

> The main task may therefore be particular survival rather than universal justice, in a world where barbarism is so palpably real...
>
> Isn't this the meaning of a "Never Again" which, in addition to genuine self-defence, justifies to the continued repression of Palestinians by Jews?

Never Again is also the title of Rabbi Meir Kahane's book, a racist-populist expression of Jewish fundamentalism. Kahane, a New Yorker, founder of the Jewish Defence League, fanatical anti-Arab zealots, and of the Kach Party, is a member of the Israeli Knesset. Kahane has been described in the liberal *Jewish Chronicle*[40] as being the nearest thing to a Jewish fascist. There have been moves to silence him, and to proscribe his party.

It is true that the 'Never Again' political philosophy is tragically double-edged. Hence Aronson's concern with a dialectics of hope emerging from a dialectics of disaster. The 'lest we forget' focuses more on memory, and how this must not be erased. Arguably, this debate has particular implications for the shaping of Jewish identity; and it is known that children of survivors have a particularly heavy burden to bear.

Both Kahane and former Israeli Prime Minister, Menachem Begin, have used the Holocaust in different ways, as have some critics of Israel's invasion of the Lebanon. It has even been suggested that the Holocaust imagery shaped the media reporting of the Lebanese war. Kahane has proclaimed a monument to the 'second Jewish Holocaust'. Using apocalyptic imagery he is referring to another Holocaust to come, that of the diaspora. Begin, on the other hand, draws on the Holocaust as an existential event to discourage criticism of Israeli policy towards Palestinians. Arguably, it has been used for demagogical ends by both politicians. It was brandished by Begin as both a political and symbolic weapon for silencing his critics abroad, including former West German Chancellor, Helmut Schmidt.[41] Some very ambiguous responses were published in *Der Speigel.*

At a 1985 London symposium[42] concerned with the meaning of the Holocaust in politics and culture after Bitburg, June Jacobs argued that it was overused politically. Jews were worrying about antisemitism while neglecting pro-Judaism. The Holocaust should not represent the sum total of our culture. Jacobs pinpoints the dilemma. However, the Jewish community itself is necessarily plural.[43] This is not sufficiently stressed. Judaism needs also to come to terms with the ethical implications of sexual politics.[44]

The taking on board of the antisemitic agenda as the cornerstone of Jewish identity is to be primarily concerned with a negative and received self-determination. At the same time, its impact is necessarily enormous in a Christian society in that the Church's teachings and practices have frequently been antisemitic (the Crusades, the Spanish Inquisition…), and its recent history linked to that of colonialism.

The London Imperial War Museum organised an exhibition on European Resistance to Nazi Germany as part of the 1984 fortieth anniversary celebrations. No specific reference was made to Jewish resistance, notably to the Warsaw Ghetto uprising. A complaint lodged by a Holocaust survivor was dismissed as 'inappropriate'. Such omissions tend to compound the myth of Jews 'going like lambs to the slaughter'. This is a Christian image often reproduced uncritically by historians. It now enjoys the status of popular myth. The truth is that there were uprisings and rebellions not only in Warsaw and Auschwitz but elsewhere.[45] For many, the mere act of survival without brutalisation is remarkable in itself.

Auschwitz as the most efficient killing centre is a category which mobilises Jewish identity. It symbolises **the** obscenity. So much depends on the construction of Auschwitz. It has been perceived as the most horrible pogrom in Jewish history. But as Bauer and others have argued, this is to ignore the specificity of Nazi ideology and the role of the bureaucratic state.

The Holocaust was not only a crime against the Jewish people: it was also a crime against humanity, a crime against 'human status', against human diversity, and hence against the nature of humanity. In other words, although undeniably part of Jewish history and culture, it is no less part of the history of western liberalism[46].

That history is now being denied. After the physical annihilation, the denial constitutes a second, symbolic Holocaust, and trivialisation is a contributory factor. Such depths of cynicism are difficult to contemplate. It requires an act of political will. Interpretations of the past, and not only those of professional historians, impinge on the quality of our present; and, in the nuclear age, on the possibility of our future. These are a focus of struggle and resistance. This largely uncontroversial claim is an underlying theme of this book. It seeks to address the different versions of the Holocaust denial as a contribution to that reflection. The Holocaust denial campaign is part of an overall neo-Nazi strategy to rehabilitate Hitler and national socialism. This political challenge must be met. Some deportees and survivors continues to dismiss the threat posed by the ultra-right revival. It is a strange paradox. Many contemporaries said the same of Hitler's party and *Mein Kampf* in the early days. Meanwhile, the Bitburg discourse and the meanings it has put into circulation in seeking to rehabilitate the SS oppressors has given the Holocaust denial a degree of credibility. That realisation is chilling.

2. The Holocaust: the Facts

How is it that one group of human beings can plan and execute the murder of another group of human beings? Whenever such barbarities have occurred, it is because the victims have been perceived as less than human, as 'not of our kind', or not like 'us'.

The Jews were the Nazis' prime target. At the same time, other sections of the population were also killed. These included political adversaries, Jehovah's Witnesses, gypsies, homosexuals, and the mentally ill. They were considered racially or genetically inferior and therefore deemed unfit to live under national socialism. The racist ideas characterising the nineteenth-century eugenics movement, the idea of racial improvement, of 'purification' of the stock, had considerable impact throughout Europe and America. The word 'eugenics' was coined by Darwin's cousin, Francis Galton, in the 1880's to refer to a 'science' which deals with all influences that improve the inborn qualities of a 'race'.[1]

The Holocaust was a product of a racist, nationalist climate fuelled by fanaticism in which widespread antisemitism was taken over and organised by an efficient totalitarian state. The 'Final Solution' (Endlösung) was the Nazi bureaucratic codeword for the destruction of European Jews. In 1939 two-thirds of the world's Jewry lived in Europe, and half of all world Jewry was concentrated in Eastern Europe. Hitler's plan to murder every Jew in Europe was a closely guarded secret, and even potential victims found it hard to believe. Every kind of deception was practised. Two million Jews were killed in their towns, villages or ghettos, others were shot at mass-murder sites, while the remaining two million were forced from their homes and taken to camps in Poland were they were worked, starved or beaten to death, shot, or gassed. There have been other genocides in history, but this was the first to be carried out by a modern, technologically advanced state.

A great deal has been written about Hitler's Third Reich and the 'Final Solution'. There are also a vast number of official documents and diaries. Because of the exposure over the years, and because it is highly emotive, many people now resist the subject. With time, certain facts have become blurred, while postwar generations have only a slight knowledge of these atrocities.

It is at this point that contemporary Nazis are trying to deny the Holocaust. The Holocaust denial as a confirmation and renewal of Nazi racist ideology is the main concern of the book. First, however, in order to counter the reticence, the ignorance and the lies, we must set the record right.

This chapter sets out briefly what happend, how it happened, and how we know about it.

Radical antisemitism

Hitler did not invent antisemitism; The term itself was coined in 1879 from the Greek by the German agitator, Wilhelm Marr, to designate the then-current anti-Jewish campaigns in Europe. Anti-Judaism is not a modern phenomenon. Historically, it has been part of Church teachings about the Jews. The phrase 'Jewish question' was used during the early Enlightenment period in Western Europe. It was a euphemism. The 'question' or 'problem' referred to the anomaly presented by Jews as a people at a time of rising political nationalism and secularism and the emergence of nation states. To refer to any section of the population as 'problem' is to dehumanise them. The geographical distribution of Jews seemed an aberration in the nationalist climate: Jews simply did not fit in.

Antisemitism was also central to a simplistic economic explanation about the rise of capitalism and the role of Jews. This was by no means limited to Germany, and was common to both right and left antisemitism. Economic antisemitism fuelled political antisemitism which was particularly virulent towards the end of the nineteenth century. Doctrines of racial superiority made racism academically respectable. The centrality of 'race' was meshed with the more romanticised notions of the *Völk* in rural Germany. The very term *Völk* is a fusion of both people and 'race'. Hitler was heir to these antisemitic and nationalist traditions and beliefs. He was able to channel them into an energising synthesis, so that 'the Jew' became not only the outsider, but the ultimate evil, the mortal enemy *(Todfeind)*.

Wer Kennt Jude, Kennt den Teufel
(Whoever knows the Jew knows the Devil)

This enemy was to be killed in self-defence.

In Hitler's *Mein Kampf,* and elsewhere, the altogether negative images of Jews were extraordinarily powerful in that he manipulated both Christian and biological discourses. These represented Jews as a satanic force and as the source of pollution and disease. Certain expressions of *völkisch* German Christianity sought to expunge any Jewish elements from their faith, opting for an 'Aryan' Jesus. Hitler himself was a pagan.

The antisemitic discourse was fundamentally contradictory in that Jews were both vermin to be exterminated and at the same time were seen to be possessed of enormous mythical power and cunning. The 'Aryan' Germans were engaged in a mortal struggle with 'the Jew'. 'Juda verrecke' ('Perish Juda') became an overworn antisemitic slogan.

In this scheme, 'war is the origin of all things' and is inevitable. War is the means to realise *Lebensraum* (living space), a concept which links racial supremacy and expansion to geopolitics. This is to be achieved by reducing the role of 'Aryan' women to breeders, and sterilising, enslaving or annihilating other women.

The German historian Karl Dietrich Bracher summarises Nazi ideology in terms of three cardinal principles proposed in Hitler's *Mein Kampf (My struggle)*:

— hatred of the Jews
— *Lebensraum* (living space), Germany's unique version of racial imperialism
— the supremacy of the Fuhrer as dictator.[2]

In *Mein Kampf,* of which the first part was published in 1925, Hitler set out his ideas of 'race' as the central principle of human existence. It formed the core of National Socialist doctrine. In Hitler's system, the 'Aryans', or German master-race, were bearers of human civilisation, and cultural development, while the 'Semites', or Jews, were the 'most diabolic creatures in existence' bent on world domination. Germany could be 'redeemed' through the annihilation of the Jews, with Hitler as the redeemer. He often referred to his messianic 'mission', and very explicitly in *Mein Kampf*:[3]

> Hence today I believe I am acting in accordance with the will of the Almighty Creator: by defending myself against the Jew, I am fighting for the work of the Lord.

History was seen as a struggle between Aryan humanity and Jewish subhumanity. The distinction between 'Aryans' and 'Semites' was crucial: the former were allowed to live while the latter were condemned to die. In another extract from *Mein Kampf* Jews are depicted as dangerous, blood-sucking parasites:

> He [the Jew] is and remains the typical parasite, a sponger who like a noxious bacillus keeps spreading as soon as a favourable medium invites him. And the effect of his existence is also like that of spongers: wherever he appears, the host people dies out after a longer or shorter period…
>
> The Jew's life as a parasite in the body of other nations and states explains a characteristic which once caused Schopenhauer… to call him 'the great master of lying'. Existence impels the Jew to lie, and to lie perpetually, just as it compels the inhabitants of the northern countries to wear warm clothing… His spreading is a typical phenomenon of all parasites; he always seeks new feeding ground for his race…
>
> Where he establishes himself the people who grant him hospitality are bound to be bled to death sooner or later… He poisons the blood of others but preserves his own blood unadulterated… To mask his tactics and fool his victims, he talks of the equality of all men, no matter what their race or colour… To all external appearances [he] strives to ameliorate the conditions under which the workers live; but in reality his aim is to enslave and thereby annihilate the non-Jewish races.[4]

For Hitler, Jews pretended to be a religion, whereas in fact they were a 'race'. The whole idea of 'race' is very problematic. Racial classification of any kind as a way of categorising people is based upon delusion. Biology gives no evidence whatsoever to support the notion of different human 'races' as distinct groups organised in hierarchical fashion with specific and unchanging cultural characteristics. However, this is not to deny that there are physical and genetic variations between human beings. The renowned French geneticist, Albert Jacquard, amongst others, put it very plainly:

> When geneticists are asked about the content of the word 'race', their answer is unequivocal: in the human species this concept does not correspond to any objective, definable reality.[5]

This has been said many times by geneticists and sociologists. But the habit of race-thinking is slow to change, as is clear from everyday speech. Because the word 'race' is common currency and is on everyone's lips, it is assumed that it corresponds to a fixed and unquestionable reality. "There must be a thing called 'race' — because you hear the term so often: 'race relations', 'racial differences', 'race riots', and so on". The relationship between language and reality is far more complex. Naming and trying to make particular meanings stick is very much a political activity. It is one which involves not merely individuals but institutions. With the focus on 'race', this 'reality' became a warrant for separation and murder; and institutions and academics played a particular role in this process.

In Hitler's Germany the primacy of 'race' was elevated to the status of 'race science'. Race-thinking, however irrational or unscientific, was part of the consensus. It was uncontroversial and informed all major issues and intellectual enquiry. In Nazi Germany and occupied Europe it spawned a series of institutions and special centres concerned with Jews and gypsies.

'Race-science' is associated with Hans F.K. Günther[6], a Nazi academic who enjoyed a popular readership and who rose to prominence under Hitler. He believed that 'race' was the key to understanding all the human sciences. He outlined theories about Nordic racial purity[7] and the perils of Jewish contamination:

> The influence of the Jewish spirit that won through economic preponderance brings with it the very greatest danger for the life of the European peoples and the North American peoples alike.[8]

Günther was considered the official Nazi race-theoretician, and his writings are still circulating among postwar Nazis.

The State Management of Antisemitism: the central role of definition

For Hitler the function of the State was to preserve 'the racial community', the *Völk*. Popular antisemitism and anti-Jewish violence were managed by the state and given legal sanction only weeks after Hitler came to power in 1933. It enacted what violence has already brought about: the removal of Jews ('non-Aryans') from the government and public life. The anti-Jewish measures which culminated in genocide were introduced in different stages; although, arguably, this was not planned from the start.

By far the most radical of these measures were the Nuremberg Race Laws of 1935. The 1935 legislation, put to the National Socialist Party (NSDAP) at its congress in Nuremberg, was adopted unanimously by the Reichstag, the German Parliament. These laws transformed the Nazi obsessions with the purity of 'blood' and 'race' into legal definitions and categories, legitimating racist antisemitism. Initially this legislation primarily defined citizenship, and affected marriage and sexual relations. Later, however, to be named a Jew, or non-Jew, was the difference between death and life. The first basic law was 'for the protection of German blood and honour':

> Deeply conscious that the purity of German blood is the necessary condition for the continued existence of the German people, and inspired by an inflexible will to assure the existence of the German nation for all times, the Reichstag has unanimously adopted the following law, which is hereby promulgated.
>
> 1. Marriage between Jews and subjects of German or cognate blood is forbidden.
> 2. Extramarital relations between Jews and subjects of German or cognate blood are forbidden.
> 3. Jews may not employ in their houses women of German or cognate blood under forty-five years of age.
> 4. Jews are forbidden to fly the German national colours. They may, however, fly the Jewish colours; the exercise of this right is protected by the State.
> 5. Infractions of (1) are punishable by solitary confinement at hard labour. Infractions of (2) will be punished by imprisonment or solidarity confinement at hard labour.[9]

Ordinances and regulations bearing on the case of **Mischlinge,** or part Jews, followed a few weeks later. Comparisons have frequently been made with South African apartheid laws.

The Nuremberg Laws were of crucial significance for the Third Reich. Within the next three years anti-Jewish laws appeared on the statute books of a number of countries, including Rumania and Hungary. In order to destroy the Jews, the state had first of all to decide on a definition of Jewry. German Jews had to be 'identified' as different from Germans before they could be rounded up, taken away and eventually murdered. The very act of imposing a legal definition provided a tangible target.

Different antisemitic legal formulae for defining a Jew were already in circulation. In legal terms, German Jews, although largely indistinguishable from Germans, as many German Jews were very assimilated, were declared non-Germans. They were 'aliens' and a threat to Germany. In non-legal documents and speeches, Jews were 'parasites', 'bacilli', 'lice' and 'vermin', as well as criminals, against whom Germany was seen to be engaged in a preventive war. In Himmler's words: 'We had the moral right vis-à-vis our people to annihilate this people which wanted to anihilate us.'[10] This legal definition, separating German Jews from Germans, laid the foundation for the liquidation of these 'parasites' who were poisoning the German blood and the German nation. Arguments invoking genocide were frequently phrased in terms of biological pollution and racial hygiene. This has a long tradition on the right. Because the body is part of nature, the fight to kill 'the Jewish bacillus' is presented as 'natural'. It follows that antisemitism itself may also be seen as 'natural'; and indeed, in *Mein Kampf,* the urge towards 'racial purity' is seen as part of 'the iron logic of Nature'. Social and political phenomena are frequently presented on the right in biological and natural terms,[11] as if biology were destiny.

The Destruction Process

Following the legal definition of Jewry which set German Jews apart from Germans, other steps were taken which led to further exclusion and, eventually, to destruction:

expropriation — the removal of Jews from professions, their dismissal from public service, and the confiscation of their belongings;

concentration and ghettoisation — the crowding of Jews into

ghettos in large cities where death by slow starvation was a deliberate policy. The average daily food ration was about 1,100 calories per person, assuming it was always available;
mobile killing operations — the sending of special mechanised killing squads of SS and police known as *Einsatzgruppen* into occupied USSR in June 1941 along with the invading army with orders to move quickly from town to town and kill all Jewish inhabitants and partisans;
deportation — ostensibly for labour purposes;
extermination — in death camps in occupied Poland.

Expropriation
As German Jews were now non-Germans, they were excluded from German public life, and their property confiscated and 'Aryanised' in the belief that everything belonged to the German Reich. It became a punishable and shameful offence to buy from Jews. Goebbels, Hitler's propaganda minister, organised 'spontaneous demonstrations', the most memorable of which began on 9 November 1938. This plunder and destruction of Jewish property became known as 'Kristallnacht' ('Crystal Night', the night of broken glass), and lasted several days. Cynically, the Jews were held responsible. Licences were withdrawn from Jewish doctors who from then on could treat only Jewish patients, and a similar decree was passed on Jewish lawyers. By 1939, those who had not been able to emigrate and were still employable could find jobs only in factories or in Jewish community organisations. The Labour ministry then introduced laws which gave separate employment status to Jewish workers. Following the introduction of special Jewish income taxes, lower wages and the obligation to accept any job offered, these laws opened the way to unlimited exploitation. Jewish workers had now the legal status of a subproletariat.

Concentration and ghettoisation
The creation of ghettos[12] was a further means of organising the *physical* separation of Jews from non-Jews, just as the Nuremberg Race Laws had defined citizenship and legislated for 'racial' and sexual segregation, and the expropriation measures had secured their social isolation and poverty.

The fate of the Warsaw ghetto has been carefully chronicled.[13]

It was set up in October 1940 in order to isolate the Jews from the rest of the population. Half a million Jews, including deportees from Germany and Austria, were forced to move inside the ghetto walls. A further 72,000 from the Warsaw region were forced into the ghetto in April 1941. By early 1942, whole groups of people were living in single rooms and dying from hunger and disease. Anyone caught trying to leave was shot.

In July 1942 deportations began to the death camp in Treblinka where the gas chambers had recently been completed. Children were the principal targets of 'flushing out' operations. By September 1942, when deportations were suspended, Nazi records show that 310,322 Jews had been deported. Among the 70,000 who remained in Warsaw, a resistance group known as the Jewish Fighting Organisation led by a young Zionist, Mordechai Anielewicz, secretly prepared bunkers linked in part to the city's sewerage system, and acquired arms from Polish resistance groups.

After this initial show of resistance, Himmler, SS chief, ordered the complete destruction of the ghetto in February 1943. The order was couched in bureaucratic language as if the Reich were contemplating a normal rehousing project. The Jews held out for nearly a month, although greatly outnumbered against heavily armed German troops. It was a heroic struggle. On 15 May, it was all over: most of the surviving ghetto population of 55,000, including women and children, surrendered. Of these, some 7,000 were shot immediately. Another 7,000 were deported to the death camps in Treblinka and a further 15,000 to Majdanek. The remainder were sent to labour camps.[14] Himmler ensured that the 'Final Solution' was given top priority; and even when the German military position was severely weakened, the deportation of Jews continued.

Mobile killing operations

The *Einsatzgruppen,* or special action groups, were first organised by Himmler and Heydrich to follow the German armies into Poland in 1939. Their object was to round up Jews and force them into ghettos. Nearly two years later, at the beginning of the Russian campaign, they were ordered to follow the combat troops in order to round up Jews and partisans for extermination.[15]

The German officers and troops were issued with ideological

guidelines. In September 1941 Field Marshal Kietel paraphrased earlier directives:

> The struggle against Bolchevism demands ruthless and energetic measures, above all against the Jews, the main carrier of Bolchevism.[16]

A German documentary film shown at Eichmann's trial in Jerusalem in 1961 recorded the horror of the *Einsatzgruppen* murders. Eichmann had been appointed to coordinate Jewish 'evacuation' to the death camps, and became an expert on the 'Jewish Question' and Jewish statistics. As Gideon Hausner, the Prosecutor at the trial, writes in his book, *Justice in Jerusalem:*[17]

> Instead of more evidence I showed a film that lasted about an hour. It contained different scenes, photographed at different times. Some of the pictures were surreptitiously taken at the time of the occurrences by Germans who could not resist the temptation to perpetuate the scene; others were taken by the Allied armies, soon after liberation. There was much in this film to give concrete shape to the preceding eight weeks of evidence; people undressing before the open pits, piling up clothes marked with yellow badges, then standing naked at the brink of the pit, their faces showing incredulity and horror. A moment later there was shooting, and they were seen falling into their graves. The camera moved to the shooting squad, immediately behind the victims, and showed the second group of naked figures being pushed forward in their turn. These were the *Einsatzgruppen* murders.

It was following the invasion of the USSR in June 1941 that Hitler order the 'Final Solution' to be implemented. The Jews were to be murdered at the same time as the Soviet Union was to be crushed (Operation Barbarossa), leading the way to racial utopia and *Lebensraum*.

Deportations

Deportations of Jews from the occupied countries in Europe was the next stage. These are shown on Map 1. After technical and administrative questions had been solved, and with the *Einsatzgruppen* still engaged in their 'special tasks' in the East, the SS directed their energies to transporting European Jews to the death camps.

MAP 1

M. Gilbert, *The Holocaust, Maps and Photographs* (London: Board of Deputies of British Jews, 1978).

Extermination

Himmler carried the operational responsibility for the 'Final Solution'. It was Göring, Air Force Commander, who authorised the involvement of the state apparatus making it a state undertaking; and the coordination of state and party agencies was organised by Heydrich, Head of the Security Police.

On 31 July an order by Göring to Heydrich marked the turning point at which a policy of expulsion became one of annihilation:

> Complementing the task that was assigned to you on 24 January 1939, which dealt with carrying out emigration and evacuation, a solution of the Jewish problem as advantageous as possible, I hereby charge you with making all necessary preparation with regard to organisational and financial matters for bringing about a complete solution of the Jewish question in the German sphere of influence in Europe.
>
> Wherever other governmental agencies are involved, they are to cooperate with you.
>
> I request, furthermore, that you send me before long an over-all plan concerning the organisational, factual, and material measures necessary for the accomplishment of the desired solution of the Jewish question.[18]

This order led to the crucial and highly secret 'Final Solution' conference held in Wannsee, near Berlin, on 20 January 1942. The meeting was due to take place earlier, but was postponed because of the Japanese bombing of the American fleet in Pearl Harbour. The crucial Wannsee conference was chaired by Heydrich. He began with a detailed and sweeping review of Jewish 'emigration' and 'evacuation' with statistics provided by Eichmann who supervised 'Jewish Affairs and Evacuation Affairs'. Heydrich then made the following statement:

> In big labour gangs with separation of sexes, the Jews who are capable of work are brought to these areas (in the Eastern European occupied territories) and employed in road building, in which task, undoubtedly, a large part will fall out through natural diminution. The remnant that is able finally to survive all this, since this is, unquestionably, the part with the strongest resistance, must be given treatment accordingly, because these people, representing a natural selection, are to be regarded as the germ-

cell of a new Jewish development, should they be allowed to go free.[19]

The language is intentionally vague, as was typical of official Nazi bureaucratic communications, but it is unlikely that the nature of the 'special treatment' was misunderstood. In official language, unlike popular language in the Third Reich, words like 'liquidate' and 'exterminate' were not usually used. They were replaced by more bureaucratic terms like 'Sonderbehandlung' ('special treatment'). In Auschwitz-Birkenau the initials SB indicated that the person after whose name they appeared had been sent to the gas chamber.[20]

Eichmann had received a more explicit order in April 1942 which he kept secret for seven months. Meanwhile, the fiction that the Jews were merely being deported for labour purposes was carefully maintained.[21] The Jews were told that they were to be 'resettled' in the East; and this became the current euphemism. 'Resettlement' began in March 1942 when Slovakian Jews were deported to Auschwitz and Jews from the Lublin ghetto to Belzec. Despite the secrecy there was little doubt about the destination of the convoys. The death camps were situated in remoter parts of occupied Polish territory: in Auschwitz, Treblinka, Belzec, Sobibor, Chelmno and Majdanek. These are shown on the second map. It is thought that they were all sited in Poland because of the well-known antisemitism of large sections of the population, and because of the convenience of the railway network. Most of the concentration camps were already functioning as slave labour camps by 1941, and the inmates included Jews. Despite the abominable conditions, which were worse for Jews than for Slavic peoples, there was a chance of survival. It is these camps which are largely featured in films and in fiction.

In 1942, following the Wannsee Conference (and earlier in the case of Chelmno, which was set up as a testing ground), killing centres were built with the sole purpose of exterminating European Jews and, later, gypsies. Initially there were four killing centres: at Chelmno, Belzec, Sobibor and Treblinka. Special apparatus for gassing Jews were introduced into concentration camps in which Jews and others were also used as slave labour, at Majdanek and Auschwitz. In these camps there was no chance of survival, except for the pitiful 'work-Jews' in the *Sonderkommando,* the special unit

MAP 2

THE CONCENTRATION CAMPS
Between 1939 and 1945, six million unarmed and innocent Jewish civilians - men, women, children and babies - were murdered in Nazi-controlled Europe, as part of a deliberate policy to destroy all traces of Jewish life and culture. As many as two million of these were killed in their own towns and villages, some confined in ghettoes where death by slow starvation was a deliberate Nazi policy, others taken to be shot at mass-murder sites near where they lived. The remaining four million Jews were forced from their homes and taken by train to distant concentration camps, where they were murdered by being worked to death, starved to death, beaten to death, shot, or gassed.
North Sea
Baltic Sea
Vaivara
Klooga
ESTONIA
LATVIA
LITHUANIA
U S S R
Stutthof
Neuengamme
Ravensbrück
Chelmno
Treblinka
Bergen-Belsen
Sachsenhausen
POLAND
Sobibor
Mittelbau Dora
Gross Rosen
Maidanek
Auschwitz
Buchenwald
GERMANY
Belzec
Flossenberg
Plaszow
CZECHOSLOVAKIA
Natzweiler
Dachau
FRANCE
Mauthausen
AUSTRIA
HUNGARY
RUMANIA
Gospič
Jasenovac
YUGOSLAVIA
Sajmište
ITALY
Adriatic Sea
Among the hundreds of thousands of non-Jews sent by the Nazis to concentration camps were anti-Nazis, Jehovah's Witnesses, homosexuals, the mentally ill, and the chronically sick. In addition, more than 250,000 Gypsies were murdered, in a Nazi attempt to eliminate Gypsies as well as Jews from the map of Europe.
Auschwitz concentration camp in which more than 4 million people were murdered between 1941 and 1944, including Jews, Gypsies, and Soviet prisoners-of-war.
Camps set up solely for the murder of Jews.
Other camps in which Jews and non-Jews were put to forced labour, starved, tortured, and murdered in conditions of the worst imaginable cruelty. Most of these camps had "satellite" labour camps nearby.
In many of the camps shown here so-called "medical" experiments were carried out, without anaesthetics, solely to satisfy the curiosity and sadism of the doctors. Hundreds of otherwise healthy "patients" were tortured and murdered during these experiments.
0 100 miles
0 100 km
© Martin Gilbert 1978

M. Gilbert, *The Holocaust, Maps and Photographs* (London: Board of Deputies of British Jews, 1978).

whose job it was to remove the dead from the gas chambers and to cremate them.

Reports of the death camps reached the West as early as May 1942, the month in which the gassing of Jews in Auschwitz-Birkenau began, though the exact location was not known. The existence of another massacre site was known, and the location was indicated as Upper Silesia, but the name Auschwitz-Birkenau was not given to the West until 1944, after 1½ million Jews had been murdered. By then it was thought too late to intervene. But this remains highly controversial.[22]

A large number of labour camps were also operating within easy reach of the extermination camps, as a cover for the implementation of the 'Final Solution'. Auschwitz, in particular, had become a concentration city, with a population of at least 15,000, guarded by more than 3,000 SS.[23] In November 1943, it was divided into three main camps: Auschwitz I, the old concentration camp; Auschwitz II-Birkenau, the killing centre which also contained a concentration camp; and Auschwitz III-Monowitz, the industrial camp. The camp divisions are important because neo-Nazi propagandists argue that Auschwitz was merely an industrial camp.

In five of the extermination camps, the gassing machinery in vans and gas chambers ran on carbon monoxide, that is, diesel fumes. The same method had been used in Russia and Serbia for killing women and children, and in the 'euthanasia programme'[24] between 1939 and 1941 when mental patients and the chronically ill were murdered. In Auschwitz, a special type of gassing operation was 'perfected'. The Auschwitz commandant, Rudolf Höss, introduced a fast working and lethal gas, hydrogen cyanide, or prussic acid, whose commerical name was Zyklon B. Used ostensibly for typhus control at Auschwitz, Zyklon B was a commercial pesticide supplied by the German Vermin Combatting Corporation (DEGESCH). Indeed, it was frequently referred to by the euphemism 'disinfectant'. It made mass killing extremely efficient and almost a batch-process. Here is an extract of a key testimony by Höss dated 5 April 1946:

> I commanded Auschwitz until 1st December, 1943, and estimate that at least 2,500,000 victims were executed and exterminated there by gassing and burning, and at least another half million succumbed to starvation and disease making a total dead of about

> 3,000,000. This figure represents about 70 per cent or 80 per cent of all persons sent to Auschwitz as prisoners, the remainder having been selected and used for slave labour in the concentration camp industries... The remainder of the total number of victims included about 100,000 German Jews, and great numbers of citizens, mostly Jewish, from Holland, France, Belgium, Poland, Hungary, Czechoslovakia, Greece, or other countries. We executed about 400,000 Hungarian Jews alone at Auschwitz in the summer of 1944.[25]

As Nazi propaganda had repeatedly stated that the Jews were parasites to be exterminated like vermin, the introduction of Zyklon B to murder Jews in Auschwitz was hardly surprising. This ambiguity of using 'disinfection' to mean killing is one which neo-Nazis are exploiting today to deny the reality of the gas chambers.

Sonderbehandlung (special treatment)

Victims arriving at Auschwitz seemed unsuspecting of their fate, and the Nazis sustained the deceit until the end. Those 'selected' for 'special treatment' were told by the SS that they were to have a bath and prepare to be 'disinfected'. They were led away to the preparation room, even given towels and soap, and told to undress. Women and children had their hair cut. They were then forced to enter the gas chambers. Anyone resisting was shot. SS guards wearing gas masks then dropped Zyklon gas in pellet form through the grills at the top which were hermetically sealed from the outside. The pellets liquified, and in half an hour it was all over. The special commandoes *(Sonderkommando)* first ventilated the chamber, then entered to search the bodies for any gold teeth or hidden jewellery. The bodies were then taken to the crematoria to be burned. The crematoria in Auschwitz catered for the disposal of some 2,000 bodies every 24 hours.[26]

Those not selected for 'special treatment' on arrival rarely survived more than a few months, weakened by hunger, beatings and disease. Subsequent 'partial selections' within the camp sent those living skeletons known as 'Musselmen' to the gas chambers. This term derived from 'Moslem' because they were seen to resemble stereotyped pictures of Arabs wrapped in a blanket. On other occasions, following illness, such as the typhus epidemic in the summer of 1942, all sick inmates were 'deloused',[27] another codeword for gassing. Since Zyklon B was also used for fumigation processes, the ambiguity was convenient. Auschwitz was also used for human guinea-pig experiments, including sterilisations. It was in Auschwitz that Josef Mengele carried out his experiments on twins with a view to doubling the 'Aryan' population. In a major BBC2 documentary, *'The Gathering'* screened in September 1982, survivors gathering in Yad Vashem, the Holocaust Institute in Jerusalem, gave accounts of the horrors they experienced.[28]

What happened at the 'selections' was recorded in a diary kept by Dr Hans Kremer, an SS captain. Here is an extract:

> **September 2nd** - Present for the first time at a special action at 3am. Compared to this, Dante's **Inferno** seems a comedy.
> **September 5th** - Present this afternoon at a special action from the women's camp... the worst I have ever seen. Thilo, the medical officer for the troops, was right when he told me this morning we are at **anus mudi.** In the evening at approximately eight o'clock present at a special action of Dutchmen. Men want to take part in these actions because of the special rations they get, consisting of a fifth of a litre of Schnaps, the five cigarettes, 100 grammes of sausage and bread.
> **September 6th-7th** - Today, Tuesday, excellent lunch, tomato soup, half a hen with potatoes and red cabbage, a marvellous vanilla ice... In the evening at eight o'clock outside for a special action.
> **September 9th** - Present in the evening at my fourth special action.[29]

The total death toll has been documented to within a few hundred thousand:

815,000 Jews from Central Europe
236,000 from Western Europe
229,000 from Scandinavia and the Baltic countries
402,000 from Southern and South-Eastern Europe
4,252,000 from Poland and the Soviet Union.[30]

Altogether, a figure close on six million out of a total of nine million Jews under Hitler's power, of whom about two million were killed by *Einsatzgruppen*. Six million was also the figure given by Eichmann at his trial in 1961. The historian and Holocaust scholar, Raul Hilberg, has recently advanced a slightly lower figure. But the statistics, however carefully researched, cannot be absolutely accurate.

There can be no doubt about the historical reality of the Holocaust and the 'Final Solution'. The documentary sources, including both official records and private papers, are very comprehensive. Nazi antisemitism was no secret.[31] The Nazis' early persecution — between 1933 and 1939 — was conducted openly, and was fully reported in German and foreign newspapers. There are also the published texts of Nazi laws and decrees, legal and business records, as well as books, magazines, leaflets and films disseminated by the Nazis.

A huge quantity of German documents provide proof that the 'Final Solution' was a goal of the Nazi war machine. Many records were seized before the Nazis were able to destroy them, which include lists of transports and exterminations. Such records were assembled by the Allies as evidence of German war crimes. In the trials of the major war criminals that followed before an International Military Tribunal Nuremberg, referred to as the IMT trials, no defence lawer ever claimed that a single document was false.

The Nuremberg evidence[32] was collected in 42 volumes known as the 'Blue Series', 8 volumes and supplements, consisting of documents not introduced as evidence. Following the Nuremberg trials, other less high-ranking Nazis were tried for crimes including murders by the *Einsatzgruppen* and for medical and economic crimes. A condensed record and selected documents were published in 15 volumes, known as the 'Green Series'. Further evidence on the numbers murdered has been compiled by comparing the number of postwar survivors with pre-war census lists. Comprehensive source lists are also available in the 16-volume *Encylopaedia Judaica*.

The victims also provided evidence in the form of documents, some of which were buried underground, and eye-witness reports. The archives, kept by the Warsaw historian Emanuel Ringelblum,[33] who aimed to record every aspect of Jewish life at the time of its destruction by the Nazis, are a major source. *The Diary of Anne Frank*, which describes a Jewish family hiding from the Nazis in Amsterdam, is perhaps the best-known young person's account. Other records were recovered from the grounds of the Auschwitz extermination camp after the war, including *Sonderkommando* eye-witness accounts buried under the crematoria.

Confirming evidence is also provided by testimonies of non-Jews who took part in the killing process, but took the risk of recording events in protest. The best-known example is Kurt Gerstein, an SS officer and a Christian, who witnessed the deaths of thousands in Belzec and Treblinka. He was made responsible for obtaining supplies of Zyklon B gas and for finding methods of 'improving' the techniques. He later risked his life trying to get the story out. He wanted to stop the genocide. But at the time he was largely disbelieved. At the end of the war Gerstein recorded his experiences in several languages.[34] He was then transferred to the Cherche-Midi prison in Paris where he was interrogated; shortly after, he committed suicide in unknown circumstances. Here are two extracts from Gerstein's testimony

> In January 1942, I was appointed head of the Department of Sanitation Techniques and at the same time to the parallel position for the same sector of the SS and Police Medical Office. In this capacity I took over the entire technical service of disinfection, including disinfection with highly toxic gases. On June 8, 1942, SS Sturmbannführer Günther [Eichmann's deputy] dressed in civilian clothes, walked into my office. He was unknown to me. He ordered me to obtain for him, for a top secret mission, 100 kilos of prussic acid and to take it to a place known only to the truck driver...
>
> I understood little of the nature of my mission. But I accepted.
>
> We were accompanied by SS Obersturmbannführer and M.D., Professor Pfannenstiel, Professor of Hygiene at the University of Marburg/Lahn.
>
> From my deliberately bizarre technical questions the people at the prussic acid plant could understand that the acid was going to be used to kill human beings. I did this in order to spread rumours among the population.[35]

The second extract is particularly revealing. It shows the concern of Hitler and Himmler, SS chief, to expedite the gassing arrangements and improve on the diesel-fume method. It also shows the attitude of a model Nazi, Globočnik, towards the Holocaust. Globočnik was Lieutenant General of Police, and in charge

MAP 3

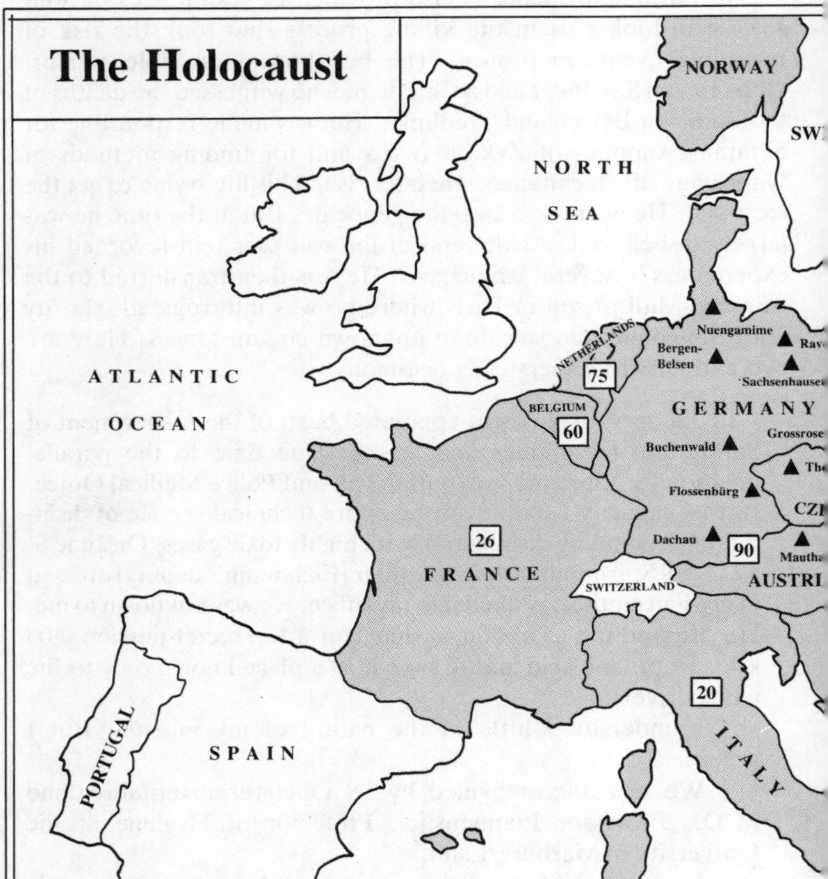

A. Ebban, *Heritage, Civilisation and the Jews* (London: Weidenfeld and Nicolson, 1985), 300-301.

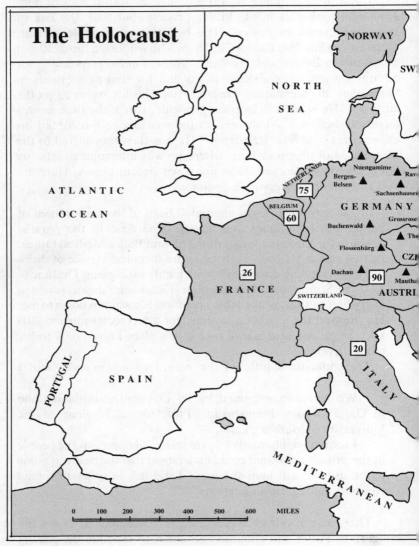

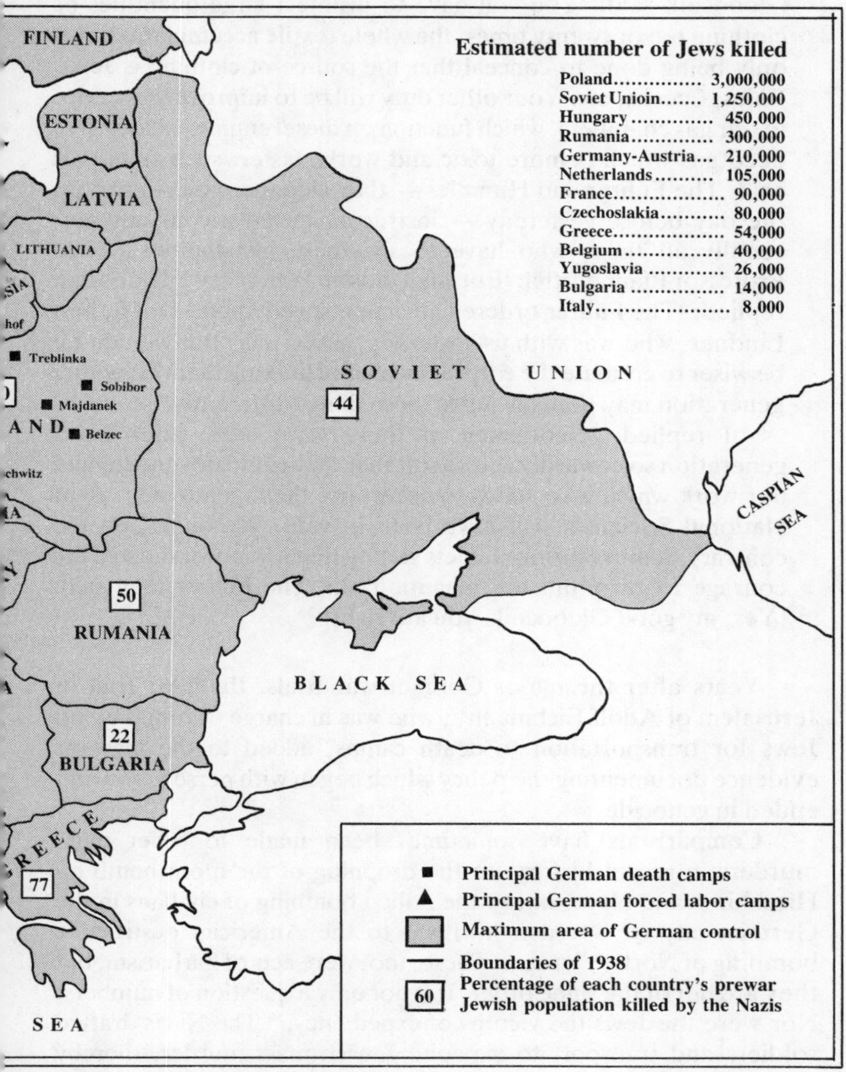
Estimated number of Jews killed
Poland.............. 3,000,000
Soviet Unioin....... 1,250,000
Hungary 450,000
Rumania............. 300,000
Germany-Austria... 210,000
Netherlands......... 105,000
France................ 90,000
Czechoslakia........ 80,000
Greece................. 54,000
Belgium............... 40,000
Yugoslavia 26,000
Bulgaria 14,000
Italy...................... 8,000
FINLAND
ESTONIA
LATVIA
LITHUANIA
Treblinka
Sobibor
Majdanek
Belzec
SOVIET UNION
44
CASPIAN SEA
50
RUMANIA
BLACK SEA
22
BULGARIA
GREECE
77
SEA
Principal German death camps
Principal German forced labor camps
Maximum area of German control
Boundaries of 1938
60
Percentage of each country's prewar Jewish population killed by the Nazis

of death camps in the Lublin area:

> Globočnik said: 'You will have to disinfect large quantities of clothing ten or twenty times, the whole textile accumulation. It is only being done to conceal that the source of clothing is Jews, Poles, Czechs, etc. Your other duty will be to improve the service in our gas chambers, which function on diesel engine exhaust. We need gas which is more toxic and works faster, such as prussic acid. The Führer and Himmler — they were here on August 15, the day before yesterday — instructed me to accompany personally all those who have to see these installations'. Then Professor Pfannenstiel: 'But what did the Führer say?' Globocnik replied: 'The Führer ordered all action speeded up.' Dr Herbert Lindner, who was with us yesterday, asked me: 'But wouldn't it be wiser to cremate the corpses instead of burying them? Another generation may perhaps judge these things differently!'
>
> I replied: 'Gentlemen, if there were ever, after us, a generation so cowardly and so soft that they could not understand our work which is so good, so necessary, then, gentlemen, all of National Socialism will have been in vain. We ought, on the contrary, to bury bronze tablets stating that it was we who had the courage to carry out this gigantic task!' The Führer then said: 'Yes, my good Globocnik, you are right!'[36]

Years after the major German war trials, the 1961 trial in Jerusalem of Adolf Eichmann[37], who was in charge of rounding up Jews for transportation to death camps, added to the mass of evidence documenting the policy which began with persecution and ended in genocide.

Comparisons have sometimes been made to other mass murders in recent history: to the dropping of the atom bomb on Hiroshima and Nagasaki; to the Allied bombing of civilians in the German city of Dresden in 1945; to the American destructive bombing of North Vietnam. These, too, were acts of barbarism, but they are not of the same order. It is not only a question of numbers. Nor were the Jews the victims of expediency.[38] The Nazis drafted soldiers and transport to expedite Jewish mass murder, thereby compromising the war effort. In this respect, any parallel with the bombing of North Vietnam, Japan, or Dresden, simply falls down. The Holocaust was a remorseless, systematic plan to annihilate an entire people. The National Socialist state set up the machinery to murder the Jews — not to hold off the Allied advance. The sole purpose was to murder this 'subhuman species' as part of the key social policy of 'racial improvement', or eugenics, supported by racial 'scientific' studies of the time. Few of us are able to comprehend the full implications of the Holocaust.[39] But we know that the world has been damaged.

3. The International neo-Nazi Network, the New Right and the Discourse of Inequality

In various parts of the world, a small but increasingly vocal minority is claiming that the mass extermination of Jews in Nazi Germany never took place; that the gas chambers never existed; that Anne Frank's diary is a fraud[1]; that the war atrocity photographs showing the heaps of bodies of camp inmates are also fakes. The Holocaust is presented as 'a gigantic hoax' and 'the myth of the century'.

Neo-Nazis are rewriting the history of the second world war. There is nothing remarkable or necessarily sinister about rewriting or revising history in itself. History is constantly being rewritten and repossessed by those excluded from power. Women's and lesbian history, gay history, labour history and records of 'third world' struggles provide poignant examples. But these are in no way comparable. The neo-Nazis are attempting to expunge history.

Why attempt to deny the Holocaust? Neo-Nazis today are trying to revive Nazi racist ideas. They are keenly aware that they must do something about their public image if they are to attract an important following. The Holocaust is the biggest obstacle in their way, so it must be explained away or denied altogether.

The attempt to rehabilitate Hitler and Nazi crimes is not new.

It began immediately after the war. At that time, however, the widespread rumours of Nazi extermination camps had just been confirmed to the world. There was not the remotest possibility of a neo-Nazi seed taking root again in the immediate postwar period. Now, some forty years on, the climate has changed. Racism is common currency, and institutional racism directed primarily against black people takes many forms. The neo-Nazis see the shift in their favour.

There is not one single version of the neo-Nazi myth denying the Holocaust and the gas chambers, but several, as we shall see. They all purport to show that Jews are liars and tricksters holding the world to ransom and continuing to extract war reparations. This is a continuation and an extension of the anti-Jewish prejudices and practices. The implication is that after all this time Jews are still liars, parasites, extraordinary powerful, and fundamentally dishonest — and that maybe Hitler was right. This is the central contradiction that lies at the heart of neo-Nazi strategy. The Holocaust denial propaganda may be seen at one level as an invitation to approve, or otherwise re-enact, the 'Final Solution' — which they deny ever took place. The idea of genocide is always present in Nazi radical antisemitism. The continuity is confirmed in the existence of the Holocaust denial literature.

It is my contention that the literature of the Holocaust denial, although produced more than fifty years later, is altogether reminiscent of the czarist forgery, *The Protocols of the Learned Elders of Zion*. This was 'proof' of a plot in which Jews conspired to take over the world. Both the **Protocols** and the Holocaust denial are part of a myth of, or false belief in, a Jewish world-conspiracy. The historical importance of this myth, which has survived many centuries in different disguises, lies in the fact that it has served as a warrant for massacre.

Radical exterminatory antisemitism can exist regardless of the real situation of Jews in society and of their number. It clearly thrives when influential Jews are in the news, and when the stereotype of the rich and powerful Jew seems confirmed, but does not automaticaly disappear where Jews are poor and powerless, as was certainly the case in many parts of eastern Europe[2] before the war.

Its specific anti-Jewish arguments will be varied to fit any perceived social problem. Dawidowicz has characterised this chameleon-like versatility of antisemitism very clearly:

> In the course of their history, Jews have been persecuted for believing in Judaism and excoriated for disbelieving; despised when poor and loathed when rich; shamed for their ignorance of the host culture and rebuffed for mastering it; denounced as capitalists and assailed as communists, derided for their separatism and reviled for their assimilationism. Whatever the Jews are to do at any particular time in history — the very nature of their existence — feed the animus of the Jew-hater and consequently serves as the 'explanation' for hating the Jews.[3]

This still holds today.

The Protocols

The influence of the *Protocols*[4] in promoting radical antisemitism was immense, and it undoubtedly influenced the course of history. Millions of copies circulated throughout the world in the 1920s and 1930s, and it remains a central reference in subsequent antisemitic propaganda.

The *Protocols* ostensibly consists of notes taken by a member of the secret Jewish government — the Elders of Zion — revealing a plot to achieve world domination. Their were a number of different versions of the forgery. The first appeared in western Europe in 1920, and was circulated among influential circles by Russian intelligence agents. One particular variant, *The Jewish Peril,* appeared in 1920. This bore the imprint of Eyre and Spottiswoode, which was in itself a triumph as they were also the publishers of the authorised version of the Bible and the Prayer Book. They were also the royal printers so that the *Protocols* were seen to have the authority of His Majesty's government.

Assisted by a long article in *The Times* on 8 May 1920, followed by *The Spectator,* a whole network of publicisers came into existence. Journals all over the world collaborated in expounding the different versions of the 'documents'. To the different German, English and French versions were added translations into Swedish, Danish, Norwegian, Finnish, Roumanian, Hungarian, Lithuanian, Polish, Bulgarian, Italian, Greek, Japanese and Chinese.

The *Protocols* soon appeared in full in the States. The newspaper owned by the automobile millionaire, Henry Ford, *The*

Dearborn Independent, published a long series of articles from May to October 1920. These were then put together as a book entitled *The International Jew: the world's foremost problem.* With the prestige of Ford's name and backed by a publicity campaign, it had a considerable impact, and half a million copies went into circulation. *The International Jew* made the *Protocols* world-famous, and was eventually translated into sixteen languages.

In Germany its influence was enormous. Hitler's thinking was permeated by the *Protocols.* It became the vehicle of Hitler's ideology and that of his most fanatical followers in the Antisemitic International, including Alfred Rosenberg, the official ideologist of the Nazi party and author of *The Myth of the Twentieth Century.*[5] The *Protocols* prepared the way for the extermination of European Jews. Hitler and the Nazi party also claimed that both communism and capitalism were Jewish, despite the obvious contradiction. The Nazi explanation for all catastrophes, including massive German inflation and the slump, was the Jewish plan to subjugate the world. The neo-Nazi Holocaust denial literature has given the *Protocols* a new lease of life.

The international neo-Nazi network

Contemporary Nazis claim to be 'revisionists' engaged in 'revising' history. These self-definitions have a neutral, academic ring. However, the term 'revisionist' is misleading and completely disingenuous. It generally refers to critical positions at variance with mainstream history which introduce new documentary sources. But these neo-Nazi fabrications bear no relation to historical data. To use their language would reproduce and lend credibility to their distortions.

The Holocaust denial is a well coordinated strategy crucial to a Nazi revival. The international networks advertise each other's publications, contribute and translate articles for fascist journals, attend fascist gatherings, attempt to penetrate other organisations and forums to gain a platform for their ideas, and are represented in international front organisations like the World Anti-Communist League (WACL). In 1979 a new front organisation was set up in the States disguised as an academic forum. It was called the Institute for Historical Review (IHR), and its specific function was to deny the Holocaust.

In the sections that follow, I shall indicate the importance of certain racist and fascist organisations, particularly in France, West Germany and Britain, and subsequently America, drawing attention to key figures and publications, and also to organisational and verbal strategies. Links between these organisations may appear somewhat tenuous. They may frequently be traced in terms of contributions of individuals, using one pseudonym or another, to particular journals. Some of these more academic-sounding journals also contain contributions from arch-conservatives with whom they share an authoritarian and racist world view. The co-authoring and prefacing of articles and pamphlets which deny or question the reality of the Holocaust, or of Hitler's role or that of the Nazi party, and contributions which question the veracity of the post-war Nuremberg trials — all contribute to antisemitism and the cooption of antisemitic stereotypes. Also relevant here are the enthusiastic reviews of such rightist literature written by intellectual fascists. The British reader may balk at the phrase 'intellectual fascists', but in France and Germany intellectual fascism has a long tradition. Although not limited to these countries, the different role and more enhanced status of intellectuals in continental Europe have given them a certain credibility. These ethnographic differences are important in understanding this phenomenon. The roots of academic racism, particularly in social psychology[6] and anthropology[7], go back to the nineteenth century, and the academic references and style are still used to make racist doctrines and policies seem respectable.

The WACL links

The World Anti-Communist League (WACL) set up in 1967 provides a key international network. At its first conference in Washington in 1978 when it received major publicity, the *Washington Post*[8] drew attention to the presence of delegations from a group of American Nazis, the National Alliance, the neo-Nazi Liberty Lobby[9], the Crown Commonwealth League of Rights, and the MSI[10], Italy's neo-fascist party. WACL has close connections with violent and fascist groups throughout the world. In the past WACL has received important subsidies from the governments of Taiwan, South Korea and Saudi Arabia.[11] Saudi Arabia has a clear connection with the neo-Nazis in that it financed a particular version of the Holocaust denial in the States.

One of the founding units of WACL is the influential Anti-

Bolchevik Bloc of Nations (ABN), a coalition of right-wing emigre organisations many of which have been publicly associated with collaboration and even war crimes during the Nazi occupation of the Soviet Union. There is evidence that these kind of fascist associations, together with direct links with anti-communist death squads in central America, are proving an increasing embarrassment to WACL. They are reported to have been at the centre of a row at the White House during discussions as to whether or not President Reagan should have sent greetings to WACL's tenth annual conference in Dallas in September 1985. The text of his greetings letter praised 'El Salvador's democracy' while the Sandinistas 'are compelled to resort to the methods of the police state'; it commends WACL for their part in promoting the 'noble cause' towards world freedom and the 'crusade for liberty'.[12] A recent WACL meeting was held in London in November 1985[13] organised by the ABN.

The Northern League

A key figure in WACL, former President of the American chapter, with unmistakable neo-Nazi connections in Western Europe is Roger Pearson. Pearson has combined extremist politics with an academic career in physical anthropology in the States. He exemplifies these complex international connections and strategies.[14] Most significantly, perhaps, Pearson was a founder of the Northern League set up in 1958. The Nazi 'race scientist', Hans Günther, was also a founding member. Its aim is to 'foster the interests, friendship and solidarity among all Teutonic nations'. There are indications that the Northern League is considered far out even by fascist groups. In his book on the National Front, Walker[15] noted the acrimony provoked within the party on the only occasion when its magazine, *Spearhead,* advertised the *Northlander,* the journal of the Northern League. This is a cycostyled magazine produced in English in Amsterdam. It has been suggested that almost all European Nazi groups have some connection with the Northern League.[16] There are also American connections.

Roger Pearson is remarkably active.[17] He is a member of the board of patrons of *Nouvelle Ecole,* one of the principal journals of the French New Right, director of the racist academic journal, *Mankind Quarterly*, since 1979, a member of the Council on

American Affairs, a branch of the better known Coalition of Peace through Security (CPS), and a member of the editorial committee of the *Journal of Indo-European Studies,* and editor of the *Northern World.* He is also a member of the American Foreign Policy Institute in Washington where, as a former member of the editorial board, he has been successful in penetrating the arch-conservative *Policy Review* of the American New Right. Although Pearson was removed from his chairmanship of the American chapter of WACL in 1981 because of his 'racist activities', in view of his other multifarious activities and contacts there is no doubt that he is an influential figure among neo-Nazis and arch-Conservatives.

The British representative of WACL is the British League of Rights, associated with Don Martin,[18] who publishes the journal *On Target*, giving WACL news. Martin also represents the Australian League of Rights founded by Eric Butler who published a version of the *Protocols*, the *International Jew*, in 1946.[19] The General Secretary of British WACL is the dowager Lady Birdwood who makes no secret of her racist opinions. She has marched on National Front demonstrations and has spoken from National Front platforms. The British League of Rights is also part of the new ultra-right anti-immigration group, WISE (Wales, Ireland, Scotland, England), which brings together racists in and around the Conservative Party with key figures of the racist, fascist right. The French section of WACL is the Association for the Defence of Culture, a satellite organisation of the French New Right. WACL's acredited German section is the German Society of Press Freedom (GFP) which has played host to the British historian, David Irving.[20]

The French New Right (GRECE)

The French New Right was officially set up in January 1969. Its real name is GRECE, *Groupement de recherche et d'étude pour une civilisation européenne* (Research and study group for a European civilisation). In the summer of 1979 it was the focus of sustained media attention ('the summer of the New Right'), and for the public the name stuck.

GRECE consists of a regrouping of ultra-right activists of the 1950s and 1960s many of whom cut their first political teeth in right-wing student activism and journalism in support of the OAS *(Organisation de l'Armée Secrète* — Organisation of the Secret

Army) in opposition to Algerian independence. They came primarily from the *Fédération des Etudiants Nationalistes* (Federation of Nationalist Students) and contributed to the racist and fascist journal, *Europe Action*. More recently they have been joined by younger activists. GRECE is primarily associated with philosopher-journalist Alain de Benoist. In the 1975-76 *Who's Who,* Benoist's entry refers to his membership of the Northern League, of the Institute of Sciences of Quebec and of Mensa. As Taguieff has pointed out,[21] the full name of the Canadian Institute is, in fact, the Institute of Psychometric, Biological and Racial Sciences. Its director, Dr. J. Bauge-Prévost, is the author of such pseudo-scientific works as *Celtism — Biological Ethics of the White Man* (1973).

GRECE's two main publications are *Nouvelle Ecole* and *Eléments*. *Eléments* was originally an internal bulletin and is the more accessible of the two. Both are now very lavish and beautifully illustrated glossy magazines. It has been pointed out that *Nouvelle Ecole* in every respect, including its interest in traditional German woodcuts, closely resembles a Nazi cultural magazine, *Germanerbe*.[22]

GRECE claims not to be concerned with activism, but with 'cultural struggle' and with metapolitics. To the dismay and discomfiture of the Marxist left, GRECE has adopted a form of 'right-wing gramscism.'[23] In particular, Gramsci's concept of cultural power and hegemony are a central reference.[24] Applying these insights, GRECE seeks to define the dominant ideas, and, subsequently, to identify those ideas which are to take their place.

Through its various publications, its satellite organisations and its practice of entryism,[25] GRECE plays a key role in promoting academic or 'scientific' racism and an interest in eugenics.[26] The importance of 'scientific' arguments as a basis for GRECE's academic racism cannot be underestimated. As M. de Guibert has noted, one of the early issues of *Europe-Action* pointed out that national socialism was destroyed because of its errors. 'Its racism was romantic, not scientific.'[27] This is a crucial reference.

Researchers have distinguished two distinct periods in GRECE's doctrinal development. The first period, 1962-1972 (which takes into account the articles published in *Europe Action* that prefigured GRECE) is characterised by biological racism. The discourse is predominantly anti-egalitarian. It is also anti-liberal and anti-Judaeo-Christian,[28] as this heritage is seen as responsible for egalitarian ideas. The second period, 1972-1982, is characterised by a 'differential racism'[29] stressing difference and the necessity of separateness for survival. The discourse is concerned with purity guaranteed by the non-mixing of cultures. It is a version of apartheid. At the same time, in this second period the public discourse of GRECE is concerned explicitly with promoting the values of the 'conservative revolution'[30] and the idea of an organic community. This is accompanied by a glorification of anything 'Indo-European'.

GRECE has ceased to be openly racist or antisemitic, though it still espouses a doctrine of race. This was not an ideological shift or reappraisal: it was merely a strategic redirection. The recommendation was put forward in their internal bulletin in February 1969. In future, they were to be more careful about the use of language, and, in particular, they should avoid 'outdated phraseology'.[31] Certain changes were effected of which the most characteristic is the substitution of 'Indo-European' for 'white' or 'Teutonic'; as found in earlier publications of GRECE, and in *Europe Action*. But the respectability they court is a poorly kept secret. Jean Mabire, former editor-in-chief of *Europe Action*, now a member of both GRECE's committee of patronage, and of the editorial committee of *Eléments*, tells it like it is: "Indo-European" really means "Aryan" for its former membership'.[32] Mabire is the GRECE specialist in Nordic myth. In a chapter of a book concerned with 'our origins', quoted by Taguieff, Michael Poniatowski, former Giscardian Minister of the Interior, actually refers to Indo-Europeans as 'the origin of white western society' and as 'the white race'.[33] The publication was enthusiastically reviewed by GRECE.

As is customary in academic journals, long articles in *Nouvelle Ecole* are accompanied by bibliographies. One way of dealing with the unmistakable Nazi influence is to include a reference to Günther in the bibliography as recommended reading. One particular issue of *Nouvelle Ecole* is even more overt. It includes a one-page laudatory obituary for Günther together with a detailed German bibliography, while indicating English and French translations. It reads very much like any *Times* obituary for an established academic.

> Born in 1891 Professor Günther is one of the most celebrated pre-war anthropological race-scientists. He made an important

contribution to one of the racial classification systems most currently used today. Through his numerous articles, monographs and essays, he made a seminal contribution to diverse fields of study, particularly physical anthropology, racial biology, racial psychology, European prehistory and archaeology, eugenics, cultural anthropology, the study of social customs, the cycles of civilisation, etc.[34]

Academic racist journals

Nouvelle Ecole is one of the main academic racist journals, along with the British *Mankind Quarterly* and its German counterpart, *Neue Anthropologie.* They maintain close connections. They draw on the same contributors, abstract and enthusiastically review one another's articles, and occasionally provide translations. Some of the older contributors for these journals either published directly in the official Nazi *Zeitschrift für Rassenkunde* (Magazine for race-science) edited by Günther (or contributed to later publications with which Günther's collaborators are associated), or have openly acknowledged the influence of German 'race-science' in their work.[35] Such works are usually presented in a totally neutral way along with other bibliographical references.

In addition to Pearson, the work of Konrad Lorenz is used in this way,[36] and, until his retirement Gayre,[37] a number of official patrons of *Nouvelle Ecole* and of two other magazines are members of the Northern League and have clear Nazi credentials. They include Jürgen Rieger,[38] editor of *Neue Anthropologie* (whose work on the 'Teutonic race' draws on *Mankind Quarterly* and is reproduced in the ultra-right *Nation Europa)* and Rolf Kosiek, leading member of the neo-Nazi NPD *(Nationaldemokratische Partie Deutschlands* — German National Democratic Party). Rieger, Kosiek and Benoist, amongst others, make frequent references to the psychological research in IQ citing the work of Hans Eysenck in Britain and Arthur Jensen in the States. Eysenck is Professor of Psychology at the Institute of Psychiatry in London while Jensen is Professor of Educational Psychology at the University of California. Jensen in particular offered a genetic explanation for 'racial differences' in IQ scores and hence contributed a genetic explanation to the nature/nurture debate,[39] that is, the importance of genetic endowment (heredity) versus social influences. But there are serious flaws in their argument and data.[40] Yet, along with

Lorenz, they continue to be quoted as legitimate scientific sources that justify racism. There is no suggestion, however, that either has expressed support for any far-right organisation. Jensen and Eysenck are also frequently cited in other extremist publications including those of the British National Party. Jensen is a member of the editorial board of *Neue Anthropologie* and a frequent contributor. Eysenck was originally a patron of *Nouvelle Ecole;* he has also been interviewed in *Neue Anthropologie* and in the British fascist journal, *Beacon.*[41] Eysenck's book, *On the Inequality of Man,* has been published in a French translation by *Copernic,* GRECE's publishing house.

The French New Right's entryism

While professing to be concerned only with cultural and ideological struggles, GRECE is remarkably well connected with leading figures among the Gaullists. This was made possible largely through an important figure on the New Right, Yvan Blot, who was formerly active in GRECE using the pseudonym Michel Norey. Blot is president of the elitist *Club de l'Horloge*[42] (Clock Club) founded in 1974 by young men in the prestigious ENA *(Ecole Nationale d'Administration),* a postgraduate Civil Service college. Whatever other membership he may currently hold, and this is uncertain, Blot is a member of the Gaullist party and held a post in the cabinets of both Poniatowski and Bonnet, former Ministers of the Interior. The *Club de l'Horloge* has attempted to coordinate French right-wing forces following Mitterrand's victory in May 1981. More recently, another forum has come into being around the Club 89 close to Jacques Chirac in which J-Y Le Gallou, General Secretary of the Club de l'Horloge, is also active. Le Gallou was a former member of the Republican Party. According to the *Le Monde* journalists, Plenel and Rollat, he is also associated with the CAR *(Comités d'action républicaine*-Republican Action Committees) formed in September 1981 and the *Association des élus pour la liberté de la culture* (Association of elected members for the freedom of culture) set up in July 1983.[43] These groups galvanised right-wing opposition forces in France in the run up to the March 1986 legislative elections.

Another coup for GRECE was the invitation extended in 1977-78 to a number of individual members and collaborators of GRECE to join the *Figaro Magazine, Le Figaro's* new weekly colour supplement with a national circulation of over 483,000. *Le Figaro* is a right-wing establishment newspaper on a par with the *Daily Telegraph*, and is owned by press magnate, Robert Hersant. It is claimed that he was a former Vichy collaborator.[46] He is now a Euro-MP. The first issue of *Figaro-Magazine* lists the names of twelve GRECE members and associates including Alain de Benoist and Yves Christen, a journalist specialising in eugenics. The chief editor is Jean-Claude Valla, one of the founding members of GRECE, co-director of *Eléments* and one of the founders of *Copernic* (Copernicus), GRECE's apparently thriving publishing house set up in 1976. In the early 1980s some members, including Valla, left to join the new right-wing *Magazine Hebdo* which has since ceased publication. The invitation to GRECE was extended by Louis Pauwels,[45] director of the cultural section of both *Figaro* and *Figaro Magazine* and a GRECE member. Pauwels has a weekly cultural column in *Figaro-Magazine* which regularly attacks egalitarianism.[46] The discourse of *Figaro-Magazine* reproduces and extends that of GRECE in a more popular cultural form making it available to a large section of the population.

Since GRECE sought respectability and claimed to be neither of the right nor the left, the journalist and philospher, Alain de Benoist, has been awarded a literary prize in 1978 by the arch-conservative French Academy for his book *Vu de droite.*[47] Clearly, this new respectable status puts an obligation on GRECE, including Benoist, to go to great lengths to disclaim any association with their French activist counterparts. At an earlier point, Benoist, using the pseudonym Fabrice Laroche (which he has never contested), collaborated with Pierre Hoffstetter, Hugo Marbach and Harold Seehase, to publish an article in *Europe Action* entitled 'Qui a déclenché la guerre?' ('Who triggered off the war?')[48] Hofstetter has also written for the PFN journal, *Initiative Nationale,* which clearly points to a link with the fascist Euro-right. He is now associated with the Institute for Historical Review (IHR) and wrote the American introduction to Rassinier's *Debunking the Genocide Myth.*[49] This article by Benoist and fellow journalists, written as early as 1964, contains some of the references to be found fourteen years later in the IHR *Journal.*

The article does not deny the Holocaust. In fact, it is not mentioned at all, even in the familiar argument on the right seeking to equate Nazi and Allied war crimes. (The Allied bombing of

Dresden and other cities are cited). However, on a more general and pseudo-academic level, the ground is prepared by questioning the historical interpretations of world war II and Germany's responsibility. It is suggested that other accounts which challenge 'official' historians have been silenced, as illustrated by the imprisonment of the French literary fascist, Maurice Bardèche, following his publication of *Nuremberg or the Promised Land.* References are made to Harry E. Barnes, since proclaimed the father of revisionism by the IHR, and to the work of David Leslie Hoggan. Hoggan has developed a thesis 'common to the entire revisionist school' which claims that 'National-Socialist Germany' was not bent on war. References are made to international opposition to the war, including that of Robert Brasillach, fascist literary figure and collaborator. It is suggested that it was the 'insidious actions of Central European emigres' which led to the 'drama of 1939 and its consequences'. One possible reading of the extraordinary statement is that 'Jews were responsible for the war': the cynical Nazi claim. 'Revisionism' is confronted with the official 'historical' propaganda machine. It has, therefore, a long way to go before it can re-establish 'the facts' and confront 'the myths'. A recommended reading list includes a book by Udo Walendy, a later contributor to the IHR, *Wahrheit für Deutschland (1964)*. The detached, academic style of writing and the mode of argument and certain key references, including Barnes, foreshadow the IHR Journal.[50] It is an illuminating find.

Links between the French and German New Right

Further connections and insights into neo-fascist thinking may be found in an article by Pierre Krebs published in 1981 in *Deutschland in Geschichte und Gegenwart* (Germany Past and Present). Krebs is thought to be a pseudonym. This article is virtually a paraphrase of an interview with Benoist 'Contre tous les racismes' ('Against all racisms') which appeared in *Eléments* in 1974.[51] Krebs condemns 'egalitarian humanism', which he claims leads to genocide and totalitarianism. This is a rephrasing of the Nazi racist phantasy, also present in the writings of philosophers associated with the 'conservative revolution' to which Benoist subscribes, according to which a multiracial society is the cause of decay and moral degeneration.

The strategy of the French and German New Right is to pretend to favour a liberal, even anti-racist stance, as Benoist's title clearly suggests. However, the underlying argument is that cultures need to develop separately to survive. As Barker and others have shown, this is also present with variations in the British New Right in a cultural guise.[52] It is the same discourse of inequality and purity based on racial or cultural separation.

We are invited to believe that egalitarian humanism implies the potential genocide of all races and ethnic groups, as the mixing of races denies individual cultures their right to be different and destroys their identity.[53] Similarly, *Panmixie* (mixing of races) leads to totalitarianism, diluting and reducing different ethnic groups to one identical model[54] *Panmixie* is a striking and scientific-sounding neologism. Significantly, it is also found in *La Politique du Vivant* published in 1979 by the elitist *Club de l'Horloge,* close to but independent from GRECE since 1978. If this is not clear enough, Krebs goes on to attack 'egalitarian humanism', preferring a vertical, hierarchical system — in short, fascism:[55]

In Benoist and Krebs the more obvious ideological links, such as references to the *Protocols,* are not present. GRECE now wishes to be more acceptable. One way in which GRECE and their associates have succeeded in gaining acceptability is by using more abstract, more 'scientific' language to lend authority to their racist doctrine. It is clear, nevertheless, despite their sophistication, that both Benoist and Krebs are concerned with racial separation and 'natural' hierarchies predicated on 'race'.

This article by Krebs is part of the Thüle Seminar[56], a 'Society for the Investigation and Study of European Civilisation' founded by Krebs in 1980. The society is concerned with '*völkisch* pluralism', a reference to the mystic, biological community of people and race, and rejects the 'totalitarian doctrine of equality'. The first publication of the Thüle Seminar (1981) is *Das unvergangliche Erbe: Alternativen zum Prinzip der Gleichheit (improbalbe Heritage: Alternatives to the Principle of Equality)*. It is a collection of essays edited by Krebs with an introduction by Eysenck and advertised by Grabert-Verlag.

The German New Right[57] does not present an organisational whole. There appear to be four groupings:

— the **neo-conservatives** who publish *Criticón* Armin Mohler and Hennig Eichberg, former German correspondent for *Nouvelle*

Ecole, are seen as the most important collaborators);
— the **biologists** centred around the academic racist journal *Neue Anthropologie* (chief editor: Jürgen Rieger);
— the **revolutionary nationalists** which is composed of several different groups, each with their own publication (including *Junges Forum* which has regularly published GRECE articles);
— the **ecologists** (the Grüne Liste, Umweltschutz — Green List, Conservation) in Hamburg and Lower Saxony;
— the **Thüle seminar.**

The Thüle seminar plays a coordinating role for the French and German new Right. Apart from its chairman, Krebs, it is also frequented by Armin Mohler, Peter Binding, Rüdolf Kunast, Jürgen Rieger and Richard Eichler as well as by Alain de Benoist, toether with a GRECE nucleus comprised of Giorgio Locchi, Jacques de Mahieu and Guillaume Faye.

It is possible that the Thüle seminar conceived by GRECE and under its influence would play a focal ideological role in a new right-wing German coalition (CDU/CSU/FDP); and in this respect it is perhaps modelled on the *Club de l'Horloge* in France.[58]

A key figure on the German 'neo-conservative' right is Armin Mohler, a Swiss journalist. Former secretary of the author Ernst Jünger after the war, Mohler was the recipient of the Audenauer prize for his anti-communist writings. The similarity between the 'neo-conservative' Mohler and the neo-Nazi apologists is apparent in his criticism of the 1979 judgment of the Federal German Supreme Court which ruled that to deny the Holocaust showed contempt for all victims of the Nazi persecution. Mohler would also seem to be echoing criticism voiced in the extremist *Deutsche Wochen Zeitung* (9 November 1979) and of the *Deutsche National-Zeitung* of the same date when, writing in *Criticón*, he asked:

> How can the revisionist arguments be subjected to a critical but matter-of-fact examination if any odd eccentric can threaten recourse to the courts?[59]

Mohler is surely justified in challenging the right of a court of law to pass judgment on history.[60] But this consideration is tangential to his main argument. His contention that 'revisionist' arguments represent a respectable, academic interpretation of history is entirely consonant with the pseudo-objective, pseudo-academic stance favoured by Butz and Faurisson. It is exemplified as a whole in the *Journal of the Institute for Historical Review,* the magazine of the antisemitic propagandists.

One of the main publishers of the German and French New Right material in West Germany is the Grabert-Verlag publishing house in Tübingen which specialises in right-wing literature. Although Nazi-type propaganda material is in fact outlawed under Article 86 of the Penal Code[61], this has not prevented a resurgence of neo-Nazi literature, which is openly for sale on news stalls. Grabert-Verlag also publishes a quarterly *Deutschland in Geschichte und Gegenwart (Germany Past and Present).* The first 1981 issue is largely devoted to Holocaust denial literature. This number illustrates the links referred to earlier in terms of themes, preface-writing and reviews. Although at one level they are merely publishing links, they are nevertheless crucial in sustaining each other and the Holocaust denial campaign.

The issue referred to includes a lengthy review of Butz — the chief American exponent of the Holocaust denial myth — by Wilhelm Stäglich, author of a similar fabrication, *Der Auschwitz Mythos (The Auschwitz Myth)* published in 1979 by Grabert.

In fact, it is a reply to a critical review of Butz which allows Stäglich to reiterate Butz's fabrications. Stäglich has also prefaced a 1973 German edition of Thies Christophersen's *Die Auschwitz Lüge,* originally prefaced by the lawyer Manfred Roeder, director of the publishing house, Kritik-Verlag, with which Stäglich is also associated. Roeder, who in 1976 launched the *Deutsche Burgerinitiative* (German Citizens' Initiative) which upholds Nazi beliefs, was accused of bomb attack murders of foreign workers and received a prison sentence of 13 years.[62] The January 1984 issue of this same journal devoted a long article to Robert Faurisson written by Stäglich. Also featured was an article by Alain de Benoist on totalitarianism in which he argued that egalitarian movements are a source of tyranny. Grabert-Verlag has also published a German translation of Benoist's *Vu de droite* which was enthusiastically reviewed in the *Deutsche Wochen-Zeitung* (24 February 1984).[63] The same Stäglich wrote a glowing review of a book by the British historian David Irving about the Nuremberg Trials. Irving became the centre of a controversy by making the extraordinary claim in *Hitler's War* that Hitler knew nothing of the Holocaust.[64] The 'sensational thesis' made front-page headlines in the *Deutsche*

National-Zietung (27 October 1978). Irving offered a reward to anyone who would prove Hitler's responsibility for the Holocaust. The IHR was to make a similar gesture. The *Deutsche Wochen-Zeitung* booklist includes Irving's *Hitler's War* and *The War Path* together with IHR publications.[65]

In Britain, the Focus Policy Group a new potential right-wing force, is centred around David Irving. In addition to promoting the organisation WISE (Wales, Ireland, Scotland, England)[66], the Focus Policy Group is attempting to regroup ultra-right wing extra-parliamentary forces in Britain. In the early 1980s evidence seemed to suggest that Irving was attempting to build a party organisation 'similar in style to the New Right in the United States and Europe',[67] and was buying existing mailing lists of right-wing organisations.[68]

The platform projected in the Focus Policy Group documents is one of anti-communism and Christian conservatism where the issue of race figures prominently. The Focus bumper sticker has changed its slogan from 'Britain: Christian-United-Safe' to 'Britain belongs to us'. Irving's own position on immigration is one of 'benevolent' repatriation. The National Front has been referred to in Focus Policy documents as one of 'Britain's budding nationalistic or patriotic movements', the euphemistic language used by the fascists to describe their own party.

Irving was reported as admitting to the *Oxford Mail*[69] that he has 'links at a low level' with the National Front. The March 1982 issue of *Focal Point* refers to a meeting between Irving and Carto, of the neo-Nazi Liberty Lobby, in Washington DC in which Irving describes the Liberty Lobby paper, *Spotlight,* as 'an excellent fortnightly paper'. Correspondents of *Focal Point* have included a number of present and former National Front members including John Tyndall of the British National Party (former leader of the National Front) and Keith Thompson of the League of St George. *Focal Point* also contains advertisements for *Excalibur* (journal of the Nationalist Party, formerly the National Front Constitutional Movement, a shortlived NF splinter group), as well as for WISE and ABEX (Association of British Ex-Servicemen). ABEX is run by Kenneth McKilliam, a leading member of the British National Party (formerly of the National Front) who has chaired meetings of WISE. At one meeting he circulated an antisemitic pamphlet describing the Holocaust as 'the greatest lie ever told'.

Irving has spoken at a number of universities in Britain. According to the far-right journal, *Nation Europa,*[70] he has also made trips to West Germany to address ultra-right wing groups. In May 1978 he spoke at Kassel for the German Society for Press Freedom (GFP), the accredited German chapter of the World Anti-Communist League. The conference theme was 'Betrayal and Opposition in the Third Reich'. Irving's contribution was concerned with the legend of Rommel. As reported in *Searchlight* in March 1982, the GFP was founded in 1960 by former SS members of the Mutual Support Association of the Waffen SS. It has provided a bridge between veteran Nazis and the new German Right. In 1979, the GFP journal, *Freie Forum,* favourably reviewed three anti-Holocaust books, including Arthur Butz's *The Hoax of the Twentieth century*.

In January 1982, Irving addressed a meeting in Hamburg of the DVU, the German People's Union. Although it claims that the Holocaust never happened, it is not a proscribed organisation. According to the *Stuttgart-Zeitung* (12 December 1981), the 10,000 strong DVU aims to ensure, thirty-six years after the second world war, that Germany's bedrock of Nazi opinion remains solid. The Third Reich is glorified, the crimes of the Nazi regime are made out to be harmless, or claimed never to have been committed. The proprietor of the DVU's newspaper, *Nationale Zeitung,* which lists anti-Holocaust books on its booklist, is Gerhard Frey, DVU leader. It was the DVU's newspaper which printed the German serialisation of *The Hoax of the Twentieth Century* by Butz, the main American exponent of the Holocaust denial.[71]

The *Deutscher-Anzeiger,* which supports the DVU, reported that Irving was to address a further ten DVU meetings throughout West Germany in March.[72] The DVU campaigns on three fronts: as *Aktion Deutsches Radio und Fernsehen* (an equivalent of the National Viewers' and Listeners' Association); as *Initiative Für Ausländeregrenzung* (Initiative to restrict foreign immigration), which campaigns against foreign workers in Germany, arguing that priority should be given to 'workers who assisted the German people and were persecuted for it during and after the war'; and, lastly, as *Aktion Deutsche Einheit* (AKON) which fights for German unification.[73] It was AKON together with the DVU that sponsored meetings in January 1982 in Hamburg and Düsseldorf to celebrate the 'Reich Foundation Day'. Gerhard Frey and David Irving were among the speakers. The subject of these DVU-sponsored meetings was a promotional tour of a book by Irving published in Germany in 1970 in a paperback edition, *Der Nürnberger Prozess (The Nuremberg Trials)*. The book claims that the Nuremberg Trials were victors' justice. There was DVU violence and a counter-demonstration in Nuremberg at the time of Irving's second DVU promotional tour in March 1982.[74] The enthusiastic review of Irving's book by Stäglich in the 1981 issue of *Deutschland in Geschichte und Gegenwart* already referred to together with his article on Faurisson provide tangible links between the German old and new Right, GRECE and Irving.

There are other ramifications of the same order. In the *Deutsche National Zeitung* (5 October 1984) Irving was cited as an authority by neo-Nazis in Germany in an attempt to rehabilitate Julius Streicher, the most notorious Jew-hater who was hanged at Nuremberg.[75] The paper cannot deny that Streicher's hate-mongering campaign in the Nazi organ, *Der Stürmer* (Stormtrooper), but suggests that the paper was 'neither a government nor a Party organ'. This is a falsification. In fact, it is listed as an official paper in the first edition of the Nazi Party's Yearbook (1927), and Streicher is actually mentioned in *Mein Kampf*.[76]

At the Sixth Annual International Revisionist Conference under the auspices of the Institute for Historical Review meeting in California in February 1985, Ingrid Weckert reproduced similar arguments. She sought to exculpate Streicher, *Der Stürmer* and the Nazi party from *Kristallnacht*, the extensive and well coordinated antisemitic pogrom of November 1938 in Germany and Austria.

The cumulative effect of these increasingly sophisticated and academic sounding discourses is to question and displace the postwar liberal and antifascist consensus. The aim is to provide an alternative authoritarian and racist framework to take its place.

There has been a marked shift to the right both in western Europe and the States. In a purely electoral perspective, this shift in public opinion is confirmed in the re-election of Ronald Reagan for a second presidential term. In western Europe it is exemplified by the return of the Thatcherite Conservative Party in Britain, the success of the Christian Democrat Coalition in West Germany; and, most recently, by the victory of the right-wing coalition in France in the March 1986 legislative elections, with the *Front National* accounting for 9.8% of the first PR ballot for the National Assembly.

This shift has resulted in the widespread circulation of authoritarian and racist views assisted by the media. There was of course a legal obligation, in the case of the *Front National*, to grant airtime to its leadership in the electoral period, but arguably much of the French press exceeded its brief with sensational headlines in the lead-up to the 1984 European elections ('Le Pen Super Star').

In countries like post-Franco Spain, even after the restoration of parliamentary democracy and the return of a Socialist majority, the Spanish public has become accustomed to the idea of fascist parties and a fascist voice as part of the parliamentary scene. With the introduction of proportional representation, this has now been extended to France. In Britain, it has been argued that the decline of the post 1975 racist and fascist vote can be accounted for by toughter anti-immigration and law and order policies introduced by the Thatcher government; and a certain two-way ideological traffic between the far-right and the Tory Party, as revealed in the secret report leaked by the Young Conservatives in 1983.

The Right in any country is not a monolith. There are ideological and doctrinal distinctions, tensions and alignments. Of more significance, perhaps, than voting patterns, the traditional measure of public opinion shifts, are the sets of meanings in circulation at any given time; and the institutions which give them legitimacy, while other meanings are ruled out of order, marginalised, and even criminalised. Hence in postwar Britain some forty years on, the British New Right, part of central government, can write that anti-racism is 'a pernicious doctrine'. This is discussed in chapter seven.

It is my contention that this shift to the right has regenerated a configuration of authoritarian meanings with very particular implications for national minorities ('ethnic' minorities) and gender roles; these impinge on a wide range of policies, including education and social policy. They constitute a discourse of inequality. Some of this discourse derives from a particular view of 'human nature' and human destiny based on spurious biological claims.[77] This was discussed in chapter three with reference to academic racism. As Guillaumin[78] has pointed out, biological determinism is offered as an explanation of women's oppression. Other oppressive models of human society are more complex still.

While different analysts may dispute the weight of social constructivism versus biological determinism in the work of certain exponents of the British and American New Right, and their even more obvious differences in economic policy, it is the shared discourse of inequality that is the main concern of this chapter.

This section examines the inegalitarian discourses of the American and British New (Conservative) Right in terms of their construction of gender, 'race' and class, the links between them, and the contribution of these discourses to the shaping of a new authoritarian morality. The British scene is further exemplified in chapter seven. This morality derives from a white, largely Christian and heterosexist vision of national identity. While the evangelist American Moral Majority is explicitly Christian, US neo-Conservatives also include a number of prominent Jews. This does not mean the absence of antisemitism within the Moral Majority, although this component tends to be ignored. I begin by offering a short descriptive note on the American New Right.

The American New Right

Since 1978 the American Conservative Caucus has succeeded in bringing together two main strands: a grouping of right-wing fundamental Christians (the religious right) and an economic and social conservative caucus (the neo-conservative right) with a certain tension between right-wing free market libertarians (represented by F.A. Hayek and Milton Friedman) and more traditional authoritarian conservatives (as exemplified by William F. Buckley of the *National Review)*. The key figures of the neo- conservatives include Samuel P. Huntingdon, Robert Nisbet, Norman Podhoretz, Midge Dector, James Q. Wilson, Nathan Glazier, Irving Kristol, and former UN Ambassador, Jeane Kirkpatrick. The neo-Conservatives' main organs are the Jewish magazine *Commentary*, edited by former liberal Podhoretz, and *The Public Interest*, edited by Kristol and Glazier. The neo-Conservatives, who lend intellectual legitimacy to Reagan's programme,[79] have built on the work of an earlier network of new right organisations set up in 1974-5 to promote conservative causes inside and outside Congress. These organisations include the Committee for the Survival of a Free Congress, the National Conservative Political Action Committee, and the Conservative Caucus. Their journal is the *Conservative Digest* published by Richard Viguerie who is at the centre of these networks inside and outside the Republican Party. Viguerie made his name by raising six million dollars for George Wallace's 1972 presidential campaign. The *Conservative Digest* is open to the ultra-Conservative John Birch society, which propagates its own particular version of the conspiracy theory, and to other ultra-conservative groups. The New Right also has a number of think tanks of which perhaps the most important in terms of promoting links is the Heritage Foundation founded by Peter Weyrich in 1974 with its quarterly journal, *Policy Review*.

A conservative majority is to be achieved in the States by forging an alliance between the business people, labour unions and the rural south, against the 'liberal establishment' and the unemployed which in the American context, clearly refers to blacks and Hispanics. Economic conservatism (anti-taxation and anti-union positions) is matched by social conservatism predominant in the South. This implies a rejection of affirmative action programmes as spearheaded by Podhoretz, together with anti-feminist and anti-welfare platforms. The policy of 'benign neglect' towards ghettos proposed by the neo-conservative Patrick Moynihan to the Nixon administration is very indicative. William Rusher, a prominent member of the Conservative Caucus active in the Goldwater campaign of the 1960s, publisher of the conservative *National Review,* and author of *The Making of the New Majority Party,*[80] put it like this: 'We might as well make up our minds that we are going to have to live, for some time to come, with many glaring inequalities'.

Despite the diversity of organisations and pressure groups, they tend to overlap in their focus on single campaigns; and the authoritarianism of the New Right most clearly manifests itself in 'moral' and 'pro-family' issues.[81]

Although the American New Right campaigns against taxation, welfare and organised unions, its most vociferous stand is against women's automy.[82] This is a constant feature of the Right. In radical feminist theory it is the defining characteristic of right-wing discourse.[83] This antifeminism is not only a backlash against women's and gay liberation movements: it is also 'a reassertion of patriarchal forms of family structure and male dominance'.[84]

The election programme of the New Right included a specific commitment to oppose abortion and the Equal Rights Amendment Act (ERA) which would guarantee equal rights for women in the American constitution. It is this fanatical anti-feminist platform which gives the best indication of its profoundly and thoroughly repressive conservatism. At the peak of the struggle for ERA, the most widely read newspapers and magazines in the States gave prominence to the view of academic biologists like Edmund O. Wilson of Harvard who assured his readers that 'even in the most free and most egalitarian of future societies men are likely to continue to play a disproportionate role in political life, business and science'.[85] Wilson is also highly regarded by the French New Right. It was perhaps Norman Podhoretz, editor of *Commentary*, who stated the biological-determinist position most plainly:

> the plague... (contemptuous repudiation of middle class values among young whites) rages fiercely... among the kind of women who do not wish to be women and among those men who do not wish to be men... **there can be no more radical refusal of self-acceptance than the repudiation of one's biological nature;** and there can be no abdication of responsibility more fundamental than the refusal of a man to become, and to be, a father, or the refusal of a woman to become, and be, a mother.[86]

This discourse is consonant with nationalist,[87] demographic[88] discourse where women as a class are encouraged to be breeders in order to fulfil their 'natural role',[89] as defined by their reproductive organs. Within this scheme, class and 'race' exclusions are operated according to the male-defined political project. The New Right's social policies are the direct outcome of a biological discourse. As Miriam David has shown,[91] increasingly these celebrate motherhood as a crucial social activity for all women. Women's 'freedom to choose' is closely circumscribed by the joint operation of social and economic policies, which also impose moral obligations of care.[92] Where anti-feminist, racist and anti-working class policies come together is the assault on welfare. The effect of the New Right's policies is to attempt to bring single parent female-headed black families regarded as deviant in line with male-headed white families, seen as the norm, in order to qualify.

In a cogently argued essay, David Edgar,[93] while not questioning the centrality of the 'pro-family' campaigns, suggests that analyses of the American New Right have underestimated 'the crucial importance of race as *a defining* issue both for the New Right and for Neo-Conservatism', and that 'the lack of direct emphasis on race is deceptive'. Among the most obvious euphemisms for 'race' in the States is the bussing question and the slogan 'states rights'. This was used by southern racists in the 1950s and 1960s to resist Federal Government's attempts to desegrate schooling and to register black votes. The 'race' issue in the States, as in Britain, is also present in the campaign for law and order, at the same time as the social theory of crime is being rejected in favour of a biological explanation. The neo-Conservative criminologist, J.Q. Wilson, promotes the 'biological factor' to explain 'predatory street crime' in Washington DC, which has a large black population.[94] Yet Wilson denies he is making a direct identification between street crime and blacks — because 'race prejudice', in his view, is little more than class prejudice. There are clear parallels here with the British New Right's dismissal of anti-racism and classism.

Edgar's conclusions are compelling:

> Once crime and welfare have become code concepts, others easily follow. If street crime is black, then state-funded abortions for welfare recipients are a black-issue too, as is government bureaucracy, and government spending, at federal and state level. It is arguable, indeed, that California's tax-cutting referendum Proposition 13 was as much a vote against black welfare as it was a vote for lower taxes. In the context of euphemism on this scale, the priorities of the New Right take on a different character.[95]

If the racism of the American New Right is underestimated, because of its coding of political issues, its antisemitism tends to be ignored altogether; and left-wing analyses are no exception. Politically, this constitutes a blindspot. The presence of many prominent Jews among the neo-Conservatives may provide an alibi, but this is misleading. As with the British New Right, antisemitism is present among some sections of Christian believers.[96]

The racism and antisemitism of the religious right may be identified in terms of both specific campaigns and in their discourse. An important overview of this Christian political fringe, their extremism, their South African backing, their connections, strategies and activities, has been provided by Derrick Knight in a very neglected study published in 1982.[97] The two main Christian allies of the neo-Conservatives are Christian Voice and Moral Majority, and they lobby extensively in election campaigns. Christian Voice was founded in 1978 by Robert Gordon Grant, formerly an assistant pastor who had links with the Christian League of South Africa. One of their first major campaigns was to try to lift US economic sanctions against Rhodesia. In 1980 an official report estimated that Christian Voice was reaching some 40 million Christian viewers through existing Christian television networks. The fundamentalist 'electronic' church is enormously wealthy and controls over 1,500 channels. Its campaign strategy is to use issue-based commercials which generate a torrent of letters, postcards and telegrams to Congress. It is therefore calculated to influence any imminent legislation. It also has a direct mail fund-raising campaign organised by Jerry Hunsinger, a former Methodist minister.

The Moral Majority was founded by a TV evangelist. It has a similar programme to Christian Voice. Its chief exponent, Rev. Jerry Falwell, is virulently anti-liberal, anti-feminist and anti-gay. Another popular evangelist is Pat Robertson who has given air time to conservative congressmen including Larry McDonald, a leader of the John Birch Society of the old right.

There are indications that the New Christian right also shows hostility to Jews, despite the commitment of some NCR members to the 'Judaeo-Christian' tradition. In a short but illuminating book Bruce[98] has shown how the same activists will modify their rhetoric depending on their audience, or readership, at any one time. He cites, for example, the retired Captain G. Russell Evans who wrote an article in the Moral Majority Report dated 24 May 1983 attacking church leaders for their pacifism. In the same month, he wrote for an extreme-right publication, *The National Educator:*

> Many Americans know today for a fact that the Zionist Jews control the media, the Federal Reserve, and most of industry. Why haven't we been told? Well, the Zionist-controlled media decided not to tell us about this diabolical plot to control the world.

Plainly, there are resonances of the conspiracy thesis as set out in *The Protocols*. 'Zionist' in Evans' article is a contemporary code-word for 'Jewish' in antisemitic texts of both the right and the far left where this lexical slippage is seen to be more politically acceptable.[99] Not surprisingly, perhaps, Evans has also written for the Liberty Lobby, the most powerful fascist lobby in the States, which claims that the Holocaust was a myth.[100]

The British New Right and American links

The American New Right has a far-reaching network of think tanks and well-financed research organisations. A number of these have counterparts in NATO countries where they organise academic programmes, and anti-communist campaigns which rely on parallel intelligence organisations. One of the most important mentioned earlier is the Heritage Foundation in Washington which has considerable influence on the Reagan administration. The Heritage Foundation itself and its house journal, *Policy Review,* provide key links between the British and American New Right. Heritage was originally funded by the Colorado brewer, Joseph Coors, who contributed funds to the extreme right-wing John Birch Society; and it has been suggested that Scalfe, a key contributor to conservative causes, has also made a significant financial contribution. As with the continental New Right,[101] it is a question of both common links and shared discourse: the discourse of inequality.

Contributors to the sober *Policy Review* have included such American conservatives as Nathan Glazer, Senator Patrick Moynihan, Barry Goldwater and the monetarist, Milton Friedman, economic adviser to the Chilean junta, to Margaret Thatcher, and, briefly, to Menachem Begin's government. It is this arch-conservative journal that has printed articles by the neo-Nazi Pearson. As already noted, Pearson is a crucial link as former member of the editorial board and former president of the North American chapter of the World Anti-Communist League. This is not to imply that all contributors are crypto neo-Nazis. Such an allegation would be unfounded and an oversimplification. Indeed, Pearson may be the only example. Even if this is the case, it nevertheless indicates that arch-Conservatives are plainly prepared to accommodate and give political space to extremists to their right. In this way tacit alliances and realignments are rehearsed and operated in the face of the common enemy: the parties and pressure groups concerned with promoting equality and social justice. The right-wing consensus may thus be enlarged to include fascists and proto-fascists. History provides examples.[102]

It was the Heritage Foundation that hosted Sir Keith Joseph's vist to Washington DC in the autumn of 1977. Joseph's elitist views are no secret in the wake of his Birmingham speech of 19 October 1974, when as Minister for Social Services in the first Thatcher government he suggested that low-income parents of large families were responsible for social delinquency. Joseph's views on social hierarchy are set down in his book, *Equality.*[103] His successor, Sir Patrick Jenkin, has made similar pronouncements on working mothers in 1980:

> Quite frankly, I don't think mothers have the same right to work as fathers. If the Lord had intended us to have equal rights to go to work, he wouldn't have created men and women. These are biological facts, young children do depend on their mothers.[104]

Policy Review has also provided a platform for other right-wing members of the establishment, British MPs, and journalists, a number of whom are connected with the *Daily Telegraph,* including T. Utley and Peregrine Worsthorne, and the *Freedom Association.* The Freedom Association is one of the many pressure groups of the British authoritarian right.[105] Recent right-wing libertarian think tanks include the Centre for Policy Studies set up in 1974, the Social Affairs Unit established in 1982, the Adam Smith Institute[106] set up in 1971, and the Salisbury Group in 1976.[107] The Salisbury Group publishes the *Salisbury Review,* a journal promoting the discourse of cultural racism, discussed in chapter seven. The Freedom Association was formed in 1975. It was a coalition of various tendencies on the Conservative right. It included Robert Moss, Director, and Brian Crozier of the cold war 'counter-insurgency' school, as well as a number of right-wing Tory MPs. Also active are Jill Knight, Winston Churchill, Rhodes Boyson and Nicholas Ridley.

NAFF's paper, *Free Nation,* concentrated on opposing 'collectivism' (a term very much in vogue on the continental conservative and fascist right, referring to socialist and communist programmes). It is also concerned with exposing alleged trade union abuses, while popularising the writings of F.A. Hayek[108] and Milton Friedman. NAFF sought to distance itself from the National Front which it identified as fascist. NAFF director Robert Moss was employed by Margaret Thatcher as a speechmaker.

It is Stephen Haseler who best illustrates these American-British links on the New Right. He was closely involved with NAFF and a member of the editorial board of *Policy Review.* In 1977 and 1978 the Heritage Foundation named him a distinguished scholar. Haseler was also Chairman of the Social Democratic Alliance which opposed the nomination of left-wing Labour MPs. Haseler since joined the policy committee of the Social Democratic Party. The

Freedom Association is also connected with the Coalition for Peace through Security set up in October 1981 to counter the Campaign for Nuclear Disarmament. The Coalition organised a conference in London in March 1982 in conjunction with members of the American New Right including Paul Weyrich, a founder of the Heritage Foundation.

An organisation which currently includes seventeen Tory MPs and which consistently campaigns on immigration issues and has been the centre of the repatriation lobby for twenty years is the Monday Club set up in 1961, and currently chaired by Harvey Proctor, MP.[109] Its positions and pro-South African sympathies have been echoed by the current extremist leadership of the Federation of Conservative students.[110] Contacts between the racist Conservative right of the Monday Club and known fascists and fascist infiltration into the Party were revealed in a report drawn up by the Young Conservatives, referred to above. The main findings became public knowledge following a 'Panorama' programme entitled 'Maggie's Militant Tendency' produced by Michael Dutfield and screened in January 1984. The Monday Club had been having joint meetings with WISE (Wales, Ireland, Scotland, England), a racist organisation set up in 1974.[111] WISE meetings have been attended by prominent members of the National Front and the British Movement; and there are British WACL connections. A former National Front member (now British National Party), Kenneth McKilliam, ex-lay Preacher and author of a series of virulently racist Christian pamphlets, chaired a WISE meeting in which Holocaust denial propaganda was distributed.

Some of the links exemplified in this chapter may appear rather arbitrary or coincidental, while other are more substantial. In any event, there is no suggestion of a conspiracy. At the same time a pre-eminently anti-egalitarian discourse is also being produced and circulated by the authoritarian right and popularised by the media; and in both cases racist and sexist discourse, biological and 'cultural', is being mobilised and backed up by racist, sexist and anti-working class legislation. Whatever the updatings, all these discourses remain fundamentally hierarchical. Right-wing discourse promotes hierarchies: hierarchies of 'race', gender and class. As I have tried to indicate, it is not always such an easy matter to decide on the primacy of these three components.[112] There is intermeshing.

4. The American scene: The Institute for Historical Review, and left-wing antisemitic discourse

Contemporary fascists are denying the Holocaust. They pose as academics, as *bona fide* historians, and wish to be taken seriously as an alternative school of history: 'the revisionists' versus 'the exterminationists'.

The Holocaust denial movement owes a debt to Harry Elmer Barnes (1889-1968), American historian and sociologist whom it hails as the father of 'revisionism'. Historically, his critique and re-examination first focussed on world war I and the official accounts of Germany's responsibility for the outbreak of war. He rejected these, arguing that America has been tricked into the war by vested political interests, and this had been extremely damaging for the States. This was a genuine historical re-assessment, and as such perfectly legitimate. However, after the second world war, Barnes and others campaigned against world war II in much the same way in a number of irresponsible writings. Indeed, as early as 1962, he questioned whether the Third Reich had committed any atrocities: and in a very rambling essay entitled *Revisionism: A Key to Peace* (1966), originally published in an ephemeral libertarian journal, he virtually dismissed the Nazi genocide. As Dawidowicz points out,[1] even neo-Nazis in Germany, including *Nation Europa* which published Barnes' articles, were not denying the facts altogether. Their strategy was to minimise them. At that point Barnes made the acquaintance of Paul Rassinier, a French socialist antisemite, and translated some of his books. He also reviewed them in the ultra-right *American Mercury*, part of the Liberty Lobby. After Barnes' death, a short book was published entitled *The Myth of the Six Million* which paid tribute to Barnes. The introduction was written by Willis A. Carto of the Liberty Lobby, using a pseudonym, and published by Noontide Press owned by Liberty Lobby.

The first international gathering of 'revisionists' met in an academic setting at the Northrop Campus in Los Angeles from 31 August to 2 September 1979. To date there have been four such conventions.

The first convention passed a resolution denying the existence of the gas chambers. This was reprinted in the neo-Nazi weekly, *The Spotlight* (24 September 1979), reproduced on page 68.

In the States this campaign has been orchestrated by the Liberty Lobby based in Washington DC, the largest neo-Nazi organisation in America. It is also an umbrella organisation for ultra-right publications and activities. Liberty Lobby produces a weekly tabloid, *The Spotlight,* which, while adopting a conservative pose and attacking disarmament, pornography and welfare abuse, promotes a conspiracy theory of history and government. Hidden forces are seen to control and manipulate events. The arch-conspirators are the Jews. *The Spotlight* has an estimated 300,000 subscribers. Behind both Liberty Lobby and *The Spotlight* is Willis Allison Carto, a former organiser of the extreme right-wing John Birch Society. In 1968 he ran a Youth for Wallace movement, renamed the National Youth Alliance, which he sought to win over to Nazi ideology. Advertisements in *The Spotlight* put readers in touch with other ultra-right racist literature, like *The Thunderbolt* of the National States Rights Party.

The focus of Carto's West Coast operations is the Legion for Survival of Freedom Inc. This company owns Noontide Press, the heart of Carto's publishing empire. It is also the proprietor of *American Mercury,* a virulently antisemitic magazine, and the Institute for Historical Review.[2] Noontide Press specialises in racist literature including Ku Klux Klan publications. Not surprisingly, it also stocks the *Protocols* together with other new and old Nazi texts.

Resolution

We, the speakers, delegates and officers of the Institute for Historical Review 1979 Revisionist Convention meeting at Los Angeles this September 2, after reviewing the evidence that the Germans killed 6 million Jews during World War II in an unprecedented act of genocide and considering both sides of the question, as well as the evidence of genuine atrocities, resolve the following:

WHEREAS, the fact surrounding the allegations that gas chambers existed in occupied Europe during World War II are demonstrably false, and

WHEREAS, the whole theory of 'the holocaust' has been created by and promulgated by political Zionism for the attainment of political and economic ends, specifically the continued and perpetual financial support of the military aggression of Israel by the people of Germany and the US, and

WHEREAS, the constantly escalating level of 'holocaust' propaganda distributed by the mass media and government agencies is poisoning the minds of the American people, especially youth, and

WHEREAS, we are conscientiously concerned that this strident hate propaganda is seriously impeding the necessary peace, unity, brotherhood and understanding that we desire among all the peoples of the Western World; now therefore

BE IT RESOLVED, that we urge that the Congress of the US investigate the whole question of war guilt, military aggression in the 20th century, the relationship of private political and banking interests with military aggression, deceitful wartime propaganda masquerading as fact, the real responsibility for war twisted history, the Nuremburg War Crime trials, proven atrocities and genocide such as the murder of thousands of Ukrainians and Poles at Vinnitsa in 1937 and Katyn in 1940 and the truth of the alleged extermination of 6 million Jews in Europe during World War II.

The booking for the neo-Nazi event was made by Noontide Press in the name of Lewis Brandon. According to *The Spotlight*'s report on the convention (24 September 1979), Brandon is the executive secretary of the newly formed and academic-sounding Institute for Historical Review. His real identity has since been claimed as David McCalden, a British neo-fascist activist who left Britain for the States in 1978. McCalden helped form the National Party in Britain in 1975, a break-away group from the National Front, on a platform of racial nationalism.[3] The National Party's international links include the German neo-Nazi party, the NPD.

The IHR 'revisionist' convention

The Institute for Historical Review held its second 'revisionist' convention in August 1980 at Pomona College, Claremont, California. The 1981 meeting took place at the University of California at Lake Arrowhead, and in 1982 in Los Angeles.

As part of the festivities, a 'revisionist tour' was scheduled to visit the major concentration camp sites. The highlight of this tour was to be the Dijksmuide festival in Belgium, the annual meeting place for Nazi groups all over Europe.[4]

As a form of Jew-baiting, the Institute offered a prize of $50,000 for proof that a single Jew was gassed by the Nazis. It also offered a $25,000 reward for a bar of soap made from Jewish fat. This jibe was taken up by *The Spotlight* (24 September 1979) in a lead article by 'Frank Tompkins', which Carto has admitted under oath is one of his pseudonyms. Mel Mermelstein of Huntingdon Beach, California, a former inmate of Auschwitz whose near relatives were gassed, took up the challenge. He has since successfully sued Carto after his refusal to recognise his claim.[5]

The Spotlight's first concentrated attack on the reality of the Holocaust appeared in its issue of 1 May 1978. It has given increased coverage to the Holocaust denial since the screening of the NBC-TV Holocaust film in 1978 and the setting up of the Institute in the following year. Following this first convention in 1979, the Institute for Historical Review launched a new quarterly, *The Journal of Historical Review*. It claims to be concerned with 'legitimate historical enquiry'. The first issue which appeared in Spring 1980 reprints the convention's main contributions. All the contributors bar Fitzgibbon are active in the Holocaust denial campaign. The papers in order of publication are by Arthur R. Butz, Robert

Faurisson, Louis Fitzgibbon, Austin A. App, Udo Walendy and Ditlieb Felderer. Carto's opening address was not included.

Butz is a lecturer in electrical engineering and computer science at Northwestern University in Evanston, Illinois. His book, *The Hoax of the Twentieth Century,* has been widely promoted in the ultra-right press. It has been chosen to play a central role in preference to other versions of this neo-Nazi myth because it pretends to present a detailed, dispassionate and independent study. For this reason *The Hoax* is a constant point of reference in the Holocaust denial literature. It has been praised by the *Journal of Historical Review* as 'the most scientific, revisionist work on the Holocaust'. Butz's main arguments and his methodology are discussed later in this chapter.

The Hoax was published in 1976 by an obscure English press in Southam, Warwickshire, for the Historical Review Press. A second edition appeared in 1977, also for the Historical Review Press at its new premises in Brighton, Sussex. It has been serialised in West Germany by the neo-Nazi newspaper, *Nationale Zeitung,* under the headline 'The Truth about Hitler's Concentration Camps' (25 February 1977). The launching was hosted by the DVU, the neo-Nazi organisation currently sponsoring Irving's book on the Nuremburg Trials.

Butz's paper for the convention is entitled 'The International "Holocaust" Controversy' and is couched in the language of academic debate. In particular, Butz claims that the gas chambers are fictitious and that the evidence of the Nuremburg trials cannot be accepted.

Also contributing was Robert Faurisson, another academic who has achieved a certain notoriety in France where he was charged and found guilty on three separate charges.[6] Faurisson's claims are no less fantastic. He argued on technical grounds that it was impossible to kill such large numbers in so-called 'gas chambers'. He maintains that Hitler never killed anyone on grounds of race or religion, and that he gas chambers never existed. According to the *Journal,* Faurisson specialises in the appraisal and evaluation of texts and documents. Until recently, when he was suspended from teaching duties, Faurisson held a lectureship in literature at the University of Lyons II.

Faurisson's paper to the convention is entitled 'The Mechanics of Gassing'. It has been reproduced in Britain in a journal of the

National Front, *New Nation,* in 1980,[7] edited by Richard Verall and Martin Webster. Faurisson has set himself up as the expert on gassing techniques, and much of his highly speculative argument is concerned with semantics. Faurisson maintain that Zyklon gas was only used for sanitary purposes and principally as a means of containing the typhus epidemic in the camps.

Another participant was Louis Fitzgibbon, author of *Katyn,* which charges the Russians with the responsibility for the murder of Polish officers whose bodies were discovered in the Katyn Forest at the end of the war.

Also appearing was Austin App, now retired, a lecturer in English at La Salle College in Philadelphia. He was one of the earliest American neo-Nazis to attempt to deny the Holocaust. App was the author of 1966 of 'That Elusive "Six Million" in the *Mercury,* and later of *The Six Million Swindle: Blackmailing the German people for hard marks with fabricated corpses.* It was first published by Boniface Press, Takoma Park, Maryland in 1973, and promoted in such publications as *The Crusader,* a Klan newspaper, and *Liberty Bell.* App has links with the German American National Congress and with the 'Ridgewood Group', publishers of the pro-Nazi *Voice of German Americans* which claimed App as its founder in an article in April 1978.

App's contribution to the 'revisionist' convention, 'The "Holocaust" Put in Perspective', argues that America entered the second world war not on the side of justice, but on the side of the Jews. Hitler, he continues, was the victim of smear on the part of world Jewry. The six million 'gassed' (App's quotation marks) is, he alleges, 'an impudent lie': 'The figure is a swindle'; 'absolutely no Jews were "gassed" in any concentration camps'; 'there is no shred of evidence.' Finally, he estimates the number of Jewish casualties under the Third Reich at 300,000 in round figures.

The next contributor, Udo Walendy, is described as the head of a 'German revisionist publishing house'. He has also translated and published Butz. According to *Searchlight,* Walendy has been active in the neo-Nazi movement since the 1960s.[8] His book, *Forged War Crimes Malign the German Nation,* originally published in Germany by Kolle-Druck in 1979, has been translated by M.S. Atoegisit (probably a pseudonym), and is distributed by the Institute of Historical Review. Walendy's contribution to the convention is entitled 'The Fake Photograph Problem' in which he alleges to 'expose' some of the more blatant forgeries. In his paper Walendy argues that most of the atrocity photographs were faked, were of communist origin, or prove nothing at all. In Walendy's opinion, these 'fakes' served a particular purpose: 'brainwashing the German people after the war'.

The last of the 'revisionist' convention contributors, Ditlieb Felderer, lives in Sweden and publishes his own virulently antisemitic 'revisionist' English-language newsletter, *Bible Researcher*. He is apparently distributing leaflets in Swedish schools and inciting pupils to ask their teachers about the 'truth' of the Holocaust. In common with Faurisson, Felderer argues that Anne Frank's diary is a fraud. He maintains that the diary contains 'literary flourishes that a 13-year old girl could not possibly use'. But he has produced no documented evidence. His claim is based purely on speculative reasoning.

Felderer's *Anne Frank's Diary — A Hoax* was published by the Institute for Historical Review in 1979, edited by McCalden, alias Lewis Brandon. Much of the material was originally published in the *Bible Researcher* in 1978. The book is distributed in Britain by Historical Review Press, and by the Australian office of the Institute for Historical Review in Melbourne. Felderer's short and quite ludicrous paper, 'Auschwitz Notebook', attempts to refute 'the Gerstein report' on the basis of similar speculations. On this occasion he attempts by the use of diagrams and formulae to show that the 'extermination theory' is 'a fiction' and 'a mental derangement'.

The Institute is clearly intended as a respectable 'intellectual' counterpart of the ultra-right campaign. This pseudo-scholarly style of *The Journal for Historical Review* contrasts with the joking, baiting tone of other neo-Nazi leaflets which peddle the same lies. The contributors to their *Journal* continually seek to elicit feedback from the Jewish community as to their reactions to the *Journal*, enclosing their booklist. Yehuda Bauer, Professor of Holocaust Studies at Jerusalem, has been besieged with invitations from Faurisson and others to engage in open debate.[9] This jokey, spurious correspondence is followed by an illustrated news sheet called 'jewish information'. 'Jew' written in the lower case is an established antisemitic stylistic feature. The 'jewish information' news sheet, which emanates from Tarby in Sweden, is extremely offensive.

jewish information

Our Ref: RH305 1 1981 POSTGIRO 86 30 32-9 Marknadsvagen 289, 2 tr S-183 34 TÄBY, SWEDEN Tel. 08-768 13 98

Please Accept This

HAIR OF A GASSED VICTIM!

● NEXT TIME YOU CUT YOUR HAIR, DO NOT DISCARD IT! NO, MAIL IT INSTEAD TO MR. SMOLEN AT THE AUSCHWITZ MUSEUM OR TO ANY OF THE ADDRESSES FOUND ON THE NEXT PAGE - TO BE EXHIBITED IN THE DISPLAY OF HAIR OF GASSED VICTIMS. YOUR HAIR HAS A MUCH BETTER CLAIM TO BE EXHIBITED THERE THAN THE PHONY SAMPLES OF COMMERCIAL WIGS AND HAIR HITHERTO EXHIBITED. ALSO COLLECT TOGETHER THE HAIR OF ALL YOUR FRIENDS, DOGS, AND OTHER ANIMALS. SEND IT ALL IN A PLASTIC BAG TO MR. SMOLEN. HE WILL REMEMBER YOU FOR IT. IT CAN BE MAILED AS "PRINTED MATTER" BY PLACING THE TERM "SAMPLE" ON THE PRECIOUS DELIVERY.

TO:
Mr. K. Smolen and Staff
Auschwitz Museum
OSWIECIM
POLAND

Dear Mr. Smolen:

In appreciation of your deep concern for gassed victims, I am hereby forwarding my personal trophy for your permanent Museum exhibits. I understand that you are intensely involved with the subject of gassing. Personally I feel rather miserable. Not even Zyklon B would cure me! This is much on account of the fact that I am getting gassed to death by a slow poison procedure. Our air is full of filth, poison, gasses, harmful chemicals and other disgusting elements. Matters are no better in your city. Your city is virtually saturated with deadly gasses emanating from your Monowitz chemical factory. In fact the place is not fit even for crows. I urge you to pay it a visit. Surely the Nazis never had a factory in such deplorable condition. But it is not necessary for you to go there as the factory's poison gasses reaches your very own office at Auschwitz which is situated close to the former Nazi brothel. In case of urgency I suggest you to put on a gas mask immediately. You may collect one at the private Museum displays in Block 24. Please be sure that it has the special "J" filter. The poison at Auschwitz is deadly. You need to take the upmost precautions.

My package of hair to you is a very personal proof of the fact that I am being gassed to death. Should you doubt it, I beg your experts to analyze it. I am therefore donating this private gift to you with the hope of that countless of your Museum's avid onlookers may gaze at it in wonder and give a solemn prayer in memory of a victim doomed to extinction due to environmental poison gassing.

With much respect for your stupendous task and your deep concern for gassed victims, I hereby solemnly, and prayerfully, deliver my hair to your loving and tender care. May it inspire you and all your visitors to a multitude of silent moments and intense meditations.

A VICTIM WHOSE DAYS ARE NUMBERED

☐ Always include this list when mailing your sample.
Get our special bulletins by sending us US $20. ALSO ORDER MORE OF THIS SPECIAL FLIER.

☐ For further details about the phony hair exhibited at Auschwitz and elsewhere, and for a general discussion, see: RH 301, 302, 303, 304. About the fake soap purporting to be "pure Jewish fat," see RH 38, 172; 313; 520:121, 125, 131-139, 184.

☐ Order our special publications ANNE FRANK DIARY - A HOAX? and SIONISMEN KAPUTT by sending us US $7. We still have a few copies left of AUSCHWITZ EXIT, Vol. 1. DO NOT FORGET TO GIVE THIS FLIER TO ALL YOUR FRIENDS AND ASK THEM TO HELP IN BUILDING UP THE EXHIBITS.

Butz and the American background

Among American neo-Nazi publications preceding the first 1979 'revisionist' convention and paving the way to it were books by Carto, App, Butz and Grimstad. The first of these, *The Myth of the Six Million,* published by Noontide Press, appeared anonymously in 1969. It is thought to be by Willis Carto, the man behind *The Spotlight* and the Liberty Lobby. The *Myth* subscribes to the classical Nazi tradition of a linked Jewish-communist conspiracy, while denying the Holocaust.

Reference has already been made to App's pamphlets. His book *The Six Million Swindle* published in 1973 presented much the same line as Richard Verrall's pamphlet *Did Six Million Really Die?* which was published in Britain under the pseudonym of Harwood a year later. This is discussed in more detail in the next chapter.

The Hoax of the Twentieth Century by Arthur Butz, first published in 1976, has been widely promoted on the far right. The 'revisionists' were no doubt hoping that Butz's academic style and the fact that he holds a doctorate, albeit in a totally unrelated area, would lend his work a measure of authority. It is the first would-be 'serious', 'in-depth' study in America to deny the Holocaust.[10] In view of the prominence given to *The Hoax,* it is useful to discuss the arguments it presents. [11] In common with Faurisson, Butz also tends to reject central archival sources on the grounds that they are communist and Zionist. Butz writes in the controlled style of academic debate; and *The Hoax* consists of 8 chapters, with some 450 footnotes and 5 appendices, including 32 plates and diagrams, amounting to a 315-page volume. In other words, the neo-Nazi myth is presented in the form of a serious investigation. The eight chapters are entitled: 'Trials, Jews and Nazis'; 'Camps'; 'Washington and New York'; 'Auschwitz'; 'Hungarian Jews'; 'Etcetera'; 'The Final Solution'; and 'Remarks'. It is argued in the foreword that the Holocaust is a 'legend' and that 'academic historians' and 'established scholarship' have avoided a critical examination of the 'holocaust, the hoax of your century'.

Butz imitates the academic style in challenging what he calls an establishment view. It is a clever pose. Later on, however, he makes the revealing link between 'establishment knowledge' (of the reality of the Holocaust) and Jews, claiming that 'leading extermination mythologists' (that is, those who assert the reality of the Holocaust in a professional capacity) are Jews.[12] It is clear that Butz is inviting the reader to conclude that the Holocaust was a Jewish invention.

Butz uses the term 'exterminationists' (to refer to those who set out the grim reality and history of the Holocaust) as contrasted with the neo-Nazi 'revisionists' as if presenting two sides of a scholarly debate. In this respect, he is anticipating the seemingly neutral, non-polemical, academic language of the 'revisionist' convention.

Chapter one questions the legality of the Nuremberg trials conducted by the 'victors'. More than 2,000 post-war trials of war criminals have taken place. The most important of these were the trials of German war criminals before an International Military Tribunal at Nuremberg in 1945-46.[13] Butz alleges that the Nuremberg 'trials' were a 'frame-up',[14] and part of the 'extermination' hoax. He records an American prison psychiatrist's admiration for Göring, Hitler's Air Force commander, who escaped hanging by taking a cyanide capsule.

Verrall, also an admirer of Göring, makes the same kind of points. Immediately after the war the French fascist, Maurice Bardèche, in more liquid prose had voiced very similar arguments in *Nuremberg ou la Terre promise (Nuremberg or the Promised Land) (1948)*.[15]

The main function of Butz's second chapter is to confuse the reader about the categories and functions of the various camps. He states that the 'proof' of exterminations in these camps (Bergen, Belsen, Dachau, Buchenwald...) were photographs of bodies lying around. But there were very few bodies, he argues, compared with the number of casualties caused by the British-American raids on Dresden in February 1945. This rehearses another fascist argument: that the Allies were no better than the Germans, and may have been even worse. This argument is developed by Harwood, McLaughlin, Grimstad and others in the English-speaking world; and in France in contributions to *Europe Action,* and by Robert Hersant, the press magnate.

The reader is thus confronted by two conflicting explanations: either these bodies at Belsen 'were a result of a total loss of control, not a deliberate policy'[16] where the guards have 'unfortunate facial expressions'[17]; or there is the typhus explanation, favoured by Faurisson and others. There undoubtedly *were* large-scale deaths due to typhus. But Butz's argument, developed by Faurisson, implies that Zyklon gas was used simply as an insecticide,[18] hence as a health measure to *save* lives. Butz is exploiting the fact that Zyklon B was also a pesticide, as did the Nazis at the time.

Butz goes on to expound a typical half-truth: 'the typical inmate of a German concentration camp was a person being detained for punitive or security reasons'.[19] Certainly, this was the case initially. But the function of the camps changed, as has been pointed out, and there were different types of camps. In either event, Butz has no political scruples about the existence of camps, whatever their purpose. He sees it as 'natural' for Jews to be segregated.

> A fraction of those interned for punitive and security reasons were Jews and under the national socialist system it was natural, in the camps, to segregate them from the 'Aryan' inmates. Thus sections of the camps could, in this sense, be considered 'for Jews'.[20]

He actually suggests that the nearest Jews came to concentration camps was in what should more properly be termed transit camps or ghettos; and Jews were only transferred to ghettos for safety reasons as the Russians were approaching the eastern front.[21] It is clear from this section that Butz is simply reiterating official Nazi propaganda of the period. He has no quarrel with the Nazi euphemisms for the 'Final Solution', or their ideology. In an attempt to show his seriousness, however, and his unbiased 'scholarship', he illustrates his text with complicated, detailed maps. It is an elaborate, cynical game.

Butz is leading up to his main argument, namely that Auschwitz had been chosen as an ideal location to set up a huge industrial operation[22] with standard working hours. According to Butz, Auschwitz had nothing to do with extermination of Jews. Indeed, in chapter two entitled 'Camps', Jews are scarcely mentioned. The industrial camp at Auschwitz is not a fiction, but, as presented by Butz, is another cynical half-truth. The fact is that Auschwitz was divided into three camps, and gassing arrangements were added to an existing concentration camp which was also a forced labour camp. This included a large industrial section located in Auschwitz III. In Butz's account, Auschwitz is an industrial labour camp, and nothing more; and where some inmates fell sick, died and were cremated.

Chapter three is quite extraordinary. It is largely concerned with technical details about the importance of Auschwitz to the

Americans because of the technological developments in synthetic rubber. Auschwitz III was indeed the base of the I.G. Farben camp, an industrial empire which included a synthetic rubber plant at Buna IV, one of the many satellite camps in the Auschwitz area. Farben, initially co-operating with the SS, adopted their methods and their mentality; and the life expectancy of a Jewish inmate at Buna was three to four months. Farben was later joined by other industries. This is how Butz 'explains' the extermination programme:

> Our ugly old friend typhus was at Auschwitz... By this time there were a number of dead which must have been a few thousand, although there is a large degree of uncertainty here. The German policy was to cremate the bodies of camp inmates who died, but the epidemic caught the Auschwitz authorities with inadequte cremating facilities. There was a small crematory at Auschwitz I but more extensive facilities at Birkenau (Auschwitz II)... were not yet under construction in 1942 and the first complete new unit, consisting of 15 conventional crematory ovens, was not to be available until January 1943. It appears that many of the victims of the epidemic were immediately cremated in pits... The buildings in which the Birkenau oven were installed had curtains, halls, room or cellars which the accusations say were the 'gas chambers'[23]

Here again Butz is repeating the Nazi claim that the places called 'bath houses' and 'shower rooms' in the killing centres, cynically labelled in this way, did indeed serve that purpose. He is also manipulating the facts by suggesting that Auschwitz deaths were typically due to typhus and that the victims were initially buried in pits and later cremated. Indeed, there were deaths due to typhus in Auschwitz and elsewhere. But Butz is trying to confuse the reader and suggests that gas chambers were not used for gassing victims at Auschwitz-Birkenau. It is true that the elaborate installations 'for the implementation of the special measures'[24] took until January 1943 to complete. But the first makeshift gas chambers were put into operation in May 1942.[25]

The Nazis' lack of emotion, bureaucratic secrecy and thoroughness in pursuing their genocidal policies are also echoed in Butz's account. It is a chilling and extraordinary revival. Butz also hints that atrocity photographs reproduced in the text have been touched up. This takes up Walendy's particular neo-Nazi version of the fantasy, but in a more elevated, pseudo-academic style.

Butz goes on:

> While the preceding adequately suggest how the Auschwitz lie originated... the claims of extermination of Jews have their origin not in Allied intelligence information but in the operations of the World Jewish Congress.[26]

The Jews are thus held responsible for the 'Auschwitz lie'. Enter the Jewish conspiracy theory. It is fleshed out as the chapter progresses with a remarkable summary of the *New York Times'* reporting of the German propaganda campaign against the Jews from spring 1942 to 1943. Goebbels' public threat on 12 June to carry out a mass extermination of Jews did admittedly mean 'extermination' etymologically[27] — shades of Faurisson and Rassinier's attempts at semantic manipulation. But then on a note of feigned academic caution Butz reminds us that one should observe that: 'extreme statements were a pervasive feature of Nazi oratory and rhetoric... It was a reaction to Allied terror bombings... people can say heated things in wartime.'

Lastly, he attempts to formulate another semantic argument claiming that 'the German word for "Jewry", *das Judentum,* is ambiguous in meaning'.[28] Although *das Judentum* can mean Jewry, it can also mean 'Judaism', 'Jewishness', or 'the idea of Jewishness'.[29] If lifted out of context, Butz argues, or interpreted literally, it can mean the killing of Jews, but it may also be interpreted as the destruction of Jewish influence and power. For example, Hitler's quite unambiguous speech of 30 January 1939, in the Reichstag, the German Parliament, called for *'die Vernichtung* (extermination) *des Judentums'* throughout Europe, or take Rosenberg's *'die Ausrottung* (uprooting) *des Judentums'*. Butz's line of argument is precisely that put forward at the Nuremberg Trials by Alfred Rosenberg's defence, as echoed by Richard Harwood and David Irving.[30]

Chapter four, 'Auschwitz', is conveniently summarised by Butz.[31] It is argued that the 'Auschwitz extermination legend' had nothing to do with extermination of people.[32] This is a reworking of the ambiguity of the uses of Zyklon B, already discussed. Once again Jews are eerily absent, except at the very end of the chapter where he comments on alleged Jewish and gypsy 'transit camps' at Auschwitz-Birkenau, the killing centre.

At this point, although he has previously stated unambiguously that Zyklon was most typically used in disinfecting rooms and barracks,[33] Butz presents the summary in such a way as to allow a dual interpretation, mimicking the academic style of argument: Butz resolves this dual interpretation in favour of the 'great hoax: the proposed interpretations of extermination are obviously lies'.[35] The truth is that at Auschwitz-Birkenau the Nazi deceit assumed such proportions that the larger underground gas chambers were indeed termed *Leichenkeller,* and the smaller ones, *Badeanstalten*.[36] Butz's summary is reproduced on page 80.

In chapter five, Butz reviews the 'atrocity propaganda' of 1944 and later claims about Hungarian Jews. He gives prominence to two postwar reports of the International Red Cross Committee and their perception of the plight of the Jews in Slovakia, Croatia and Hungary. There are a number of references to extermination, but Butz dismisses these claims. He argues that large numbers of Hungarian Jews could not have been exterminated as late as 1944 because of the strain that would have put on the rail system.

As Höss testified, some 400,000 Hungarian Jews were indeed exterminated at Auschwitz-Birkenau in the summer of 1944 alone. And no doubt this did put particular demands on the rail system. But Himmler, Minister for the Eastern Occupied Territories, had stated more than once the priority of the destruction process: 'Economic questions should not be considered in the solution of the Jewish Question'.[37] The destruction of the Jews came first, regardless of the war effort.

Butz also argues that the lack of American response, the failure to bomb the rail links[38] at the gas chambers, and the 'insufficient evidence' from photographs, 'compel the conclusion that nothing resembling or approximating extermination actually happened to the Hungarian Jews'.[39] Major works like Braham's *The Destruction of Hungarian Jewry* (1963) are ignored. Other sources like the journal *Nation Europa* and Thies Christophersen's *Die Auschwitz Lüge (The Auschwitz Lie)* are cited instead.

Chapter six, 'Etcetera', is, as the title implies, merely a rounding-off of the 'extermination legend', or, more specifically, of the 'Zionist hoax', 'since the proposed justification for the reparations has been invalidated'.[40] Already the language is bolder: the

1. The Zyklon was employed for disinfection and also allegedly for exterminations.
2. The 'selections' were necessary by the nature of the operations at Auschwitz and also allegedly for exterminations.
3. It would not have been inaccurate (although perhaps somewhat misleading) to call Birkenau a 'death camp', especially at certain times (and especially when the Baruch Committee was in existence and immediately thereafter); it was also allegedly an 'extermination camp'.
4. Disrobing-showering procedures were followed for delousing and also allegedly for exterminations.
5. Conventional crematoria existed for accommodating both the death camp role and alleged extermination camp role of Birkenau.
6. Some *Leichenkeller* ('Mortuary Chapels') were mortuaries while it is alleged that others were, in reality 'gas chambers'. The two types of *Leichenkeller* were in proximate locations at Birkenau.
7. Some *Badeanstalten* ('bath houses') were bath establishments while it is alleged that others were, in reality, 'gas chambers'. The two types of *Badeanstalten* were in proximate locations at Birkenau.
8. The stench that the people of the area experienced was due not only to the hydrogenation and other chemical processes at Auschwitz but also allegedly to the cremations.

Actually, in view of the points made in the analysis it is only charity to say that there are proposed dual interpretations of fact in connection with these eight points. The proposed interpretations of extermination are obvious lies and the last, concerning the stench, is the 'excess fact'; the authors of the hoax should never have used the fact of the stench in their story.[34]

A. R. Butz, *The Hoax of the Twentieth Century* (California Noontide Press and Historical Review Press, 1977), 131.

world has been presented with 'a fabrication constructed of perjury, forgery, distortion of fact and misrepresentation of documents'[41]: the victims are presented as the perpetrators of crimes. This is a familiar reversal.

This chapter contains more number-play based on the function of the *Einsatzgruppen*. It was they who controlled partisan activity in occupied Russia. And they had been ordered by Hitler to round up and execute Jews and gypsies, as well as Soviet political commissars and partisans. The documentary evidence for these exterminations, Butz writes, is 'simply funny'.[42] To accompany this lie he injects an oblique argument intended to deflect from the function of the *Einsatzgruppen*. In another context this might suggest a progressive stance: 'I suspect that every accuser of the *Einsatzgruppen* would have obeyed orders to participate in the air raids on Hamburg, Dresden, Hiroshima and Nagasaki'.[43] The function of this apparently humanitarian, anti-authoritarian argument, common in fascist rhetoric, is to confuse the reader, to make us hesitate. The function is to absolve the Third Reich of genocide.

Chapter seven, preceding the conclusion, sets out what in Butz's view *did* happen to the Jews, as he has already shown that 'the exterminations are a propaganda hoax'.[44] At this point, his stylistic and other defences are abandoned;

> To answer the question in general [of what happened to the European Jews] all one needs to do is consult the relevant German documents. What the German leaders were saying to each other about their policy is obviously the first authority that one should consult.[45]

Here Butz is acting unmistakably as a mouthpiece of the official Nazi line. This requires no further comment except that he confidently repeats the performance at the end of the chapter. Concluding that gas chambers were 'wartime propaganda fantasies comparable to the propaganda produced in World War I' (another common Nazi 'explanation' of the Holocaust), Butz looks to an extraordinary authority. It is none other than Heinrich Himmler, head of the Gestapo, the most dreaded police force in all Europe. Butz writes:

> The factual basis for these ridiculous charges was nailed with perfect accuracy by Heinrich Himmler in an interview with a representative of the World Jewish Congress just a few

> weeks before the end of the war... That Himmler's assessment of the gas chambers is the accurate one should be perfectly obvious to anybody who spends any time with this subject.[46]

Butz has already echoed Rosenberg's defence, and revived Nazi explanations and codewords for mass murder. It is perfectly consistent that he should now refer to Himmler's denial of the gas chambers as a legitimate source. There can be no doubt whatsoever about the ideological nature of Butz's enterprise. Indeed, it is altogether consonant with the Nazi vision, as illustrated in the following extract of a speech made by Himmler. He is addressing high-ranking SS officers in Poznon on 4 October 1943, when Germany was under severe pressure, and some five million Jews had already been murdered.

> I also want to make reference before you here, in complete frankness, to a really grave matter. Among ourselves, this once, it shall be uttered quite frankly; but in public we shall never speak of it... I am referring to the evacuation of the Jews, the annihilation of the Jewish people... Most of you must know what it means to see a hundred corpses lie side by side, or five hundred, or a thousand. To have stuck this out and to have kept our integrity, and this is what had made us hard. In our history, this is an unwritten and never-to-be-written page of glory.[47]

This text eventually found its way into SS files; and later, along with other records, fell into Allied Hands.

William Grimstad: popularising Butz

After Butz, the next move was to produce a more readable, glossy version of the neo-Nazi myth aimed at a more popular readership. *The Six Million Reconsidered* appeared the following year, published by the Historical Review Press as a Special Report for the Committee for Truth in History for Media Research Associates. A British edition marketed by the Institute for Historical Review appeared in 1979. The black and white cover features a 'mix' of Jewish deportees, some from the Warsaw ghetto, and scenes of sado-masochism showing uniformed Nazi soldiers whipping chained, half-undressed women, in the form of a comic strip.

The author of this vile book has since been revealed as William Grimstad. Grimstad, a journalist, first appeared in the American Nazi movement in 1971. In 1972 he became a managing editor of the American paper *White Power*, a publication of the Nazi National Socialist White People's Party. Grimstad later worked for a Klan paper, *Crusader*, and for David Duke, head of one of the many Klan branches, and who subsequently visited Britain.[48] The American-based Anti-Defamation League previously exposed Grimstad, a San Diego journalist, as a registered Saudi Arabian agent No. 2849. In June 1977, Grimstad received 20,000 dollars from the government of Saudi Arabia in appreciation of *Antizion*, published in 1974. It is dedicated to the late King Feisal who was also a distributor of antisemitic literature, including the infamous *Protocols*. The dedication in *Antizion* reads: 'To the memory of a distinguished statesman and humanitarian, who in this New Dark Age never lost insight into the hidden causes of world upheaval.' This is a veiled reference to the Jewish conspiracy theory. A party of religious scholars from Saudi Arabia distributed copies of the *Protocols* at the Constituent Assembly of the Council of Europe in Strasbourg in December 1974[49];and Saudi Arabia has also distributed *The Protocols* through its own embassies.

Antizion is distributed by Carto's company; by Jame Madole's neo-Nazi National Renaissance Party in New York; by Patriot Press, the literature side of David Duke's Klan Knights, in Louisiana; and by Liberty Bell publications run by George Dietz, a former member of the Hitler youth. *Antizion* was first published as *The Jews on Trial* in Washington DC by Aryan Press. It was subsequently revised and published by Noontide's Press, Carto's organisation. *Antizion* is advertised as an anthology of anti-Jewish quotations, some of which support 'Zionist imperialism: the explosive idea whose troubled time has come'. This squalid little book includes quotations from Hitler, a 'twentieth-century statesman' whose writings and speeches are described as examples of 'moderation'.[50]

The British Prime Minister, Margaret Thatcher, and the Queen both paid courtesy visits to Saudi Arabia in 1981 as an indication of the desire to cultivate a more cordial relationship. It is sobering to know that the government of Saudi Arabia, often considered the leader of the more conservative Arab states, actively finances Holocaust denial activity on a world scale.

It would appear that some reactionary forces from other middle and far east states are assisting. A package containing Grimstad's *The Six Million Reconsidered* together with his earlier publication, *Antizion,* was posted in the summer of 1981 from Pakistan by the World Muslim League to more than a thousand prominent British politicians, trade unionists and industrialists.[51] The marxist arabist scholar, Maxine Rodinson[52], suggests that in the Muslim world it tends to be Muslim fundamentalists and obscurantists who relate Zionism to popular antisemitic beliefs. However, there is, of course, nothing intrinsically antisemitic about the Muslim religion.

As the first popular American version of the Holocaust denial, Grimstad's book merits closer attention. It is dedicated: 'To the Unknown Hundred Million, killed in this century by Marxism, Zionism, and the winless wars of International Finance.' This is echoed by McLaughlin's British pamphlet discussed in chapter six. The dedication sets the tone and gives an intimation of the dishonest techniques used not only to deny the Holocaust, but also, classically, to blame the victim. The case for historical antisemitism is set out, with quotations from Voltaire, Napoleon and other not-so-enlightened figures — the conclusion being that if Jews were so feared and hated in so many civilisations and historical epochs, then there must be a very good reason for it: 'Jewish spokesmen will never publicly admit that Jews *as a group* are anything less than blameless as the driven snow' (emphasis added).

To begin with, it is argued that 'antisemitism' is meaningless — because Jews, (regularly referred to as 'Zionists'), are not really Semites, but oriental 'Khazars', descendants of Mongolians from Central Asia.[53] 'Neo-Khazars' (the reference being to European Ashkenazi Jews) have 'seized control of world Jewish affairs, largely through the financial activities of the Rothschilds and the half-dozen banking dynasties allied with them.'[54]

This is an argument also found in virulently antisemitic British publications associated with the Christian and former National Front figure, McKilliam.[55] But as well as being part and parcel of international capitalism, symbolised by the Rothschilds, Jews are also responsible for communism. This is a familiar Nazi argument, complete with references to New York bankers Schiff and Kuhn Loeb, also found in National Front literature, reviving yet another antisemitic myth. The contradiction of supporting both capitalism and communism only 'makes sense' in the context of a Jewish conspiracy, of which the 'six million myth' and 'Zionist imperialism' are an integral part. 'The evil Marxist monstrosity unleashed on the world by the same 'Khazar' element... spawned its Siamese twin of Zionist imperialism.'[56]

In the usual twisted logic, Jews are seen as reponsible for two world wars; and Czarist pogroms are largely an invention on a par with Nazi genocide. The Jews, or as Grimstad would have it, 'Khazars', are arch-criminals wherever they are; they are also Zionist imperialists, world bankers, and communists. All these 'Khazars' have an obsession about annihilation of themselves and others, which is born out in their obscene scriptures.

The Six Million Reconsidered is a lavishly illustrated publication offering few variations on the basic neo-Nazi themes. Perhaps the greatest emphasis, backed up by photographs, is placed on the alleged atrocities in the 'slave labour empire of Soviet Russia'. In the chapter entitled 'Jews and Communism', the Nazis' 'supposed "Six Million" victims' are constrasted with the murder of millions under communism in which Jews are seen to have played a central part. This is another echo of the *Protocols* suitably updated.

The figure of 45 million victims of communism is advanced,[57] in which Bolshevism is invariably seen as consonant with Judaism and Palestine — even prior to the foundation of the Israeli state. The text is accompanied by a large number of gruesome photographs intended to identify the real criminals. These are, of course, the Jews, indistinguishable from the communists...

This concludes the survey of the neo-Nazi Holocaust-denial literature in the States.

Left-wing antisemitism: the case of Lenni Brenner

A very particular variety of left-wing revisionism may be exemplified by the American trotskyist journalist, Lenni Brenner, in *Zionism in the Age of the Dictators: A Reappraisal* (1983).[58] Brenner does not deny the Holocaust, or seek to minimise it. His intervention is of a different kind. Rather, on the basis of skewed and irresponsible interpretations of particular documents, the existence of which are not in dispute, he claims that the Zionist movement in general not only collaborated with the Nazis, as if that allegation were not disturbing enough, but that Zionism and

Nazism are entirely congruent; and that Zionism, by implication, bears responsibility for the Holocaust. His hypothesis echoes that of the British Anti-Zionist Organisation (BAZO) in such pamphlets as Tony Greenstein's 'Zionism: Antisemitism's Twin in Jewish Garb' and the pamphlet of the fanatical Neturei Karta sect, 'The Holocaust Victims Accuse', distributed through BAZO;[59] and these have their counterparts elsewhere within different sections of the left. This pernicious charge of Zionist-Nazi collaboration is a variation of the UN 1975 resolution 'Zionism equals racism' which, as Bryan Cheyette[60] has pointed out in his review of Brenner, has continued to generate its own discourse, and is in effect writing a fictionally 'revised' world. Brenner's depicts Zionism as a modern racist ideology of Jewish separation based on *Blut und Boden* (Blood and Soil), the title of his second chapter, hence its symbiosis with Nazism. In so doing, he completely ignores the origins of Zionism as a nineteenth century European ideology of nationalism and self-determination. Other nationalisms are learned about, but there is widespread ignorance of the early history of Jewish nationalism. Antisemitism was clearly significant, but Zionism was also a messianic movement which drew on Jewish traditions and aspirations. The complexity is captured by Shlomo Avineri:

> Jewish nationalism was then one specific aspect of the impact of the ideas and social structures unleashed by the French Revolution, modernism and secularism. It was a response to the challenges of liberalism and nationalism much more than a response to antisemitism... It substituted a secular self-identity of the Jews as a nation for the traditional and orthodox self-identity in religious terms... As such, it is as much a part of the Jewish history of liberation and the quest for 'self-identity'.[61]

Brenner then goes on to argue that accommodation with antisemitism became a central stratagem of the Zionist movement, implying that the Zionists did not, indeed, could not organise against antisemitism. He then proceeds to exemplify this extraordinary thesis citing cases of alleged collaboration. Brenner's view of Zionism is reductionist and a-historical. Obviously it is legitimate to criticise Zionist policies, but the grounds Brenner chooses, those of collaboration, are simply not appropriate.

One particularly dramatic example of alleged collaboration

concerns the so-called 'Transfer Agreement' (the Ha'avura) of June 1933 between the Nazis and the Zionist officials of the Jewish Agency, with British acquiescence. This is the focus of Brenner's chapter six. Interestingly, this is also the subject of a book by Edwin Black, *The Transfer Agreement: the Untold Story of the Secret Agreement between the Third Reich and Jewish Palestine* (1981).[62] A second example is a document produced by the radical extremist Irgun Zvai Lemi in January 1941 proposing their participation in the war on the German side.

The transfer project itself was widely discussed and debated in the contemporary press. In particular, it has been addressed in Lucy Dawidowicz's authoritative study of the Holocaust, *The War against the Jews*. It is therefore no secret.

What was the purpose of the 'Transfer Agreement' of 1933? The date is important for interpreting motives. Under the terms of the agreement, wealthy German Jews could deposit up to four thousand British pounds in German banks. This money would be used to buy agricultural equipment and other necessary goods to be shipped to Palestine to help build up the economy of the Jewish 'national home'. The German Jewish participants would then be admitted to Palestine over and above the quota, and emigrants could later reclaim their money (although, in fact, a large proportion was lost in the transfer process). In effect, this plan helped some twenty thousand Jews flee from Hitler Germany.

The plan was widely discussed. It was critically reviewed by some Jews outside Germany for whom it caused some distress for obvious reasons. It raised both political and ethical problems. Opinions were divided. But it saved lives. The debate could not ignore that the transfer agreement afforded an opportunity not only for capitalists but also for oppressed German Jews to emigrate at a time when Western Europe and America had shut their doors to Jewish immigration.

Brenner attacks the arrangement itself as 'collaboration'. He focuses on a related memorandum sent by the Zionist Federation of Germany to the Nazis in June 1933 requesting a meeting with the Nazis to work out a *modus vivendi*. Brenner claims that this document remained buried until 1962, suggesting a cover-up. In fact it was mentioned a quarter of a century earlier in an article by

Joachim Prinz, a young German Zionist leader. Prinz wrote:

> The Nazi attitude towards the Zionists was only a facade. In reality, Zionists were and are miserably treated... this seeming pro-Zionist attitude of the German government is not an expression of, and should not be confused with, cooperation on the part of one side or another.[63]

Brenner does not quote this part of Prinz's article which makes a case against any charge of 'collaboration'. Brenner refers to the same source, but by selective quotation interprets it in such a way as to convey the opposite meaning.

As the German historian, Alexander Schölch, quite correctly emphasises in his essay 'The Third Reich, the Zionist Movement, and the Palestinian Conflict'[64] — it was not the Zionists who finally succeeded in convincing the German Jews of the need to emigrate, but rather the Nazis who forced this 'insight' upon them. It was not the Zionists who led the Nazis to decide to force German Jews to emigrate; rather, the Nazis used the Zionists. The Zionists tried to organise the emigration in the way that was most favourable to them.

Because of the balance of power — and it is surely an anti-semitic thesis, and part of Jewish stereotyping to suggest that Zionists enjoyed power, particularly under Nazi Germany — this arrangement at that time coincided with the interests of the Nazis who wanted to make Germany 'Judenfrei' (Jew-free).

Underlying this and other interpretations of alleged collaboration is a very particular hypothesis that such behaviour is somehow part of the inner logic of Zionism. So the interpretation is strangely circular and self-fulfilling, as in all conspiracy theories. In this respect, and this respect only, his book has a certain inner consistency and compelling quality.

The second example concerning the Irgun illustrates a different technique, but within the same interpretative frame. The document to which Brenner refers is certainly extant, and, like the Transfer Agreement, is not a revelation. It has been published in Israel as part of the official history of the Haganah. It has also been referred to by Yehuda Bauer in his book *From Diplomacy to Resistance, a History of Jewish Palestine, 1939-1945 (1973)*[65]; and in Walter Laqueur, *A History of Zionism (1982)*.[66]

In Palestine still under British mandate, the Jews did not have a single, united leadership. The Zionist movement and the Jewish people as a whole were very fragmented.[67] There was no one authority but perpetual conflict and many different voices. For this reason it is extremely difficult to talk of Jewish foreign policy, or, indeed, Jewish power, in the years leading up to the Holocaust and afterwards.

In Palestine from 1940 mass Jewish resistance to the British occupying force was organised by the Haganah, a militia of the Mapai (Labour) Party. It was part of the Zionist movement and subject to the authority of a civilian committee. In 1937, there was a split in the underground, more right-wing organisation, Etzel, which had been formed in 1931 as a breakaway group from the Haganah. Half of Etzel, known as 'Irgun B', rejoined the Haganah. The remainder, now composed chiefly of Revisionists (their titular leader was Vladimir Ze'ev Jabotinsky) whose party, the Union of Jewish Revisionists, was outside the Zionist movement, formed a new Etzel organisation the Irgun Tsva Leumi. They were responsible for a number of acts of terrorism, both against the Arab population and against British soldiers. Unlike the Haganah, it was not answerable to the Zionist movement.[68]

In the summer of 1940, with the external threat growing, and following the Arab revolt of 1936-39, there was an absence of unity both in the Haganah and in the rival underground movements. The question they were asking was 'Who is the real enemy — the British or the Germans?'. Jabotinsky had been pro-British. Leaders of Etzel, including Avaham Stern (hence the name Stern gang) who had been imprisoned by the British in 1939-40, and Menachem Begin (still in Poland at that point, but later leader of the Stern gang from 1943), held the view that Britain was a hostile force. Stern, however, went much further by suggesting that Britain's enemies should become their allies, that is, Germany and Italy.

On Stern's release from prison with four other comrades, there was enormous confrontation within Etzel which split along pro-Stern (Lehi or 'Etzel in Israel') and pro-Revisionist lines ('Etzel in the hand of Israel') in favour of the latter. At this point Lehi consisted of a maximum of 50 hardcore Revisionists.

Lehi established contact with the Axis powers through an emissary via Lebanon. Contact was made through Roser, a local German intelligence agent, and Otto van Hentig, who sent a memorandum to the German representative in Turkey. Lehi also drew up a document suggesting that they were prepared to enter the war on the side of the Germans.

The document, which purported to emanate from the Irgun and not from a miniscule splinter group, is called a 'Proposal of the National Military Organization (Irgun Zvai Leumi, IZL) concerning the Solution of the Jewish Question in Europe and the Participation of the NMO [the Stern gang] in the War on the Side of Germany'. The Ankara document is dated 11 January 1941 and was lodged in the German Embassy in Turkey. No reply was ever received.

A leader of Lehi since 1935 when he arrived in Palestine was Yitzhak Shamir, Foreign Minister of Israel under Begin. Shamir is currently joint Prime Minister with Shimon Peres in the present coalition, and leader of the right-wing Likud party. The details of Shamir's relations with the Nazis were published in the respected Israeli daily, *Ha'aretz*, on January 31, February 3 and 6, 1983.[69]

There are a number of points to be made here. The first concerns the Jewish Revisionists. They were a fringe party. The break-away Lehi was even more marginal. It is estimated as a group of forty five or fifty at the most. This makes the claim that modern-day Israel is run by Zionist Nazi collaborators a patent distortion.

The fact remains, however, that this document is absolutely authentic; and it testifies to a minor, but nevertheless shameful, episode of Jewish resistance in Palestine. However, the history of world war II resistance movements is often clouded. The political irresolution and ambiguities of the French resistance were captured in two highly controversial films, *Lacombe Lucien*[70] and *Le Chagrin et la Pitié*.[71] Yet diaspora Jews and Israelis, (the two are often conflated in ignorance), are expected to have a higher moral standards — as if they were a people, or a 'race' apart. This in itself is antisemitic.

This same antisemitism allows Israel to be judged by altogether different criteria from other nation states. This is further discussed in chapter seven. This chain of reasoning is part of the more diffuse political and moral delegitimation of Israel to which Brenner makes a significant contribution. It is no surprise that Brenner's works are advertised by the IHR.

The second point concerns the timing. In 1941 Hitler's genocidal policies had not yet been put into operation, although of course his radical antisemitism and antisemitic policies were public knowledge. It is cynical in the extreme to appear to blame the Zionists for not foreseeing the 'Final Solution', an accusation that could just as easily be levelled at the Allies, or the German population. Any claim that this extremist group, or the German Zionists in general, not only collaborated with the Nazis but, by implication, colluded with the plans for genocide is based on ludicrous hindsight. It is an anachronism. As Schölch[72] has shown, realistic alternatives must be demonstrated if the writing of history is to remain meaningful. And it is also extraordinary and 'a pecular inversion of logic'[73] to blame the Jews for the fact that the British government or the colonies did not open their doors to Jewish refugees. The Zionist resolve to establish a Jewish 'national homeland' was therefore hardened after 1939.

The virulently antisemitic thesis of Brenner, like the neo-Nazi Holocaust denial literature, can be found in a number of variations both on the marxist and anarchist left.[74] Apart from the BAZO publications referred to earlier, they include East German sources like Klaus Polkehn, 'The secret contacts: Zionism and Nazi Germany, 1933-41' published in the *Journal of Palestine Studies,*[75] and an earlier article reprinted from the GDR's weekly magazine, *Horizont.*[75] In the Soviet Union, the disturbing antisemitic, anti-Zionist trend present in both scholarly and popular publications is represented by Lev Korneev in such books as *Klassovaya Sushchnost sionizma (The Class Essence of Zionism)* (1982)[76]. Korneev appears to have taken over from Evgeny Evseev, a staff member of the Soviet Academy of Sciences' Philosophy Institute. This book presents a panoramic view of Jewish history from Biblical times. Korneev describes the process by which, supposedly, Jews have over centuries gradually and systematically accumulated financial and political power on a world scale, anticipating the rise of Zionism. The Talmud is referred to as a religious work in which 'money is the criterion not only of material but also of spiritual values and the basis of human intercourse, morality and history'.[77] He also asserts that Jews also controlled Russia's banks, natural resources as well as the media, banks and the military industrial complex in the West at the present time.

Regarding the Holocaust, Korneev claims that the Jews deliberately exaggerated the number of victims to suit their own cynical ends.[78] In a passage in bold type he writes 'Were it not for the

Zionist-Nazi alliance the number of victims in the Second World War would of course have been less'.[79]

He would appear to be saying that Jews are at least partially responsible for the murder of Russians and other Soviet nationalities by the Nazis. This is a very serious charge indeed in a country which suffered such enormous losses and where the Soviet war dead are a constant point of reference.

The Class Essence of Zionism was favourably reviewed in the Soviet Government newspaper, *Izvestiya*[80], and the Communist Party Central Committee organ, *Soveskskya Kultura.*[81] On a more positive note, however, at the Moscow book launch on 6 June 1983 a split occurred between members of the newly-formed Anti-Zionist Committee of the Soviet Public;[82] and in the latter half of 1983, Ivan Martynov,[83] a non-Jewish bibliographer, together with Leningrad Jewish 'refuseniks' have been conducting an anti-Korneev campaign.

Much the same set of neo-Nazi arguments present in the IHR, and, no less frighteningly, albeit in a somewhat different form, on the predominantly marxist left, are advanced by a different set of actors in France where Robert Faurisson has been cast in the leading role. His publisher has left anarchist credentials.

5. The French scene and the Faurisson Affair

Robert Faurisson, whose story is told below, is not the first French neo-Nazi apologist of the post-war period; nor is he an isolated case. A French version of the neo-Nazi myth was propagated by Maurice Bardèche, a leading fascist theoretician and literary critic, in his book *Nuremberg ou la Terre Promise (Nuremberg or the Promised Land)* published as early as 1948.

Before looking in detail at Bardèche and later neo-fascists we need to consider some disconcerting facts concerning antisemitism in France.

French antisemitism

The horrors of the 'Final Solution' tend to have put the Vichy anti-Jewish policy in the shade. Vichy is the French spa town where Marshal Pétain set up his collaborationist government from 2 July 1940 to August 1944, after signing an armistice with Hitler's Germany on 22 June 1940 offering a pledge of cooperation. The Vichy government assisted the Germans in their deportation and extermination policy more than any other European country. This assessment includes the fascist regimes of Hungary and Roumania.[1] On 3 October 1940 a major anti-Jewish statute was passed, and on 20 March 1941 a General Commissariat for Jewish Affairs was set up to prepare further anti-Jewish legislation and to take police measures. By the end of 1944 some 76,000 Jews had been deported.[2] Their fate was reported in the clandestine press. Some 2,500, less than 3%, survived. The destination for the vast majority, 70,000, was Auschwitz. Most were gassed on arrival. The remainder were sent to other camps: to Maidenec and Sobibor, and a handful ended up in Buchenwald in August 1944. These are the statistics given by the official German archives complemented by lists established by the Ministry for ex-Servicemen.[3]

It is reassuring for leftists to assume that antisemitism, like the history of Zionism, is exclusively of the right. This would not merely be an oversimplification: it is incorrect. Historically, antisemitism in France, including in its heyday in the 1890s, the time of the Dreyfus affair, has been fuelled by nationalist elements from both ends of the political spectrum. Antisemitism has that in common with sexist ideology and misogyny: it transcends the traditionally conceived divisions of right and left.

The classical antisemitic work of Drumont, *La France Juive (Jewish France),* first published in 1885, was the best French seller of the second half of the twentieth century, running into 200 editions.[4] Its appeal may in part be explained by his manipulating categories of left- and right-wing antisemitism. On the left, Jews were equated with the evils of the capitalist system, which must be replaced by 'state socialism'.[5] On the right, in the anti-Dreyfusard tradition, antisemitism is a crucial component of the 'integral nationalism'. This was the platform of the nationalist and Catholic traditionalist *Action Française,* founded in 1899, for whom a Jew is a threat to France and the symbol of perversity. It has been argued that *Action Française*[6] was a model for subsequent, more successful fascist movements.[7]

The main inspiration of *Action Française,* which was also anti-German, was the prolific novelist, Maurice Barrès, one of the most influential writers of his day. For Barrès, Dreyfus[8] was capable of treachery, that is, of handing military secrets to the Germans, by virtue of his race.[9] The man largely associated with *Action Française,* Charles Maurras, was a Vichy supporter. In terms of racist nationalism, including its home-grown theoreticians and intellectuals, France had little to learn from Hitler Germany.[10]

As in the 1890s, antisemitism and antisemitic culture is today present across the political structure. By antisemitic culture I refer to unquestioning belief in, and uncritical transmission of, negative Jewish stereotypes. In a Christian culture, these are not entirely unconnected, in my view, with the rejection of the 1964 Vatican II proposals by an extremely right-wing section of Catholic opinion because of Vatican II's withdrawal of the millennial charge of deicide against the Jewish people. For many Christians, Jews still represent anti-Christ.

Maurice Bardèche

The neo-Nazi myth was further propagated by Maurice Bardèche, a leading fascist theoretician and literary critic who founded *Défense de l'Occident (Defence of the West),* the theoretical journal of French fascism, in December 1951. Bardèche enjoys the dubious distinction of beginning his book, *Qu'est-ce que le fascisme?*[11] *(What is fascism?)* with the statement: 'I am a fascist writer'. Most of the arguments are rehearsed in his book *Nuremberg ou la Terre Promise,* in which he writes: 'For three years we have been duped by history.'[12]

The same set of arguments are on offer some thirty years later. The continuity is striking. And the line from Bardèche to Rassinier and Faurisson is strongly suggestive.[13] Bardèche's fascist positions in *Nuremberg* may be summed up as follows:

1. History has been falsified, but not everyone has accepted the verdict of the victors at Nuremberg;
2. The Allies were also guilty of war crimes, particularly bombings;
3. Photographs of concentrations camps proving the bestiality of the Germans are 'too good to be true';
4. The Nazis were engaged in a preventive war;
5. The Treaty of Versailles was tantamount to German slavery;
6. Gas was used in the camps for disinfection purposes: 'extermination'
7. While not denying the existence of concentration camps, it is suggested that the evidence is flimsy, second-hand and probably faked — deaths in the camps were primarily due to food shortages and epidemics;
8. Atrocities were committed by the Allies, including the French underground and the Soviet troops in Germany;
9. 'The solution of the Jewish problem' simply referred to the establishment of ghettos in the East;

10. It was morally wrong to suggest Germans should disobey orders in that morality was not on the side of 'democracy' as practised in Washington or London. A strong state is essential to combat communism;
11. It was also wrong to be concerned with Jewish dead, since it was the Jews who caused the war…

Paul Rassinier

Bardèche's apology for fascism was echoed by Paul Rassinier but, whereas Bardèche's contribution to the contemporary fascist 're-visionist' scene is not publicly acknowledged by his fellow fascists — this would not be politically expedient as his fascist views are well known — this is not the case with Rassinier. However, as the quotations clearly illustrate, it is frankly absurd to pretend that Rassinier was anything but antisemitic. Rassinier was Faurisson's mentor. He is also an important reference in English-speaking fascist circles: he is constantly cited by both Butz in the States and Verrall, alias Harwood, in Britain.

Rassinier's importance for the fascist propagandists stems from the fact that he was a socialist, a member of the social-democrat party, the SFIO, the forerunner of the present Socialist Party. He was deported to Buchenwald and Dora for resistance activities. After the war he became a socialist deputy and served for one year before retirement. Give his different political pedigree, Rassinier's denial of the existence of the gas chambers offers far greater mile-age in terms of fascist strategy.

Rassinier was quite prolific. His books include *Le Passage à la ligne (The Crossing of the Line)* (1950), *Le Mensonge d'Ulysse (The Lie of Ulysses)* (1979, 6th edition), *Ulysse Trahi par les Siens (Ulysses Betrayed by his own People)* (1962), *Le Véritable Procès Eichmann (The Real Eichmann Trial)* (1962), and *Le Drame des Juifs européens (The Drama of European Jews)* (1964). Two of these, *The Lie of Ulysses* and *Ulysses Betrayed,* were reissued by Faurisson's publisher, La Vieille Taupe, in 1979 and 1980 respec-tively.

Rassinier's books are remarkably repetitive and bristle with antisemitism. He blandly argues, for example, in *Les Res-ponsables de la seconde guerre mondiale (Those Responsible for the Second World War),* published in 1967, that the misfortunes of the Jews under Hitler were largely a consequence of their own doing:

the Jews were foreigners, and there was simply no room for a national minority. According to Rassinier's account, it was the Jews and the international Jewish community who declared war on Hitler Germany — so he had to defend himself. All Rassinier's books were combined in one, in an English language edition entitled *Debunking the Genocide Myth* (1978) published by the Historical Review Press. The first eleven chapters consist of the bulk of the first three books, and *The Drama of the European Jews* makes up the final four chapters.

This short extract from chapter fourteen, 'Statistics: Six Million or...' gives the flavour:

> After some fifteen years of historical research, I have come to the following conclusion: it was in 1943 that National Socialist Germany was accused for the first time of the systematic mass extermination of the Jews in the gas chambers. The author of this first horrible and infamous accusation was a Polish Jew.[14]

Implicit here is a Jewish conspiracy. Referring to the Gerstein report about use of Zyklon B gas in the camps, he comments on the outcry provoked by this 'immoral forgery',[15] evoking the satanic power of Jews:

'In the world press the gas chambers mythology began its dance to every tune and diabolical rhythm; that unrestrained saraband full of missteps has not stopped since.'[17]

Other quotations confirm his rabid antisemitism and racism within a familiar Nazi, conspiratorial view of the world:

> There is no doubt that twentieth-century humanity is faced with a racial problem: the relations that can or should exist between the white race and the coloured races. It is a problem that exists both on a physical level and on an intellectual level...
> But, concerning the Jews especially, it is not a race that today they represent, but a way of life and its aspirations. And, it is not a racial problem that they pose, as the State of Israel proves so well, but an economic and social problem, of such dimensions that... it envisages the setting up of a mercantile feudal system, which, as we have said, would take in the whole world.[17]

The American translation by Adam Robbins, with an introduction by Pierre Hofstetter, includes notes and references which clearly postdate the original. Hofstetter was a former contributor to the racist and fascist *Europe-Action,* together with Alain de Benoist of the French New Right, as discussed in chapter three. Articles in *Europe-Action* also stressed Allied 'atrocities' — a key fascist argument[18] which implies that Allies were no different from Hitler Germany.

Rassinier is a recurrent reference in the Holocaust denial literature and, partly because his work is little known, and the left association is confusing, he tends to constitute a marginal myth in his own right. But Rassinier falls into the same category as the other fascist manipulators, sharing the obsessions of his admirer, Faurisson.

The Darquier interview

In November 1978 Robert Faurisson wrote a letter on the 'problem' of the gas chambers. Its timing was important. Its publication in *Le Monde* followed close on the heels of a scandalous interview with Darquier de Pellepoix in the weekly magazine, *L'Express.*[19] Darquier was the Vichy Commissioner General for Jewish Affairs.[20] Darquier has been described as the 'French Eichmann' — though even Eichmann, the architect of the 'Final Solution', did not seek to deny its reality.[21] Darquier, edited the *Anti-Juif (Anti-Jew),* which blamed the Jews for the world's troubles. He also wrote an introduction to a French edition of the *Protocols* published in 1939. He argued, as did Hitler, that whether they were true or false was not important: it was their vision that counted.[22]

Darquier was the second director of the Commission, created by the 1941 Vichy Law. He occupied the post for nearly two years. He was obsessed with the notion of race, and his propaganda machine spawned a pyramid of racist institutions. Whereas his predecessor, Vallat, played down the Nazi racist abuses of biology and physical anthropology, leading to the matching of physical types with intelligence and genetic desirability, Darquier had no such scruples.[23] He made a radio statement in December 1942 suggesting that the deportation of Jews was a question of 'public hygiene'. The vocabulary of pollution is significant. Darquier made a number of proposals which went even further than those proposed by the Germans.[24]

The interview with the war criminal Darquier was a shocking event. It provoked a wave of indignation. It had been assumed that he was long dead, having been condemned to death in his absence on 10 December 1947. In fact, like the Nazi Belgian Rexist, Léon Degrelle,[25] he was enjoying military protection in Spain. Clearly, no effort had been made by the Giscardian government to extradite him, and the Gaullist Minister of Justice, Alain Peyrefitte, lost no time in making a statement to the effect that extradition orders were not made on political grounds. Yet there are obvious counter-examples on the left, like the Stuttgart lawyer, Klaus Croissant, whose only crime was to defend his clients, the Baader-Meinhof urban guerrillas, who later committed suicide in the Stannheim top security prison under suspicious circumstances.

In his *Express* interview, Darquier sought to deny both the Holocaust and the gas chambers ('There was no genocide — you must get that out of your head'). He claimed that only lice were gassed in Auschwitz. He also denied his own responsibility in the formulation of anti-Jewish legislation and in organising mass deportations. And he expressed no regrets.

If this were not enough, the interview also gave offence because of its racist vulgarity and innuendo. The images of Jewry are reminiscent of the classical antisemitic work of Eduard Drumont of the Dreyfus period.

For Darquier, Jews are typically liars: the six million dead? — 'devilish Jewish propaganda'; 'a pure invention'; 'Jews will do anything for publicity'; 'Jews only have on idea in their head: to make a fuss wherever they are. And their aim? To make Jerusalem the capital of the world'. This war criminal went on to suggest that the photographs of gas chamber victims are 'Jewish fakes', and that the responsibility for the war lay with the Jews.

The Faurisson affair

The Holocaust denial in France has become synonymous with the Faurisson affair. What is more, it has become embroiled with Noam Chomsky, the distinguished American linguist and staunch opponent of the Vietnam war.

Faurisson's book is entitled *Mémoire en Défense — contre ceux qui m'accusent de falsifier l'histoire. La question des chambres à gaz (Testimony in Defence: Against those who Accuse me of Falsifying History. The Question of the Gas Chambers)*. It is Faurisson's answer to the accusation of falsifying history. *Testimony in Defence* was published in Paris by Pierre Guillaume for the left anarchist publishing house, La Vieille Taupe (The Old Mole), in 1980. It boasts a preface by Noam Chomsky, an impassioned if ill-placed defence of free speech. It was this and no more. Chomsky most emphatically has no sympathy with the Holocaust denial propagandists.

Securing a preface by Chomsky was quite a feat. It was not what he said that was significant but the face that the book was now closely associated with such a well-known and respected intellectual. It guaranteed Faurisson a measure of authority and a following largely, of course, on the fascist right, but also among some sections of the anti-imperialist, anarchist left. At the same time it gave him access to the media.

Faurisson's denial of the Holocaust first appeared in the satirical *Canard Enchaîné* on 17 July 1974. It subsequently gained public attention in December 1978 when the influential Paris daily, *Le Monde,* published a letter from Faurisson headed 'The problem of the "gas chambers" or "The rumour of Auschwitz" '. He wrote with calculated cynicism: 'The non-existence of the "gas chambers" is good news for poor humanity. Good news like this should not be suppressed any longer.'[26]

Robert Faurisson is not a historian. He belongs to a long line of antisemitic academics and literary critics. Until recently, he was a lecturer in twentieth-century French literature at the University of Lyons II. He specialises in revealing 'the real meaning' of texts. In Faurisson's view, texts have one particular meaning, or none at all, an approach to stylistics he calls 'the Ajax method' — because 'it scours as it cleans as it shines'.

Faurisson has 'demystified' or otherwise cleaned up a whole series of French authors in this way. He exposed the 'fabrications' and 'falsifications' of previous interpretations of which readers were 'dupes' and 'victims', a deception which in some cases had gone undetected for a hundred years. He then turned his attention to other types of text, including Anne Frank's *Diary*[27] and the Gerstein report. With characteristic repetitiveness and thoroughness, the Ajax method having done its work, he informed the world that, in his view, the *Diary* was a 'fabrication' and the gas chambers an 'enourmous hoax'. This is the 'good news for humanity' announced in his letter to *Le Monde*.

Being such a benefactor of humanity, Faurisson had been itching to impart this news for some time. Over a period of four years he had written to *Le Monde* 22 times about the gas chambers. *Le Monde* finally conceded after Faurisson had commented approvingly on Darquier's allegation in a letter dated 10 November 1978, and published in *L'Express*, which he circulated to a number of newspapers. Following this letter, he was contacted by the socialist daily, *Le Matin*. In an Interview in *Le Matin* of 16 November 1978, he expressed the hope that the *Express* interview:

> will help the public to realise that the alleged massacres in the 'gas chambers' and the alleged 'genocide' are part of same lie which, unfortunately, has hitherto been sustained by official history (that of the victors) and by the considerable power of the media. In common with the Frenchman, Paul Rassinier (a former member of the resistance and a deportee), with the German, Wilhelm Stäglich, [author of the *Auschwitz Myth*], the Englishman, Richard E. Harwood, the American, Arthur R. Butz (author of the *Hoax of the Twentieth Century,* such a remarkable work that clearly no one has been able to reply to him) and twenty other authors who are either ignored or calumnied as I hereby proclaim… that the massacres in so-called 'gas chambers' are a historical lie… The drama documentary 'Holocaust' will not shed any light on this question, nor will LICA [League against Racism and Anti-Semitism, now known as LICRA]… We can only make sense of it by examination of the different arguments.

Amidst the outrage provoked by the Darquier interview and in discussions about the screening of the 'Holocaust' film, which was eventually shown in France in February 1979, Faurisson's letter came under fire. He used this pretext to demand his legal right to reply and to impart his good news to an even larger section of the French reading public. It was at this point, between Darquier and the 'Holocaust' film, that *Le Monde* gave in.[29] A full version of Faurisson's text had previously been published by Bardèche in the June 1978 issue of *Défense de l'Occident.* As the fascist *Défense* has a limited circulation, Faurisson sent copies of the text to a number of public figures. The letter was accompanied by the following typed note:

Conclusions (after thirty years' research) of revisionist authors:

1. The Hitler 'gas chambers' never existed.
2. 'Genocide' (or 'attempted genocide') of Jews never took place; more precisely, Hitler never gave the order (or would never have approved it) that anyone should be killed on the grounds of their race or religion.
3. The alleged 'gas chambers' and the alleged 'genocide' are part of the same lie.
4. This lie, which is essentially Zionist in origin, has allowed a huge political and financial swindle of which the state of Israel is the principal beneficiary.
5. The principal victims of this lie and of this swindle are the German and Palestinian people.
6. The tremendous power of the official media has hitherto ensured the success of this lie and censured the freedom of expression of those who denounced the lie.
7. The supporters of the lie now know that their lie has only a few more years to run: they are distorting the objective and the nature of revisionist research; what is simply a concern with a return to historical truth they are calling 'resurgence of Nazism' or a 'falsification of history'.[30]

This produced explosive reactions and a blaze of publicity, which Faurisson had sought for so long. It was at this juncture that the Dean of Lyons University decided to suspend Faurisson's lectures following hostile demonstrations.

How is it that Chomsky and the left-wing French sociologist, Serge Thion, became involved in the Faurisson affair? The association is highly disconcerting for anyone on the left. Chomsky and Thion are friends. They were both prominent in the anti-imperialist struggle in South East Asia.[31] They are much admired on the left for their outspoken and courageous stand. What happened?

Chomsky was one of the first to sign a petition in defence not of Faurisson, he insists, but of civil rights. An 'opinion' (*un avis*) originally solicited by Thion which Chomsky emphasises was intended simply as an 'opinion', nothing more, was published as preface to Faurisson's *Testimony in Defence*. Yet Professor Arno J. Mayer of Princeton University talked with Chomsky about his preface one month before it was published so that he knew exactly in what context it was being used.[32] Faye's version, however, is slightly different. According to a letter sent to his friend, the French writer, Jean-Pierre Faye, which Faye made public in a televised interview, Chomsky sought to retract this 'opinion', but too late. Convinced by Faye, Chomsky wrote to Thion requesting him either not to publish his statement on civil liberties, or to publish it as separate document. Thion also issued a communiqué, quoting from the letter in question.[33] But the deed was done. However, this does not square with other information. Other Chomsky interviews, like the one given to the Italian newspaper, *La Stampa,* published on 18 December 1980, give a different impression. According to the report of the interview, he stated that, even with hindsight, his 'opinion' was not misused.

Chomsky's 'opinion' published in *Testimony in Defence* is entitled 'Some elementary comments on the right to freedom of speech'. In the second paragraph, Chomsky advises the reader that he has no particular knowledge of the subject, that is, of the gas chambers. This impression is confirmed when, towards the end of the preface, he tells us he is not very familiar with Faurisson's work. In fact, there is no evidence that Chomsky had read anything at all by Faurisson when he wrote this piece. What he had read, at least in part, was Pierre Vidal-Naquet's scholarly and detailed demolition of Faurisson's argument in 'A Paper Eichmann'.[34] That surely was sufficient. Yet Chomsky does not address himself to Vidal-Naquet's arguments. He restricts his comments to Vidal-Naquet's reaction to the petition referred to in 'A Paper Eichmann'.

The petition itself speaks for a man at the butt of persecution. But his defence of free speech knows no bounds. He writes:

> I should like to add a final remark about Faurisson's alleged 'anti-semitism'. Let it be said that even if Faurisson were a rabid anti-semite or a fanatic Nazi supporter — and these are accusations levelled at him in letters I have received... — that has absolutely no bearing on his legitimacy of the civil rights' defence... On the contrary, that would make the defence of these rights all the more imperative since, once again,... and history shows this, it is precisely the right to express the most dreadful ideas freely which must be most rigorously defended...
>
> Leaving aside this central question, one may wonder whether Faurisson is really an anti-semite or a Nazi. As I said before, I am not very familiar with his work... but I am in

possession of no evidence which would support any such conclusions... As far as I can judge Faurisson is a kind of relatively apolitical liberal.[35]

That anyone can describe Faurisson as a 'kind of relatively apolitical liberal' after reading his *Testimony* and other essays conveniently reproduced by Thion is quite extraordinary. It is my considered view that Chomsky committed an act of gross irresponsibility.

Taking an extreme anarchist position on free speech may appear attractive in theory. In practice, however, it usually involves making judgements. In this case, Chomsky has made a judgement about Faurisson by characterising him as a 'kind of relatively apolitical liberal'. As this is clearly far from being the case, it could be said that this political *laissez-faire* position leads to fudging.

Thion's part in the Faurisson affair is quite different from Chomsky's in that he has willingly assumed the role of Faurisson's spokesperson. His book, *Vérité historique ou vérité politique? (Historical Truth or Political Truth?*. 1980) published by la Vieille Taupe, reproduces a number of Faurisson's hitherto unpublished essays and letters.

In a forceful introduction which strikes an urgent, personal note, Thion invites historical debate on the question of the gas chambers as a fundamental academic principle. He is undecided himself whether they existed or not. This open and questioning disposition is typically part of a certain academic training. In Thion's case, as in Chomsky's, it is no doubt shaped by his profound distrust of 'official versions' of history, whatever their political colouring. The stubborn refusal of sections of the official communist left to admit to the grim reality of Stalinist excesses, put out at the time as CIA fabrications, is part of this resistance to 'official history' which is widespread on the left.

It would be mistaken, in my view, to assume that Thion's involvement is an act of political bad faith. As I see it, Thion, in encouraging a thousand versions of history to bloom, while refusing an acceptable label to any one, replaces a state view of history (which he is surely right to reject) with a range of undifferentiated, equally weighted accounts. The difficulty is that such a range ignores power relations. It is a kind of free-market version of history.

Thion would seem to have fallen into the trap of reproducing

Faurisson's arguments as if they were disinterested contributions to a historical debate. It is tragic that Thion's uncompromising radical commitment to both free speech and academic debate ('we have no desire to discuss his [Faurisson's] intentions')[36] does not allow him to see, even less accept, that Faurisson and others are bent on replacing the present anti-Nazi climate with a Nazi consensus, and that, in order to do so, they are playing intellectual games using academic, anti-authoritarian language. To talk of defending free speech in what is clearly a profoundly racist context can only be attributed to naïveté or bad faith.

For Pierre Guillaume, the proprietor of La Vieille Taupe, in a letter published in *Libération* on 7 March 1979,[37] this constant over-exposure of Nazism is politically undesirable. Guillaume admits that he prefers the reaction 'that's dead and gone', or 'Hitler, who's he?'

Furthermore, in his view, it is 'an attempt to assume ideological power' and a substitute for the analysis of 'real problems'. It was on these dubious grounds that Guillaume was opposed to the screening of the 'Holocaust' film. He argued that deportation and torture are features of war everywhere (an argument also present in Bardèche and comparable sources), and drew attention to the undeniable atrocities committed by the French army during the Algerian war.[38] This lead to an exchange of letters in *Libération* which refer derisively to the Holocaust as the top of the 'horror hit parade' and to 'the great holocaust laments'.[39]

A number of leaflets appeared from the extreme left in support of Faurisson following the LICRA accusation of falsifying history. One such leaflet originally produced in June 1980 by *La Guerre Sociale (Social War),* associated with La Vieille Taupe, was entitled *Qui est le Juif (Who is the Jew?).* It seeks to draw a clear distinction between Darquier and Faurisson, and argues that the doubts about the existence of the gas chambers originated on the left with Rassinier, and the left must be concerned with the truth. The truth, it claims, cannot be antisemitic, even if it contradicts the 'mythology of the holocaust'.

It further argues that 'the legend' of the 'gas chambers' was made official by the Nuremberg Tribunal where the Nazis were judged by the victors. If the function of these trials was to distinguish 'democratic stalinist' camps from the Nazi camps, then it follows that the functions of both anti-fascism and anti-Nazism are comparable in that they serve to justify their own war crimes. The leaflet goes on to proclaim that there is one enemy, namely, the relations of capitalist production. This enemy is not to be confused with a single social group, like the bourgeoisie or the bureaucrats. The tract concludes by supporting Faurisson on the grounds of freedom of expression: it claims that he is being attacked for having looked for truth. Finally, it is stated that the struggle against racism of any description is both shortlived and superficial if it is not a struggle against capital. This is a striking example of dogmatic, maxist reductionism where oppressions are conflated to those of capital and class. It is not merely simplistic: it is also racist in that it ignores other specifities, other patterns of exploitation and exclusion.

These arguments are set out more fully in a 1979 issue of *La Guerre Sociale*[40] produced in association with La Vieille Taupe. The second part has assumed the proportions of a hundred-page book entitled *De L'Exploitation dans les 'camps' à l'exploitation des camps (From the Exploitation in the Camps to the Exploitation of Camps)* which also reprints a number of earlier leaflets.

In May and June 1981, Faurisson stood trial at the Palais de Justice in Paris. There were three separate charges. The first was brought by the eminent historian, Léon Poliakov. Faurisson had accused Poliakov of manipulating and fabricating his sources with particular reference to the Gerstein report.[41] This first charge was a straightforward slander case, but given the charged political context, it carried particular overtones. The second case to be heard, and the only civil charge, was concerned with the social responsibility of the historian. Under Article 382 of the Civil Code, Faurisson was accused of wilfully distorting history. The third charge, relating to an antisemitic radio statement which Faurisson had made on 17 December 1980, was for incitement to racial hatred according to the 1972 French Race Relations Law. Faurisson had stated:

> The alleged gassing and the alleged genocide of Jews are part of the same historical lie which has been the basis of a huge political and financial swindle of which the principle beneficiaries are the State of Israel and the principal victims the German people, not its leaders, and the Palestinian people.

It is a shocking reversion of roles in which the Jewish people are accused of perpetrating crimes of which they were the victims. The reference to Palestinians is no less misleading and cynical. The reality of the gas chambers bears no relation to Palestine or the Palestinians. It is a confusing, diversionary tactic, and one which has had some support on the left. Indeed, there is a certain congruence with left-wing 'revisionism' of the Lenni Brenner variety discussed in chapter four. This argument, together with most of those reproduced and expanded by Faurisson, had been formulated by Rassinier in *Debunking the Genocide Myth*,[42] who uses much the same phrasing. Faurisson only appeared for the first trial, and was found guilty on all three charges. The three cases were reported in *Le Monde*.[43] The trials were reported in the British press by Gitta Sereny in the *New Statesman*,[44] and in the French anti-fascist press.[45] A full legal report was published in *Le Monde* on 18 July 1981, which has been translated in *Patterns of Prejudice*.[46]

We shall begin with the last case. This case, in which the prosecution called on a number of expert witnesses, including historians, was particularly revealing in terms of fascist language and argument. Le Goff, medieval historian, illustrated how over centuries, going back to the year 1,000, a systematic association has been constructed linking Jews with 'fraud' and 'deception'. An understanding of the historical dimension of antisemitism is vital. In his own experience, Jewish teachers are persecuted in present-day Poland in the name of 'anti-Zionism'. For Faurisson, antisemitism and anti-Zionism are synonymous. Madeleine Rébérioux, social historian, referring to Kant, the nineteenth century idealist philosopher, characterised the phrase 'international Zionism' as 'a concept devoid of content'. Whereas the Nazis of the Third Reich referred to 'Jews' and alleged 'Jewish plots', contemporary Nazis refer to 'Zionists' and 'international Zionism'. The same is true in Britain.[47] It is essential to realise that this strategic vocabulary shift is a feature of postwar fascist movements. The equation of 'Jews' with 'Zionist' is not just a facile and misleading formula but part of a well-planned strategy which attracts the allegiance of non-fascists, including uncritical section of the far left.[48]

The second trial for falsification of history was the most remarkable. The charge itself is quite extraordinary. It was a civil case brought by two anti-racist organisation, LICRA (League against Racism and Antisemitism) and MRAP (Movement against Racism and for Friendship among Peoples), together with groups representing former members of the resistance and deportees.

Neither side was inviting the court to rule on historical fact, or for or against a particular interpretation of history. This would have been crass and in any event unacceptable in a liberal democracy. It was Faurisson's methods that were under attack, not the right to express or publish his fundamentally antisemitic views. It was not the Inquisition trying to silence Galileo, as Faurisson's lawyer would have it. The case was based on a new interpretation of Article 382 of the Civil Code which is concerned with civil responsibilities. This new reading focuses on the social responsibility of the historian not to ignore or distort key documents.

In a sense this is somewhat paradoxical since Faurisson claims to be reinterpreting existing documents, a normal part of academic reappraisal. But it is Faurisson's claim to academic status which is at the heart of the trial. Faurisson, Butz and others, as we have seen, go to great lengths to be accepted as genuine academics concerned with the advancement of knowledge. This strategy is evident in the creation of the Institute for Historical Review and its journal.

The lawyers were conscious of the paradox, and addressed themselves to the distortions and gaps in Faurisson's arguments. Another dimension of the paradox was that in order to highlight these distortions it was necessary to contextualise and therefore provide the court with data concerning the gas chambers and the methods of extermination. The prosecution lawyers, in particular Bernard Jouanneau representing LICRA, had taken two years to prepare the case, working with and as historians. The documentation was as voluminous as it was horrifying, its main focus being the Kremer diary. Johann Paul Kremer was an SS doctor who had been transferred to Auschwitz on 30 October 1942, ostensibly to solve the typhus epidemic. On arrival, he was given secret instructions by the doctor in charge. The Kremer diary gives detailed account of gassing arrangements, of the selection and preparation of victims, the removal of hair and gold teeth.

In his books Faurisson argues at some length that the Kremer diary entry in which he records his first participation in the 'special action', describing Auschwitz as an 'extermination camp'[49] has been misinterpreted and manipulated by postwar 'Polack-Stalinist' commentators. He alleges that the term 'extermination' *(Vernichtung)* has nothing to do with gassing, but relates to the typhus epidemic which was raging throughout the camp. He goes so far as to provide a definition of typhus from the Larousse dictionary suggesting that the Greek etymology explains the term *typhos* as a kind of inertia.[50] It is clear that the 'special actions', at which Kremer was present on 15 occasions, coincided exactly with new arrivals at Auschwitz. This further coincided with new, increased deliveries of Zyklon B gas. He maintains that the new arrivals represented an increased health hazard, and hence the gas — for delousing purposes only. Faurisson's other arguments, concerning mistranslation and omission addressed by the prosecution council, are of the same order.

Ostensibly and superficially, the trial was about writing history, about historical method. There are, of course, conventional historical methods, and a historiographer entertains a particular relationship with history. The selection or elicitation of evidential material is intimately tied up with a particular construction of reality: any history, is typically a social construction in narrative form. This construction is eminently political and ideological, and involves categorisation.

To erect categories is to establish the central characteristics of an object. For example, to talk of Jews as a 'problem' is to give a further lease of life to the dehumanised stereotype sustained by Nazi propaganda. This is also how blacks tend to be categorised in the media. And, indeed, all dominated groups. Reference has already been made in chapter two to the manipulation of the category of the natural. Also, the content of what one believes shapes one's stand, and this stand shapes what one sees. Belief in a Jewish world conspiracy[51] will 'explain' or twist events, including the Holocaust, in which Jews are again the arch-conspirators, and the gas chambers a myth of their own making.

Paradoxically, the charge, much of the prosecution and part of the defence, were seemingly apolitical. A number of the prosecution lawyers rejected the political in favour of the 'technical'. The 'technical' arguments amounted largely to detail accounts of the techniques of gassing based on SS diaries and testimonies, particularly the Kremer diary. These were counter-arguments to those advanced by Faurisson in his *Testimony* — but they were not answered by the defence. It made more strategic sense to shift their terrain and construct a defence on the grounds of civil liberties and the limits of knowledge.

This was political — at different levels. It was ostensibly politicised in that Faurisson was portrayed as a victim of a repressive system. It was also a very acceptable liberal and left argument in terms of freedom of speech. The argument about the limits of knowledge was unanswerable. Eric Delcroix, Faurisson's lawyer, began: 'I am not brilliant. I don't claims to know everything. Who can claim to know everything about the truth?' Unimpeachable. Here was the 'revisionist' defence making skilful use of liberal arguments with the knowledge on both sides that fascism is as inimical to liberalism as it is to Marxism.

It was political, too, at another level: in moving from and re-defining the original charge (distortion of history), the defence effectively and radically changed the rules, though this was, of course, still within the juridicial rules and conventions for conducting a defence.

I have referred to the weight of the technical arguments which Bernard Jouanneau and Charles Korman of LICRA presented to the court, through a mass of documents which they had assembled over a two-year period with the help of historians. Jouanneau spoke at some length in an appropriate monotone about the production and use of Zyklon B gas in the camps, and Auschwitz in particular.

Korman's presentation was more personal in tone. He addressed himself to the conditions of the victims in Auschwitz prior to gassing, and to the case of three Dutch women who were recorded as shot — precisely because they rebelled against the 'special action'. In Faurisson's construction, prisoners were typically shot, never gassed.[52] Korman had calculated how many Jewish victims had to be squeezed into the limited area of each chamber so that they remained wedged upright although dead. Young fascists in the courtroom sniggered and poked fun at the apparent impossibility of such maximisation of dying-space.

Other lawyers for the prosecution made complementary points. These included Robert Badinter, former Minister of Justice in the Mitterrand administration, whose vibrant testimony led for the prosecution. It was as if the prosecution felt it incumbent upon them to advance the proof of the Holocaust — as if the neo-Nazi fabrication had to be taken seriously, as if it called for serious rebuttal on behalf of historians. Arguably, this was secondary. However, a prosecution cannot plead distortion in the abstract — data must be provided. This was another paradox of the trial.

As Apfelbaum has commented,[53] the insidious effect of

reading the Holocaust denial literature is to lose one's own identity as a survivor, and, more generally, as a Jew. The experience is comparable to psychological disorientation or sensory deprivation. After the physical genocide, this desire to destroy a people's history and identity represents a symbolic genocide. These were certainly the feelings I experienced during the trial,[54] and I felt nausea then and now.

My precise political assessment of the trial has not wavered: I agree wholeheartedly with Vidal-Naquet[55] and others that it was an aberration. How can a court of law be invited to pass judgement on a version of history? It is unthinkable. At the same time, and I can stand the contradiction, I have an enormous sympathy, and, indeed, an enourmous admiration for lawyers, like Jouanneau and others, who spent two years preparing the trial and who, like me, had been exposed daily to the Holocaust literature and its effects. Some must have entertained doubts about the advisability of this trial.

The case was heard under the Giscard government. I can easily understand how anti-fascists, including Jewish anti-fascist activists, given the complicity of members of the police and high-ranking government officials, were determined to use every means at their disposal, and in this case, the legal system, to control and expose antisemitic activity and attacks. The trial also raises a fundamental problem for liberalism and the limits of free speech.

Arguments in Britain about the pros and cons of banning the National Front produced similar divisions and uncertainties on the left. It would be widely accepted that fascism or fascist presence stifles free speech. Conversely, it is argued that moves to proscribe rightist organisations would certainly be used to ban the revolutionary left. Such moves are common in France against fringe groups, (who immediately regroup under another name), and are operated in Britain to ban both fascist and unemployment marches. Also, since courts would tend to be seen on the left and certainly by most black people as part of a repressive state system used to strengthen and, indeed, administer institutional racism, they cannot be considered as vehicles in the anti-racist struggle. On the other hand, race relations legislation, however toothless, uses the court of law. Clearly, this is a very vexed question.

6. The British Exponents of the Holocaust Denial Myth

The Historical Review Press

In Britain as elsewhere, the neo-Nazi denial of the Holocaust is portrayed by the myth-makers as fact. These pamphlets denying the Holocaust are distributed by the Brighton-based Historical Review Press (HRP). They masquerade under the general title of *Historical Fact.* The HRP list does not merely circulate among Nazi côteries: it is sent out to British universities. In the early 1980's, anyone placing an order was put on a mailing list that was also used by the *Sussex National Front.*

A copy of the HRP wholesale catalogue contains both Nazi and neo-Nazi titles: *Mein Kampf* figures along with Harwood's *Six Million Lost and Found*, referred to below; there is no doubt about the ideological continuity. This is not all. As proof of their links with neo-Nazi activists, they also advertise incendiary devices (for '*bona fide* dealers only'). The address on the form is that of Anthony and Alan Hancock, father and son, who are at the centre of the Holocaust denial strategy in Britain. Anthony Hancock was also a member of the Northern League.

The HRP list of publications advertise titles by the National

Front in the conspiracy tradition, like books by Nesta Webster and Revilo P. Oliver,[1] and also Günther, the official race theoretician of the Third Reich. It is now diversifying and currently offering reproductions of woodcuts in the tradition of national socialist art as originally produced by Sluyterman, and books on the Vikings, seen as part of the 'Aryan' heritage. As has been noted, these are also a feature of GRECE publications. This focus on the traditional is an unchanging dimension of radical antisemitism. Jews are identified with everything that is modern: industrialism, capitalism, pornography, and, of course, money, and liberal democracy.

HRP also publishes *Historical Facts* Nos 1 and 2 by Richard Harwood. The allegation that Harwood is really Richard Verrall, formerly of the National Front, has never been challenged. His pamphlet, *Six Million Lost and Found: The Truth at Last* is undated, but was probably produced in late 1977 or in 1978. It is a reissue of *Did Six Million Really Die?* (1974), the original title, since translated into a number of languages, and which was the subject of a court case in South Africa.[2] This was followed by Harwood's *Nuremberg and Other War Crimes Trials; A New Look* (1978). *Historical Fact* No 3 (1979) is by Michael McLaughlin, leader of the even more hardline British Movement until 1982. All rely heavily on Rassinier,[3] as did Faurisson. They are virtual plagiarisms, with the odd quotation added here and there from British sources together with references to the British war scene.

This flurry of *Historical Facts* has been suceeded by a four-page illustrated newsletter, *Fact Finder, Britain's No. 1 Lie Detector*. It is aimed at school students and distributed by the British Movement from its address in Clwyd, North Wales. There have been four issues to date. The first appeared in November 1980, and circulation has been very limited. Headlines include 'The Hushed-Up Holocaust' and 'New Book Tells the Truth about Hitler's Germany'. The new book is McLaughlin's pamphlet. Issues two and three make the typical Nazi identification between communists and Jews. The last issue is largely concerned with alleged Israeli atrocities. Issue two is particularly revealing in terms of fascist strategy. The headline reads 'Communism; the facts behind the fiction'. It focuses primarily on alleged communist atrocities. The gruesome photographs include two purporting to show corpses of children in 'Soviet slave camps' before Hitler came to power. The caption reads 'This four-page broadsheet turns history upside down. Pictures of Hitler's concentration camp victims carry captions saying they were *Russian* captives'.[4]

The intention is obvious: not only to absolve Hitler and the Third Reich of the Holocaust, but to blame camp deaths on the Russians. In this way, atrocities will be associated only with communism. Since there is ample 'proof' in the *Fact Finders* and in other Nazi literature that communism is Jewish, the reader is left to draw the obvious conclusions. This type of reversal is a central feature of neo-Nazi strategy. However, it is also a broader phenomenon increasingly found on the ultra-conservative right where 'red fascism' and 'fascism of the left' are gaining acceptance as part of anticommunist discourse.[5]

There are other significant connections both with the antisemitic American propaganda concerned with the Holocaust denial, and with the *Protocols*. The same photographs of horribly mutilated individual corpses shown here have also appeared in *The Six Million Reconsidered,* thought to be written by Grimstad.[6] As in Grimstad, the corpses are typically attributed to communism. There is an example of direct borrowing, with appropriate updating, from a section of *The International Jew,* a version of the *Protocols*. It appears on the front page:

> Each time we pick up a newspaper we read of Jews being persecuted in the USSR and how the Jews are fleeing abroad. How strange that the same Press never mention that Soviet dictator, Leonid Brezhnev, is not only married to a Jewess, but is bringing his children up as Jews speaking the Yiddish language.

In *The International Jew* we are given a picture of Lenin and his wife, who were childless and were not Jewish, chatting away in Yiddish to their children.[7] This example, too close to the original to be a coincidence, illustrates the remarkable continuity between Nazis and neo-Nazis, and stresses the key role still played by the *Protocols* today as the 'documentary proof' of Jewish conspiracy.

Another highly controversial British figure with a fascination for the second world war and Nazi Germany is David Irving, a freelance historian. I shall refer to these different positions and the 'hard' and 'soft' variants of the 'revisionist' myth. Irving's books are discussed and assessed in terms of the 'soft' variant.

The 'hard' variant of the 'revisionist' lie

Given their political and intellectual history, it is not difficult to predict the main arguments of the Holocaust denial in the British 'hard' variant. They are based on an implied conspiracy of Jews, who seek to dominate the world. It is these 'enemy aliens' who make totally false claims about the gas chambers and the numbers of Jewish dead, in order to get rich from German war reparations: According to *Did Six Million Really Die?*, 'It is the most profitable atrocity allegation of all time'.

In Harwood's second pamphlet, *Nuremberg* (1978), he offers a few updated variations on the same recurrent themes. It makes for remarkably monotonous reading. A number of his early comments concern the OSS (Office of Strategic Studies), a forerunner of the CIA. Harwood claims that the OSS was a participant in the promotion and administration of the Nuremberg trials. He begins by identifying the prominent advisers as Jewish, another Nazi habit. He also emphasises the wealth of the Jewish OSS advisers as another dimension of the stereotype. The Morale Operations Unit, he informs us, also employed 'many left-wing Hollywood Jewish scriptwriters'.[8] This is the familiar identification of Jews with communism.

Also present is a coded reference to bankers, common in neo-Nazi literature, linking Wall Street bankers with the Russian Revolution.[9] Any reader exposed to Nazi ideology is able to put the pieces together in such a way as to identify the full-blown Jewish conspiracy, as in: 'Columnist Drew Pearson commented that the (OSS) staff was mostly made up of "Wall Street Bankers" '.[10]

Harwood's comments on the Nuremberg defendants show unreserved admiration. He has enormous respect for Göring, Hitler's Air Force Chief, and Rosenberg, the Nazi Party's leading specialist on racial questions and author of the virulently antisemitic *Myth of the Twentieth Century*.[11] Harwood refers to the defendants' 'crimes' in quotation marks to indicate his disbelief.

Göring is shown as a controlled, altogether admirable adversary. His health problem and his addiction to morphine are seen to add to his heroic stature. Harwood's comments on Rosenberg begin with typical Nazi categorisations, showing his eagerness to distinguish between Jew and non-Jew; 'Despite his Jewish-sounding name, he was a German through and through, although born and brought up in Estonia'.[12]

Later in the exposition, there is a characteristic example of Nazi semantics. This is concerned with the translation and decoding of the word *Ausrottung* (extermination), central to Rosenberg's defence, and echoed in Butz:

> The prosecution also alleged that Rosenberg had advocated in a speech the 'extermination of the Jews' *(die Ausrottung des Judentums)*. But Rosenberg was able to show that *'Ausrottung'* had been mistranslated; in fact it meant uprooting. Likewise, *'Judentum'* did not mean 'Jews' as individuals, (this would have been *Juden*), but should be translated as 'Jewry' or 'Jewish power'.[13]

Harwood is clearly in sympathy with Rosenberg's counsel and reproduces his arguements. In so doing he provides other examples of semantic distortion. He suggests that the term *'Sonderbehandlung'* meaning 'special treatment', and generally applied to Jews as a Nazi bureaucratic code-word for extermination, should really be understood as 'special privileges', like receiving a bottle of champagne every day.[14] This extraordinary lie is echoed by Faurisson who alleged that *'Sonderaktion'* (special action), the selections which preceded the gassing of Jews, bear no relation to extermination by gas.

Harwood's distortion is amplified later in his comments on the Eichmann trial in Jerusalem in 1961.[15] Adolf Eichmann, the Reich's expert on Jewish Affairs, was responsible for organising the mass deportation of Jews 'necessary for the accomplishment of the desired solution of the Jewish question'.[16] He was acting on an order signed by Göring on 31 July 1941, six weeks after the invasion of the USSR. The recipient was Heydrich, head of the Reich operations and Hitler's deputy. This order, as we have seen,[17] marked a turning point in anti-Jewish history and the inauguration of a new policy of annihilation with the 'Final Solution' conference on 20 January 1942 at Wannsee. In Harwood's version, Eichmann was 'merely an unimportant administrator'. 'His office was responsible for the internment of enemy aliens.'

This argument rests on the distortion that it was perfectly normal practice in wartime to detain enemy aliens in the same way as the British and Americans detained Germans and Japanese at home. It denies that Jews were murdered in millions for no other reason than that they were Jews. This same argument is used by Faurisson.

Another macabre semantic game is rehearsed when Harwood discusses a Nuremburg document detailing the number of Jewish murders carried out by Eichmann's Action Group in occupied Russia. The Jews in question were 'resettled' *(angesiedelt)* and receiving 'special treatment' *(sonderbehandelt,* a variant of *sonderbehandlung).* Neither of these terms, in Harwood's view, indicated extermination.[18]

Harwood is echoing the Nazi totalitarian language used in official bureaucratic correspondence. The Jews were 'evacuated' *(evakuiert, ausgesiedelt)* and 'resettled' *(umgesiedelt).* They wandered off *(wanderten aus)* and disappeared *(verschwunden).*[19]

Another dimension of Harwood's arguement is common to both neo-Nazi antisemitic literature and versions of anticommunism. The thrust of their argument is that the Allies, and particularly the Russians, were also war criminals of comparable stature. These Allied 'war crimes', which include the destruction of German cities and the alleged Soviet brutality towards their prisoners, receive considerable exposure. Harwood includes a photograph of bodies heaped on railway lines. He claims that this is a photograph of victims of Allied bombing, and that Allied propaganda used such scenes as fake concentration camp photographs.[20] The destruction of German cities, including Dresden in February 1945, was certainly a reality. However, the function of Harwood's argument is to try totally to expunge Nazi guilt, or if this fails, to equate it with Allied responsibility. Similar arguments have been noted in *Europe Action,* the forerunner of GRECE publications, and in *Figaro Magazine.*[21]

In Harwood's pamphlet, Nazi Germany emerges as the unfortunate victim on whom the alien Jews and the Allies declared war, and proceeded to destroy Germany which fought back in a defensive action. And even today Germany continues to pay the cost of crippling war reparations for about '1,200 Jewish casualties of war'. The figure of 1,200 is from Rassinier.

The historian Trevor-Roper made the following comment on Harwood's *Did Six Million Really Die?:*

My judgment of it is that, behind a simulated objectivity of expression, it is in fact an irresponsible and tendentious publication which avoids material evidence and presents selected half-truths and distortions for the sole purpose of serving anti-semitic propaganda.[22]

McLaughlin's pamphlet, *For Those Who Cannot Speak* (1979), covers much the same ground as Harwood. It is perhaps even more virulently racist and antisemitic. This is quite in keeping with the British Movement.

The cover photograph, a picture of war dead in Allied cemeteries, sets the tone. The caption reads: 'Victims of real holocausts 1914-1919 and 1939-1945'. The problem for McLaughlin is that Nazism has had a bad press: 'No period in history and no people has been so misrepresented'.[23]

Later, he defines national socialism in positive terms, using the formulation of William Joyce (Lord Haw Haw), the British Nazi, whose voice was heard regularly on Nazi news broadcasts. It was also a formulation of the British fascist leader, Sir Oswald Mosley. 'If you love your country you are a nationalist, if you love your people, you are a socialist. Put the two together and you have National Socialism.'[24]

Since McLaughlin explicitly loves his 'Race and Nation' more than anything else on earth,[25] there is arguably a certain logic in his admiration for Nazism. Those who oppose Nazism, 'anti-National Socialists', simply perpetuate wartime propaganda. These anti-Nazis are not ordinary people, but those who claim to speak on their behalf. They are backed by 'internationalists' who are allowing Britain 'to be colonised by the coloured invaders'[26] and who seek to impose 'a huge malevolent minority of aliens'.[27] It becomes increasingly clear as the pamphlet progresses that 'internationalists' and 'Zionists' are code-terms for Jews, who are still out there conspiring against the white race.

Echoing Nazi wartime propaganda, McLaughlin argues that it was the Jews who declared way on Germany.[28] The Jews were an 'alien minority' who had taken control of Germany: 'The German people virtually lost control of their own affairs; they had become outcasts in their own land'.[29] Jews completely controlled the international banking system, the media, the economy, trade and industry, the professions, the Social Democratic Party, not to mention pornography, international drug traffic, and white slavery.

Making reference to the 'Jewish control of the media', a common theme in Nazi Germany, as in neo-Nazi literature today, he informs us that 'Jews have an unhealthy obsession with the alleged murder of their people'.[30]

> If there was any doubt as to who controls the media, its obsession with Jewish suffering to the exclusion of all others should dispel it. Whenever we turn on the television or read a newspaper, we are assaulted with wailing on behalf of international Jewry who, true to form, tend to get a bigger slice of the sympathy cake out of all proportion to their numbers in our society.[31]

In view of this exposition complete with the stereotype of the malevolent, alien and powerful Jew, it is not surprising for it to be followed by denial of the Holocaust. The Holocaust is characterised as 'the biggest rip-off in history',[32] and 'the gassed six million yarn'.[33] If this were not offensive enough, there is also an implied threat as if to rehearse a second genocide. Referring to the 'Holocaust' film, he writes that the 'propaganda film "Holocaust" will only hasten the day of the big reckoning'.[34] It makes chilling reading.

The Nuremberg trials, in McLaughlin's view, were 'a legal farce',[35] like the Moscow or Khomeni show-trials. As regards 'the alleged extermination of Jews', 'the six million hoax',[36] it is 'Zionist propaganda'.[37] It is strange, he observes, that the 'white man' should accept this.[38] Followers of Islam, he suggests, do not. One possible reading is that he is attempting to appeal to sections of right-wing anti-Khomeni Muslims.

In common with Harwood, McLaughlin goes on to argue that, in contrast with the much maligned Reich, the Allies committed, mass murder both before and after the war: in the Katyn Forest in Poland; in Hiroshima and Nagasaki; in Dresden; and in Mai Lai, a scene of massacre by American troops in South Vietnam. Here McLaughlin is using liberal and left-wing sounding arguments in an attempt to exonerate Hitler's Germany.McLaughlin's assessment of Hitler echoes Goebbels, his propaganda minister and creator of the Hitler myth: 'He [Hitler] died as he had lived — a griant among pygmies'.[38]

The remaining elements are already familiar. Anne Frank's *Diary* is a 'soft sell' and a 'tear-jerker'. It is a fake which spearheaded the propaganda of the Zionist political machine.[40] Faurisson has also gone to great lengths to invalidate Anne Frank's *Diary*, perhaps because it has introduced postwar generations to the reality of the Holocaust. McLaughlin refers to the violently anti-semitic journalist Felderer as 'the Swedish investigator' as if he were a neutral scholar. There are also references to 'mass murders by the Jews in Palestine' with a particular mention of Deir Yassin in 1948. Although this was a guerrilla war with cold-blooded murders carried out by the nationalists on both sides, the equation is avoided.

McLaughlin makes his own addition to anti-Jewish and anti-Zionist propaganda in suggesting that the IRA learned the techniques of letter bombs from the Jews who used booby trap bombs against the British occupying forces in Palestine prior to the creation of Israel. This links the Nazi stereotype of Jewish communism with the contemporary British and Irish scene where both the British Movement and the National Front are violently opposed to the IRA and have links with extremist Ulster Protestant organisations.

The final 'Why?' section is particularly illuminating in terms of the Nazi belief in 'race and nation'.[41] It is grounded in a conspiratorial view of the world. To summarise the argument, McLaughlin is suggesting that any anti-nationalist programme spells disaster for the 'white race'. He talks of the 'racial cowardice' of 'white peoples of the world' and 'their womenfolk' 'collaborating sexually with the dark-skinned alien invader' — rather than standing up to anti-Nazi propaganda which supports black nationalism and labels opposition as racists or fascists.[42] Those who gain from denouncing 'white anti-communist nationalists' (McLaughlin's euphemism for Nazis), are 'those who colonise Britain ... seek to impose upon Britain a huge malevolent minority of aliens'.

From the previous analogy with Germany, purportedly colonised by the 'alien Jewish minority', it can be deduced that this is also part of the Jewish conspiracy to dominate the world, first by taking political and economic control, and, second, by 'race-mixing',[43] seen by the Nazis as the root cause of racial decay and hence of cultural decay and decadence. This overall theme is clearly set out in *Mein Kampf* in the chapter on 'Nation and Race'. It is the main focus of the propaganda of the British Movement and the National Front; and it is also present, as we have seen, in the writings of the French and German New Right in a more sophisticated form.

Finally, McLaughlin delivers an apocalyptic message: Europe may only be saved from 'alien squatters', 'racial inundation and political death' if 'National Socialism, or something akin to it, will divest itself of its colonisers' and 'forestall the designs of World Communism'.[44] This is an unambiguous statement of his desire to restore Hitler's 'New Order' in Europe. The Holocaust denial is a crucial part of that struggle and a means to that end.

A strategy of the British National Party of John Tyndall (a new regrouping of the National Front) is not to deny the Holocaust (though it has done so in its magazine, *Spearhead*), but to deplore the morality of those who find genocide reprehensible. The American Nazi leader, William Pierce, writing in the March 1982 issue argues that 'a newer and higher morality' must be found.

> The 'revisionist', the conservative, and anti-semite who cannot face the Holocaust squarely and judge it on the basis of a higher morality, according to which it is only the upward cause of Life which is sacred, also cannot solve the other moral problems of the day; he cannot, for example, cope successfully with challenges to the white future which are presented by non-white immigration and by a high non-white birthrate.[45]

The shift follows on the successful court case in America brought by Mel Mermelstein in which it was ruled that the Holocaust was proven fact. It also echoes extreme right-wing novels like *Le Camp des Saints* (1978)[46] by GRECE's Jean Raspail, a chilling and brutal racist fantasy, and marks a return to the unadulterated Nazi racist obsession, which also has clear implications for gender construction. The reference to a new morality is also present in the pseudo-scholarly writing to the IHR Journal, where the new 'body of morality' based on 'constructive myths', the factor of unity, is essentially antisemitic.[47]

The 'soft' variant: the contribution of David Irving

David Irving makes a very decisive contribution to the 'soft revisionist' literature on the second world war. His sober writing contains nothing of the vulgar racism which permeates the pamphlets of McLaughlin and Harwood. He does not deny the Holocaust. He does not suggest that the Jews were responsible for the war. Rather, on the basis of documentary scraps and by editing documents, Irving claims that Hitler knew nothing of the 'Final Solution', and that his aides carried out the killings behind his back. This is the thesis of his most controversial book, *Hitler's War* (1977)[48], published in Britain by Hodder and Stoughton.

Irving's use of documentation and this extraordinary assertion has guaranteed him negative critiques by four of the world's leading specialists on Nazi Germany: Alan Bullock, Hugh Trevor-Roper Eberhard Jackel and Martin Broszat. In 1978, Irving also suffered the acute embarrassment of being severly criticised by a panel of eminent West German historians on German national television.

The book received considerable critical attention in the press. Relying on a controversial note of a phone call between Himmler and Hitler made on 30 November 1941, prior to the Wannsee Conference in which Hitler called for a halt to one particular transport of Jews, Irving has argued that not only did Hitler *not* give the order to exterminate the Jews, but he actually vetoed it.The extermination was carried out by Himmler's SS who unquestioningly obeyed the Führer.

It would be absurd to suppose that the policy was carried out in violation of Hitler's orders, which is what Irving tries to suggest. Typically, Irving seizes on a small, dubious particle of 'evidence' and builds general conclusions from it. The weight of evidence against this note referring to all the Jews is simply overwhelming, despite the secrecy surrounding the 'Final Solution'. Irving refers to Goebbels's diary entry for 27 March 1942, but fails to quote it. It stands as an indictment of Irving's own position:

> It is a pretty barbarous business, and it is best not to mention details but the Führer's threat of 'annihilation' was to be realised in the most dreadful manner. We must not be sentimental in these matters. It is a war to the death between the Aryan race and the Jewish bacillus. Here, too, the Führer is the inflexible champion of a radical solution.[49]

Irving was universally condemned by the West German press, with the exception of the Nazi fringe. Yet, in Germany, *Hitler's War* proved to be a best-seller. It is not difficult to explain its appeal. The argument of the book may be summed up as 'If only the Führer had known about the murder of the Jews, he would have stopped it'. For West Germans who do not want to face up to the past, it was easy to be persuaded that if Hitler did not know, then neither did the person in the street.[50]

Irving's thesis, claiming Hitler's ignorance and therefore innocence, together with his original allegation that Anne Frank's diary was a fake, has since been withdrawn after a successful suit filed by the late Otto Frank, Anne Frank's father.[51] It suggested a significant overlap between 'hard' and 'soft' revisionism.

The argument, alleging Hitler's ignorance, is undoubtedly the most sophisticated contribution to the 'revisionist' arsenal. In my view, it is a more subtle, more refined version which encourages a reappraisal of Hitler, although not of the Nazi party as a whole. Indeed, the portrait of Hitler which emerges from *Hitler's War* is of a man of enormous sensitivity and charm, a man of courage and principle, despite the corruption and rivalry in his entourage, a man who made antisemitic speeches — but apparently didn't really mean it.

Hitler's January 1939 Reichstag speech, in which he said that if the Jews provoked a world war, it would end with their destruction *(Vernichtung)*, is pinned to Irving's wall. He made this singular admission in a public student meeting in Birmingham in February 1981. Yet Irving continues to reiterate that after his rise to power in 1933, Hitler simply paid lip-service to antisemitism.[52] Irving's books are slanted in such a way that they may be seen as a very sophisticated attempt to rehabilitate Hitler. It is often difficult to see where the views of the Führer, or those of his private secretaries, end, and those of Irving begin.[53]

Irving is remarkably prolific. To date he has produced ten full-length works, not including three translations. This does not include his German publication on the Nuremberg Trial. All of these books have necessitated long, arduous and immensely detailed archival research largely in Germany and the States, which also required finance. For reasons of space, I shall limit the discussion to four of his books: *Hitler's War* (Hodder & Stoughton, 1977), *The War Path* (Michael Joseph, 1978), *The Destruction of Dresden* (Kimber, 1964) and *Uprising* (Hodder & Stoughton, 1981). *Hitler's War* is perhaps the best known because of the controversy it provoked. Its companion volume, *The War Path,* charts Hitler's progress towards world war.

It is in *Hitler's War* that Irving argues that there is no documentary link between Hitler and the murderous atrocities of the SS task forces in the extermination camps in the East,[54] as if the absense of a written order from Hitler were sufficient proof. Broszat has carefully demonstrated that this absence of a written order by Hitler is neither surprising nor significant. The command system in the occupied Eastern territories and the complex evolution of Nazi antisemitic measures combined in such a way that an oral order from Hitler to Himmler and Heydrich was a more natural development than a written authorisation through bureaucratic channels. There are other examples of oral orders. It has also been noted elsewhere, and documented in detail, that a basic feature of Hitler's dictatorship was a preference for oral instructions rather than written directions to Bormann, Himmler, Heydrich and Goebbels, especially in secret, sensitive matters.[55]

However, the absence of a written authorisation ordering the extermination of Jews is argued elsewhere, notably by Butz, as 'proof' of the 'hoax'. This is where the 'hard' and 'soft' versions of the revisionist argument appear to meet.

Irving gives a brief, misleading version of the most crucial Wannsee conference on the 'Final Solution',[56] which he even fails to index. According to Irving, Heydrich simply briefed 'the leading government officials in Berlin' to the effect that 'the Führer had sanctioned the evacuation of all Jews to the eastern territories', where 'they would build roads until they dropped'. What Heydrich actually said was that in the east those Jews *fit for work* would be divided by gender into huge labour gangs to build roads, during the course of which the great majority would expire naturally (from overwork and undernourishment). The surviving Jews, Heydrich continued, would undoubtedly be those who were the strongest and most capable of offering resistance, and therefore 'would have to be handled accordingly' *(entsprechend behandelt werden müssen,* meaning 'liquidated'), since they would otherwise form the nucleus of a new Jewish race.[57]

Irving apparently has privileged access to primary Nazi sources. Comments in his foreword to *Hitler's War* help us fill out this picture. They, too, are intended to be subtly persuasive. He writes that: 'too many postwar books contain pitfalls for the historian', referring to various doctored diaries and memoirs written in Allied captivity. These he regards as spurious primary sources. Irving has spent years searching out buried documents at great personal inconvenience. Many of these authentic records were in the hands of well-placed Nazi widows. These include the widow of von Ribbentrop's state secretary, von Weizsacker, whom Irving looked for and found.

This is not all. Other little-known but authentic diaries of people in Hitler's entourage were produced for him alone.[58] No other established historian of the second world war has been rewarded by such a remarkably rich find in terms of primary sources. It was also Irving who unearthed the hitherto unpublished versions of Hitler's *Table Talk* in Munich. This is acknowledged by the historian, Trevor-Roper, in his preface to *Hitler's Table Talk, 1941-44; his private conversations* (1983).[53] This pattern of finding new, abundant documentation is also a feature of Irving's other books. Some interesting hypotheses may therefore be considered.

Also worth noting in this same connection is Irving's emphasis on the need to use primary, unpublished material, rather than merely relying on Nuremberg documents. He is making a valid and quite uncontroversial academic point — but one which is anchored in a very particular chain of reasoning:

> And who are these emotional historians of the Jewish holocaust who rely on the printed Nuremberg exhibits, and have never troubled themselves even to open a file of the SS chief Heinrich Himmler's own handwritten telephone notes or to read his memoranda for his secret meetings with Adolph Hitler?[60]

It is the foreword to these companion volumes, more than the main body of the texts, which allows us to glimpse his ideological position, together with the main thrust of his argument. Yet the reference to sources is put over as an authoritative, academic stand arguing the necessity to treat the Nuremberg trial documents with caution and, by implication, any official version of the second world war.

The Destruction of Dresden (1964),[61] although narrower in scope than the books about Hitler, is closely researched and draws on interviews with British and American bomber crews and with some Luftwaffe pilots. The importance of *Dresden* is the argument it rehearses, echoed elsewhere on the ultra-right. Basically, it is this: the Dresden bombing carried out by the Allies resulted in 135,000 casualties in a premeditated strike against non-military targets, despite the fact that Dresden was recognised as a refugee city.[62] There were some 71,000 dead when the Allies dropped the atomic bomb on Hiroshima. A little over 13,000 were killed at German hands in the blitz on Britain by 1940. On the scale of war crimes, the bombing of Dresden looms large. It must be considered in the same light as the excesses of the belligerent pro-Nazi powers. Irving quotes Goebbels' statement at the memorial service to make his point: 'this kind of aerial terrorism is the product of the sick mind of the plutocratic world destroyers'.[63]

The figures are disputed. Irving uses German sources for the number of Dresden victims, but it is a grossly inflated figure. The figure has been refuted in a scholarly work by Gotz Bergander, *Dresden im Luftkrieg* (1977), and, in fact, has since been retracted by Irving.

We are invited to ask what right the Allies had in judging other war crimes. In short, it is an argument of relativism which makes a moral or political judgment impossible. Yet it is also a persuasive argument with a liberal ring, which echoes the leftist positions of La Vieille Taupe and *Libération* suggesting that Jews do not have the monopoly of suffering. The function of that argument, however, is to deny the specificity of the Jewish genocide; to deny that Jews were first identified by the Nuremberg Race Laws of 1935, rounded up, transported and murdered *en masse* for no other reason than because they were Jews; and that this was part of a systematic plan of extermination of an entire people. *The Destruction of Dresden* is a persuasive book, but in the context of Irving's other writings and other arguments in circulation, it is highly ambiguous.

Uprising (1981)[64] concerned the Hungarian revolution of 1956 and has no obvious bearing on the Holocaust denial. It is pertinent, however, in that it illustrates Irving's antisemitism. It also provides a very particular slant on the alleged relationship between antisemitism and anticommunism in the eastern bloc which surfaced again in Poland.

Irving's thesis is that October 1956 was not a revolution, but an uprising sparked off by antisemitism. He sets the scene with a three-page list, 'Who was Who in Hungary'.[65] Here is a brief extract:

ACZEL, Thomas — 35, Jewish, Stalin prize-winning author, journalist and Communist Party Secretary to the Writers' Union; escaped to USA.

ANDICS, Elizabeth — 54, Jewish, dialectician, director of the

Party School, married to Andrew Berei, 56, Jewish, economist, chairman of the Planning Office. Both alive in Budapest.

APRO, Antal — 43, Jewish, Communist trades unionist who became deputy prime minister. One of Hungary's most durable politicians. Still serving.

BATA, Stephen — 46, former bus conductor, chief of general staff from October 1950 to July 1953 when he became minister of defence.

BENKE, Valeria —36 Jewish, director of Hungarian radio broadcasting; now Politburo member, Budapest.

BENJAMIN, Ladislav — 41, Jewish, former factory worker, poet.

On the basis of the word-count alone, 'Jew' and 'Jewish' would emerge high on the list. He even identifies 'former Jews'. It is surprising, therefore, not to find the entry 'Jew' in the appendix, since it is a key word and clearly a key concept for Irving in his account of the Hungarian revolution. In Irving's view, this is largely a pogrom of Jewish-Communist officials for which he uses offical Hungarian casualty figures.

The argument may appear superficially more complex, but there is no shortage of illustrations to support his antisemitic thesis. What is usually associated with fascism, particularly the physical repression of the opposition, is depicted by Irving as an integral element of communism. This is enforced by Jewish Soviet-trained puppets who are torturers in the AVO secret police. Treatment meted out in the camps is described in graphic detail.[66] What is significant is that antisemitism and anticommunism are seen as one and indivisible.

In *Uprising!* Irving continually uses quotes from emigrés to disseminate antisemitic views. Jews are referred to as 'exploiting other Jews';[67] 'holding the key jobs';[68] 'controlling the Social Democrat Party';[69] 'not working';[70] and one quote claims: 'The regime was *theirs,* it was the Jews who caused the greatest trouble in Hungary'.[71]

Irving uses the literary and sociological device of making others speak. In this way the virulent antisemitism is seen to be expressed by the refugee interviewees, and not by Irving himself. Irving sums up the interviewees' comments by explaining that to a significant extent the refugees interviewed after the uprising were anti-Jewish.

As in Nazi propaganda about Germany, and in antisemitic French leaflets in the 1930s,[72] Jews are seen to occupy all the key positions. It is a remarkable anaology, with Hungary in the place of Germany.

Jews and communists are represented as a twin evil, a now familiar category, which we have already identified as a feature of radical antisemitism since the *Protocols*. There is no doubt how Irving's books are being interpreted and used by apologists of Hitler and National Socialism.[73] *Hitler's War* and *The Warpath*, in common with Lenni Brenner, are advertised by the IHR.

7. Conclusion: Contemporary Antisemitism and Racism

The Holocaust denial: a new version of the Protocols

The *Protocols,* the czarist forgery, became in Cohn's phrase 'a warrant for genocide'[1] in the hands of Hitler and the Nazi party. Fascism as a totalitarian system does not necessarily imply either antisemitism or genocide. With Nazism and Hitler, it did. The *Protocols* provided a sanction for the Holocaust. But the *Protocols* and antisemitism did not die with Hitler or the defeat of Nazism. In a 1981 study carried out by the Institute of Jewish Affairs in London, 42 postwar editions are reported in 21 countries. The obsession with the myth of Jewish conspiracy continues to provide a system of thought and an overall explanation for all possible crises. Contemporary neo-Nazis, joined by sections of the anarchist and marxist left for whom antisemitism is not an integral part of their world view, are shaping a new warrant in the form of the Holocaust denial.

The range of the neo-Nazi Holocaust denial arguments and distortions of the second world war can be summarised under four main headings:

1. **The Nuremberg trial conducted by the Allies at the end of the**

war to judge Nazi war crimes was a 'kangaroo court' because prisoners were tortured to obtain confessions; and the judiciary were Jews or communists, or under their influence. It was therefore a case of 'victors' justice'.

This view of the Nuremberg trials is perfectly consistent with a Nazi position, since, in the Nazi view, communism is Jewish and all anti-fascists are communists or fellow-travellers by definition. Nazism represents a negation of both marxism and liberalism.

2. **The Holocaust is a 'hoax', a 'swindle', 'a multi-million dollar racket' to make Jews rich (at the expense of Germany through war reparations) and to justify the Jewish state at the expense of Palestinians.**

The language is significant—'hoax', 'swindle', 'racket'—all in themselves implying 'Jew' through the historical accumulation of antisemitic connotations (money grabbing, Jewing, Shylock, etc.).

The neo-Nazi onslaught on Zionism is not intended to be read as an attack on Zionism as an expression of Jewish nationalism. In the circumstances it would be an unlikely reading for a movement in which nationalism is viewed as positive; and because an influx of Jews to Israel would reduce the number of Jews in other territories. Rather, it is a code-word, or euphemism, for Judaism. Whereas it is more politically acceptable and politically credible to be anti-Zionist, both on the far right and on the left, in view of the increased militarisation of the Israeli state and its controversial left bank policies, it is less acceptable to be seen as anti-Jewish. But this perception is changing.

3. **Allied bombings and atrocities, particularly crimes against the civilian population, like the bombing of Dresden, were on the same scale as, or even exceeded, alleged German atrocities.**

This a common thesis on the far right, argued from Bardèche onwards. It is also echoed on the anarchist left by the associates of La Vieille Taupe in Paris.

4. **Zyklon B gas was used in the camps, but only as an insecticide, principally to contain the typhus epidemic. 'Extermination' is a mistranslation: Jews died, but they were merely victims of war.**

The gassings were carried out in the strictest secrecy. The

bureaucratic language of Nazi Germany also aimed at concealing the truth. Code-words like 'bath-houses' for gas chambers were an essential part of the process. Neo-Nazis now claim that such euphemisms correspond to reality. Faurisson has set himself up as an 'expert' in semantic and technical translation arguments.

Having summarised the arguments, it is critical to consider the political context in which the new *Protocols* are being published. These postwar variants of the *Protocols* are making their appearance during a period of recession and profound social unrest accompanied by a major shift to the right in most of Europe and America.[2]

The amount and vehemence of antisemitic literature in Arabic has no parallel in the postwar era, and the *Protocols* has been distributed in the Arab states for a number of years. It has gone into nine editions in the Arab and Muslim world between 1951 and 1970. It was recommended by President Khadafi of Libya as a 'most important historical document' when addressing western journalists in 1972, and a party of religious scholars from Saudi Arabia distributed copies at the Constituent Assembly of the Council of Europe in Strasbourg in December 1974.[3] Saudi Arabia has distributed the *Protocols* through its own embassies and, as we have seen, has played a prominent role in financing Grimstad's version of the Holocaust denial and the World Anti-Communist League.

Another element in the Holocaust denial arguments is the overlap between the neo-Nazis and a section of the anarchist and marxist pro-Palestinian left. Some of the overlaps have been identified with reference to the French anarchist scene; and, on the marxist left, Lenni Brenner in the States and Lev Korneev in the Soviet Union are reproducing and circulating a patently antisemitic discourse. In Korneev's case, the stereotypes of Jewish power are those of the *Protocols*. Although not strictly part of the neo-Nazi strategy of the Holocaust denial, they are significant in that they prepare the ground for making antisemitism 'acceptable'.

Trivialisation of the Holocaust

Another tactic of those who deny the Holocaust is to trivialise it. A particularly offensive example on the anarchist right appeared in the French satirical monthly, *Hara Kiri,* in June 1981. It was reproduced in the July-August issue of *Droit de Vivre,* the LICRA

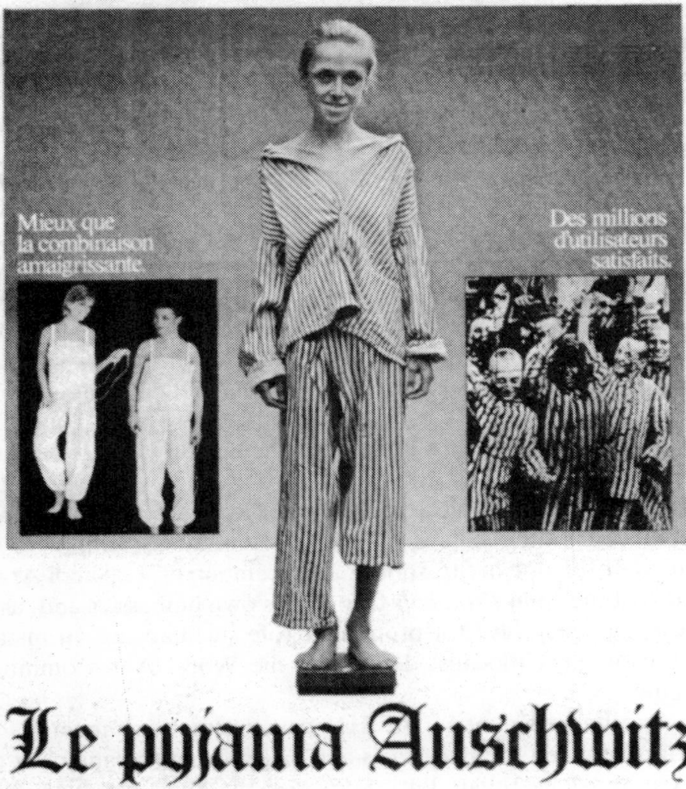

anti-racist monthly (League against Racism and Antisemitism). It shows women modelling striped pyjamas, the prisoners' uniform in the camps, advertising their slimming appearance.

The tone of the *Hara Kiri* piece is not radically different from the mocking 'jewish information' letters sent by the Swedish neo-Nazi, Ditlieb Felderer, some of whose posters have turned up in Poland. It is also reminiscent of the antisemitic cartoons which appear in National Front and British Movement publications.

A British commercial example of annexation of Nazi themes has been operated by the rock industry and record companies, which draw on Nazi symbolism.[4] Certain songs like 'Kill the Reds',

Master Race', and 'White Race' explicitly encourage violence. One Decca label record popular among Skinheads, 'Strength thru Oi', since withdrawn, is clearly reminiscent of the Nazi youth slogan 'Strength through Joy'. On its sleeve was the photograph of a vicious-looking skinhead sporting a British Movement emblem. Television presenter, Tony Wilson, one of the proprietors of a Manchester night club which shows all-night videos featuring Nazi rallies and ceremonies has denied that they promote fascism. Wilson also runs the company Factory Records which owns the club and manages the former 'Joy Division', now called 'New Order'. This political mood, its musical meanings and its savage male culture have been dramatised by Trevor Griffiths in his remarkable television play, 'Oi for England'. But it was critically received on the grounds that it gave racists a voice.

Sadomasochism as a public and private performance would appear to be taking on different forms from the late 1970s com bining the use of chains with Nazi symbolism. Certain claims are advanced for sadomasochism using the language of liberation. It is as if oppression were a game in which oppressors and oppressed, Nazis and their victims, are basically one and the same; and the confirmation of these skewed meanings are renewed and celebrated through the aesthetics of brutality. Sadomasochism is a kinesic representation of Bitburg semantics.

Current fashions also trivialise Nazism. The sight of bikers, Skins and others, sporting the death-head symbol of concentration camp guards on helmets and T shirts, is commonplace. 'Heil Hitler' is standard graffiti for West German Skins. Punks and other Young fashion trends are promoting repro Nazi badges and iron crosses in brilliant diamante. This pick 'n' mix symbolism may appear creative to some, and exemplify a plurality and free play of meanings. To others, it is deeply offensive and contributes to a denial of meaning and of history.

In Britain the Anti-Nazi League was remarkably successful in mobilising young people against racist and fascist groups like the National Front, not least because of its imaginative response to the punk phenomenon and the drawing power of organisations like Rock against Racism. In France, SOS Racisme, primarily a young black organisation, is having a similar success with its campaign slogan 'Touche pas à mon pote' ('Hands off my pal'). It also links different oppressions. In a recent issue of their journal it was pointed out that immigrant women are the object of double discrimination on the grounds of gender and origin.[5]

In West Germany and elsewhere in Europe, the early 1970s saw a 'nostalgia vogue' expressed mainly in the collection of second world war bric-a-brac and militaria. Books and films exploited the 'Hitler Wave' and a number of these were clearly nostalgic. In contrast with the 1960 Erwin Leiser Film, *Mein Kampf,* which denounced Nazi crimes, Joachim Fest's 1975 film biography of Hitler is very ambiguous, and makes only brief reference to the murder of Jews. With Fassbinder's play, 'Rubbish the City and the Death',[6] written in 1976, there is little ambiguity. It features 'the rich Jew' as its arch-criminal to whom a number of Germans fall prey. One of the victims, a Nazi criminal, delivers an antisemitic speech expressing regrets that the Jew had not been gassed by the Nazis. The text of the play was immediately attacked.[6]

A former West German policeman invented a board game called 'Jew, don't get angry'. It is based on a popular dice game. Designed in the hexagonal shape of the Star of David, it features the names of six major Nazi concentration camps. The first player to get their counters round the board and back into the corner, symbolising the extermination of six million Jews, is the winner. The game provoked sharp protest from Jewish organisations. The inventor was acquitted on the grounds that 'thoughts are free'.[7]

The 'Holocaust' film in West Germany and France

In West Germany, the 'Holocaust' television film, screeened in January 1979, attracted an estimated 20 billion viewers and had a considerable impact as a national catharsis. Former Chancellor Schmidt commended the series as essential viewing in view of the controversy over the statute of limitations. *Der Spiegel* devoted much of the February and March 1979 issues to questions related to the Holocaust. It has been said of this Americanised television drama that it succeeded in bringing home to Germans the real horror of the Nazi murder of Jews *because* it trivialised it: the film reduced it to a scale and presented it in a form which was comprehensible and which made the guilt psychologically bearable.[8]

Both the anarchist left and the far right in Germany and elsewhere saw the 'Holocaust' film as serving contemporary American and Israeli, and hence capitalist, interests. Comtemporary antisemitism in Germany is complicated by the fact that the right-wing Springer press combines reactionary domestic policies with an unqualified support for Zionism, coupled with unbridled admiration for Israeli military prowess. Following the Six Day War, Israeli General Dayan was portrayed in Springer's *Bild Zeitung* as the new Jewish 'desert fox'. This totally uncritical pro-Israeli nationalist stand of the reactionary Springer press may at one level appear to be unreservedly pro-Jewish, where Israeli military leaders are mirror images of other martial heroes, as part of a nationalist macho ideology.

For a section of the West German anarchist left, the 'Holocaust' television film provoked discussion principally around two themes: first, that 'Holocaust' was to be located as 'a point of intersection of capitalist interest and Zionist ideology', and, second, that the Holocaust itself may be compared to Vietnam: 'Ten years ago there was a second Auschwitz'. Both these examples are taken from *Pflasterstrand,*[9] a journal written by and for the 'sponti-scene' in Frankfurt and edited by Daniel Cohn-Bendit, former student leader of the Paris 1968 revolt.

Dany Cohn-Bendit's analysis of the 'Holocaust' film as a product of capitalism and Zionism offers a number of analogies with the arguments put forward by La Vieille Taupe with which his brother, Gabriel Cohn-Bendit, is associated. Dany Cohn-Bendit's comment also overlaps with Faurisson's statement on French radio, the basis of the third court case, in which he characterised the Holocaust (the extermination of European Jews, not the film) as a 'political, financial swindle' and a product of 'international Zionism'. The statements are not identical, but they are remarkably close. They both contribute to antisemitic discourse.

In France, in view of the opposition of Robert Hersant, French newspaper magnate, it was a triumph that the 'Holocaust' film was shown at all on state television network. An article was published in the Hersant-owned *Figaro Magazine,* the newly created weekly supplement to the daily, only a few days before the screenings. It was entitled 'Holocaust: Hitler, Stalin and the Others', and is dominated by two photographs: one of bodies piled high at Buchenwald and the other of bodies piled high at Dresden after the largest ever raid on that city. It draws a parallel between the two, explaining that the Buchenwald inmates died of typhus in the last days of the war while the Dresden raid was undertaken solely as an exercise in terror. Having established that there was really not much to choose between the two sides, it goes on to say that the film can only serve to 'feed an anti-German campaign prejudicial to the creation of Europe'. The article is signed by a Frédéric Toulouze, which may be a pseudonym for Hersant.[10]

The desire to relativise the Holocaust and to compare it to another Vietnam, is also voiced quite genuinely on the left as an expression of outrage against the atrocities committed in the name of democracy and western values. It is a view with which I have some sympathy, but is nevertheless a position which blurs the political vision and stands in the way of a clear political analysis of National Socialism and of the centrality of racial politics. American imperialism (or any other agressive imperialism) and National Socialism may have features in common, but this does not mean that they are identical. We are dealing with different social formations.

The relativist position is also used by the ultra-right in order to suggest that the Allies were also guilty of crimes like the wartime bombing of civilians in German cities, or the excesses of the Stalinist gulags. The line of argument advanced by the British historian, Irving, as we have seen, in *The Destruction of Dresden*, is part of this framework. The ultra-right would claim the Allied acts of this kind 'cancel out' Nazi war crimes. A version of this argument is to be found in the political programme of the neo-Nazi NPD Party of West Germany:

> For the sake of its future Germany needs a true picture of its history. We oppose the glorification of treason and the assertion that Germany is solely responsible for all the misfortune in all the world, which have led to the moral self-destruction of our nation. Therefore we demand that there be an end to the lie of sole German guilt for the war and to the blackmail which is costing our people millions of Marks in reparations.
>
> The brave conduct of German soldiers throughout the ages must serve as a model for our armed forces today. Military service is an honour... As long as the fathers are branded as criminals publicly, and with impunity, the sons cannot be good soldiers.

With the media increasingly soft on the Nazi record and the general ignorance of the Holocaust among young people everywhere, despite some educational initiatives,[11] it is not surprising that the crucial political and moral issues it raises are generally lost.

Sexism and Racism: relations of domination

Fascism has traditionally taken root during a period of slump and exacerbated social tensions. Despite its radical rhetoric, one of the main components of fascism has been the emphasis on traditional values. These stem from a traditional view of manliness and gender roles; these are accompanied by a blind obedience to authority grounded in a mystic, biological concept of the nation. Such practices have been summed up for the favoured group of women as: *Kinde, Küche, Kirche* (children, kitchen, church).[12] For 'non-Aryan' women the prescribed role was very different, though equally biological. For Jewish women it included sterilisation and genetic experimentation. They were offically untouchable by 'Aryan' men except to be worked, beaten, shot or gassed to death.

The New Right today, in America and western Europe, is profoundly antifeminist. Roger Scruton, editor of the British New Right quarterly, the *Salisbury Review,* has also pronounced on the biological definition of gender roles:

> a woman's body has a rhythm, a history to fulfilment that are centered upon the bearing of children: this is what it means to be a woman.[13]

In the States, the 1980 Reagan campaign was fought around the explicit engagement to repeal the Equal Rights Amendment Act. The Moral Majority in the States and, to a lesser extent, pressure groups inside the present British Conservative government are attempting to reconstruct a social and moral order though policies on sexual morality and religious and sex education in schools. David has argued that it is these moral issues that distinguish the new from the old right.[14] They are new in so far as they are thrust on the public agenda, though of course the issues themselves are not new.

Anti-racist feminists need to theorise the relation between sexism and racism. Most studies of racism speak with a traditional male voice and do not share these concerns. Griffin has observed in her remarkable study on pornography and silence that:

> ... almost everywhere that one finds a virulent form of racism, one also finds an idea of traditional roles oppressive to women.

This was as demonstrably true in the American South as it was in the Third Reich, and as it always is in reactionary political movements.[15]

Griffin's analysis of pornography and its analogies with sado-masochistic racist phantasies is original and compelling. She argues that the objects of pornography are separated and dehumanised, and hence no longer seen as part of 'us', in the same way that German Jews were separated from the rest of the German population.

The construction of Jews as 'other', the anti-Jewish violence, the subsequent legislation and ghettoisation 'confirmed' their outsider, subhuman status already 'justified' academically by 'race science'; given the technology and the state organisation, it was possible to 'play out' the racist, sado-masochistic phantasy to its conclusion. In examples of hard porn, women, black and white, are also humiliated, tortured, and eventually killed in a number of ways. Jews are murdered *qua* Jews; women *qua* women are attacked and humiliated, and killed, in a nationalist and hetero-sexist culture where neither can fully 'belong'.

The British New Right's emphasis on cultural differences

The Thatcherite New Right has no bearing on the Holocaust denial. Why, therefore, include this section? The discussion is relevant in that it contributes to an understanding of how 'otherness' is constructed today as part of an authoritarian political project. This has implications for all minorities; and, indeed, for the very fabric of British society. In the present nationalist climate in Britain the government is enacting further legislation to define who 'we' are, with implications for 'race' and gender. The 1981 British Nationality Act is the latest of these legislative measures.[16] Earlier anti-immigration legislation was introduced by both Tory and Labour governments. This was both racist and sexist. The Nationality Act sets out in legal categories who is British, and who is not; or who 'belongs' and who does not. Despite its bewildering complexity, the definition of British, which hinges primarily on parents' birthplace, largely operates on colour lines. Britain's first anti-immigration legislation was enacted in 1905 to halt futher Jewish arrivals, and was called the Aliens Act.[17] This Act separated Jewish families in much the same way as black, particularly Asian, families are separated today.

In Britain a whole set of meanings is being put into circulation which seeks to define what it means to be British. The agencies include central government and right-wing pressure groups assisted by the media. In the present Thatcher administration it was the Prime Minister herself who set this culturalist discourse[18] in motion in her widely reported 'swamping speech' of 1978:

> If we went on as we are, then by the end of the century there would be 4 million people of the Commonwealth of Pakistan here. Now that is an awful lot and I think it means that people are really rather afraid that this country might be swamped by people with a different culture. And, you know, the British character has done so much for democracy, for law, and done so much throughout the world, that there is a fear that it might be swamped; people are going to react and be rather hostile to those coming in.[19]

It was in the same speech that she castigated the National Front.[20] At the time, the journal CARF (Campaign aganst Racism and Fascism) produced a front page 'mix' of Thatcher and Tyndall, National Front leader.

The New Right in Britain and elsewhere is increasingly making interventions into culture.[21] This is a particular forcus of the *Salisbury Review,* a quarterly journal of the new Philosophy Group edited by the philosopher Roger Scruton, Professor of Aesthetics at Birkbeck, a constituent College of London University. Many of the contributors to the *Salisbury Review* have some connection with Peterhouse, Cambridge, and Scruton is a former Fellow. The meetings of the Conservative Philosophy Group have been attended by Conservative MPs, including Enoch Powell, prominent right-wing journalists, media personalities and communicators.[22] According to a *Times* article on 31 January 1980 entitled 'Who speaks from Mrs. Thatcher?', Prime Minister Thatcher has been a keen participator. The Prime Minister is therefore associating with a number of avowed repatriators.

The idea of 'Britishness'and British culture is being increasingly defined by the New Right in such a way as to exclude 'foreign' accretions. At the same time there are 'good' and 'bad' foreigners: those who try to be like 'us' and the others, the out-group, who celebrate a different set of identities and cultural values (Rastas, Sikhs...).

The ethnocentric way in which culture is being defined as one disintegrating under foreign influence not only denies the history of colonialism: it also constructs British identity as white in the context of shared institutions and kinship. A black anti-racist response put it very succinctly: *We* are over here, because *they* were over there.

In an important article in the first issue of the *Salisbury Review* entitled 'One Nation — the Politics of Race',[28] John Casey, Cambridge don, argues the case for repatriation of black people, and retrospective granting of 'guest worker' status to black citizens following the West German model. The article is ostensibly concerned with *cultural* differences, where 'culture' seems to stand in for 'race'.

Casey quotes Conservative sources in his discussion of culture: Edmund Burke, the founder of modern intellectual Conservatism, the Anglo-American poet and dramatist, T S Eliot, and Enoch Powell. Casey's article as a whole may be seen to paraphrase three major speeches by Powell in 1968 when he became a pariah of the Conservative Party under Edward Heath. Powell's first speech on 9 February was an invitation to discuss immigration statistics and to play the numbers game; the second, in Birmingham on 20 April, contained the 'rivers of blood' metaphor; and the third address at Eastbourne on 18 November linked black people with criminality and referred to 'dislodging the indigenous population ('the people of England'). The Powell quotation here is ostensibly concerned with culture, as was Thatcher's 'swamping speech'.

> There is a problem when we come into contact with a lower culture for the first time. There is another problem when a native culture has already begun to disintegrate under foreign influence, and where a native population has already taken in more of the foreign culture than it can expel. There is a third problem where, as in some of the West Indies, several uprooted people have been haphazardly mixed. And these problems are insoluble.[24]

Casey's cultural discourse includes frequent references to British history, echoed recently by Lord Elton;[25] to the English language and to 'shared institutions' and 'kinship' as indicators of

'Britishness'. It is these which set the parameters for a discussion of 'race'.

> There is no way of understanding British and English history that does not take seriously the sentiments of patriotism that go with a continuity of institutions, shared experience, language, customs, kinship... English patriotism... has at its centre a feeling for persons of one's own kind.[26]

He goes on, and clearly the text really needs to be cited in full:

> Now one very respectable way to refer to all this is to talk of the sense of *race*. Unfortunately, in the nineteenth century 'race' became the name of a scientific theory, rather than of a political and moral idea.[27]

Casey here would appear to be distancing himself from any nineteenth century *scientific* theory based on race. But he continues rather paradoxically:

> I have no option about race as a scientific theory except that it seems no sillier than many more fashionable theories in the biological and social sciences.[28]

This is something of a throw-away statement. Yet there is no doubt that Casey does not espouse any theory of biological racism. What is interesting, however, is that he then attempts to change the negative connotations surrounding 'race' and to rehabilitate it as part of political, 'moral' and, indeed, 'noble idea':

> But it ['race'] stands proxy for that feeling for loyalty to people of one's own kind that I have been trying to describe and as such expresses a moral idea and a noble one.[29]

Implicit in this posture, and more explicit elsewhere in the *Salisbury Review,* is the denial of institutional racism. There is also an attempt to remake and galvanise a discourse imbued with moral authority that would justify action, symbolic and perhaps physical, as a legitimate white self-defence of a culture under attack. Indeed, the remainder of Casey's article discusses the 'possible destruction of life in the centres of the big cities', and the '*profound* difference in culture' of black communities, in which both West Indians and Asians are stereotyped in recognisable ways. The radical solution to the presence of black communities is repatriation:

> The West Indian community is *structurally* likely to be at odds with English civilisation. There is an extraordinary resentment towards authority — police, teachers, Underground guards — *all* authority... Then there is the family structure which is markedly unlike our own: educational standards that are below those of all other racial groups... and the involvement of West Indians in a vastly disproportionate amount of violent crime... The West Indian life style... seems to include drugs and unlawful activities...
>
> What is finally at issue comes out more clearly with the Indian community or communities — industrious peaceful people, with most of the domestic virtues. Nevertheless by their large numbers, their *profound* difference in culture, they are most unlikely to wish to identify themselves with the traditions and loyalties of the host nation...
>
> I believe that the only radical policy that would stand a chance of success is repatriation.[30]

The other more publicised contribution to this ostensibly culturalist debate are the articles of Ray Honeyford published in the *Salisbury Review*. The choice of the *Salisbury Review* was politically significant in view of the thrust of Casey's article. Honeyford was the former headmaster of Drummond Middle, a predominantly Asian middle school in Bradford, West Yorkshire, which in 1981 adopted an all-party policy on multi-racial education. Honeyford wrote articles criticising these guidelines and 'multiculturalists' in general, claiming that white children were disadvantaged in a largely black school. The *Salisbury Review* published his articles which resulted in him being labelled as a racist. It was Roger Scruton who used his Tuesday *Times* column to campaign for Honeyford's views and who turned a local controversy into a national campaign.[31] The tabloids, led by the *Mail*,[32] popularised the arguments making Honeyford into a martyr of free speech.

Community relations were irreparably damaged, and a parents' action committee was set up to campaign for his dismissal. Inspections, boycotts, a week-long school strike and court cases ensued. In October 1985 Honeyford was invited by Mrs Thatcher to a high-level meeting in Downing Street concerned with multicultural education, and which was chaired by the Prime Minister.

This lent his arguments both recognition and legitimacy.

The New Right argument is not only about cultural difference, but cultural hierarchies. In a pamphlet produced by the New Right's Centre for Policy Studies entitled *The Trials of Honeyford,* its author argues that 'the slogan "no culture is superior to any other" would... make education impossible'.[33] Honeyford's position was echoed in a Monday Club Policy Paper of May 1985 by Simon Pearce, 'Education and the Multi-Racial Society', in which it was argued that 'anti-racist policies create strife while advancing malign political forces'.

More recent issues of the *Salisbury Review* include a very focused attack on anti-racists in which black experience is trivialised or dismissed, as exemplified in an article by David Dale.[34] It is blacks and multiculturalists who are portrayed as totalitarian, and it is they who are seen to promote social unrest.

Racism, earlier characterised by Casey as 'decadent' and as a 'vulgar and banal catch-phrase',[35] is redefined in such a way as to mask the unequal power relationship so that blacks are also presented as racists. This is not a new argument. It is as if the position of blacks and whites in British society were symmetrical or even reversed. Racism is not seen as a *structural* relation:

> Through a combination of facile argument, political opportunism and moral intimidation, the Left, under the specious banner of 'anti-racism', has succeeded in forcing 'institutionalised racism' onto the legitimate agenda of politics and, in the process, is fostering the very racial disharmony it purports to condemn.
>
> The anti-racists... employ... a form of covert blackmail of which the late Senator McCarthy would have been justifiably proud... This moral Scargillism, with its language of intimidation and character assassination, is designed to blur objectivity...
>
> ...anti-racism rests on a demonology which no amount of evidence could ever refute. The fundamentalist fervour which accompany its unexplained concepts - 'institutionalised racism', 'black identity', 'the experience of being black' and so on — is calculated to inspire moral inferiority and guilt in those whom, by definition, the concepts exclude...
>
> Racism is not the exclusive property of white people... Anti-racism is a pernicious doctrine.[36]

Campaigning against anti-racism is part of the morality of the New Right. On the campuses, this is spearheaded by the Thatcherite Federation of Conservative Students whose leadership is currently dominated by the 'libertarians' and supporters of the Monday Club.[37] Anti-racist policies and teaching packs of the Inner London Education Authority, of the recently dissolved Greater London Council, and anti-racist booklets produced by the (non-governmental) Institute of Race Relations, are singled out for attack.

The construction of the totalitarian 'other' as 'the enemy within' is falling into place. This was clear from the Prime Minister's 'enemy within' speech in July 1984 concerned with 'the rule of law'.[38] The relationship between discourse and policies is increasingly apparent. The talk of tougher law and order measures has been recently translated into even more authoritarian legislation[39] in which the police define acceptable political activity. Law and order is generally recognised as synonymous for 'race relations'; and a response to the more militant demands of the black community. The police may now penalise demonstrators for 'disorderly conduct'.

Although part of a process which shapes meanings and values, there are nevertheless significant points or events within that process. A striking example was the police publication in March 1962 of criminal statistics usually released by the Home Office equating certain types of crime, particularly mugging, an ill-defined category, with black people.[40] As I have pointed out elsewhere,[41] this was the specific focus of the National Front campaign in 1976 when a National Front poster depicting a black as a mugger was banned under the Race Relations Act. It is clear that both fascist parties and extremists in the Thatcherite government are contending for the same political and racist space. Despite widespread criticism, this pattern was repeated in 1983 and taken up again by the tabloids:

BLACK CRIME: NEW FIGURES (*Daily Mail*, 23 March 1983)

These same patterns were present in the tabloids' reporting of the September 1985 rebellions in Handsworth and Tottenham, complete with animal imagery. Despite the disturbing increase in racist attacks and harassment, where entire black communities live in fear, there seems to be no way in which established media patterns can portray blacks as victims.[42]

The British New Right's focus on cultural differences combines an emphasis on numbers with that of 'alienness'; and these representations are a constant feature of media reporting. The stereotyping of West Indians (of men — women are largely absent) is more clearly recognisable as part of a discourse of order. Cultural racism does not require the notion of biological inferiority. This was central to the racist doctrine of the old right. Biological racism was discussed earlier in connection with the academic racism of *Nouvelle Ecole, Mankind Quarterly* and *Neue Anthropologie,* which has nineteenth century roots. Cultural racism simply requires the notion of difference and separation.

The notion of cultural difference and of 'Britishness' is being constructed within an authoritarian and racist framework as part of a mystical notion of national identity. This has implications for all minorities and non-conformists. And this includes self-identifying Jews.[43] The standard white practice of referring to black citizens as 'immigrants' is to question their status and rights under English law, as if their real home were elsewhere. There is a parallel here with antisemitic language in which the labelling of Jews as 'Zionists' suggests an uncertain loyalty; in both cases it also suggests impermanence — as if neither group were 'here to stay'.

Antisemitism as anti-Zionism

Antisemitism has taken on new forms since the foundation of the state of Israel in 1948. Increasingly, antisemitism is being coded as 'anti-Zionism', as this is seen as politically more acceptable. This coding is to be found at both ends of the political spectrum. The extreme 'anti-Zionist' refuses to recognise the Jews as a people, the existence of antisemitism as a legitimate concern, or Israel as a nation. The equation between Zionism and racism voted in 1975 by the United Nations, and symbolised visually in posters superimposing the swastika on the star of David, has traumatised a whole generation of Jewish students. Some cartoons in the Arab press of Menachem Begin, former Israeli Prime Minister, are also disturbing. They depict him as a blood-sucking vulture accumulating US dollars, and part of a larger media and international capitalist network run by international Jewry. Such cartoons are reminiscent of Streicher's *Der Stürmer.* They are putting the same set of meanings into circulation.

In Israel, where the media is relatively independent, despite the usual political appointments, there has been large-scale opposition to the Lebanese war. It is generally recognised in all but the most hawkish circles that this war has no bearing on Israel's legitimate and very real concerns with secure frontiers. The terrible bombing of Beruit was unjustifiable in terms of Israeli security. The attitude of the Jewish press in Britain, which fiercely rejects any critism of Israel, and is predominantly conservative, is also tending more towards this view.

Successive Israeli governments have denied Palestinians human rights, including the right to self-determination. Israel has a right-wing government pursuing aggressive imperialist policies, and is currently engaged in an aggressive war in occupied territories. However, this is not the sole prerogative of Israel. Britain recently fought an imperialist war in the Falklands. Britain is also engaged in an imperialist war in occupied Northern Ireland. All persons identifying with the 'Troops Out' movement, or with the Irish independence struggle, are under constant surveillance, and may receive heavy sentences as criminals under the draconian Prevention of Terrorism Act. Prior to Algerian independence, France was fighting a barbaric and protracted war. And what of the involvement of the Reagan administration in financing death squads in El Salvador; and of Reagan's war against the democratically elected government of Nicaragua, which he recently characterised as an 'outlaw state', or the US raid on Libya in flagrant contravention of international law.

These wars and the governments who wage them have been justly condemned by the anti-imperialist left. Yet there has been no movement to make Britain, France or Reagan's America into international pariah states. There has been no political campaign to drive Britain into the sea, or to question the legitimacy of its people as a nation. Nor is it ever suggested that France, as the country of revolution (even less the Soviet Union), should have different moral standards. Yet this has been said of Israel — as if nation states themselves can be 'good' or 'bad'. It is absurd. It is also very significant. It is quite clear that Israel's actions and policies are judged differently from those of any other state *because it is a Jewish state*.

Traditionally the charge against Jews was that they were rootless and cosmopolitan, as were gypsies. The French New Right continues the ultra-right Catholic nationalist tradition through the nineteenth century novelist, Maurice Barrès, of celebrating all values 'rooted' in 'Indo-European culture'.[44] As one of their members, Jean Mabire, has shown, by Indo-European, they really mean

'Aryan'.[45] In the *Meaning of Conservatism,* Scruton also talks of 'the need for roots'.[46] It is significant, too, that it was the two 'rootless' peoples, the Jews and the gypsies, who were sent to the gas chambers.

'Anti-Zionist' politics has also penetrated the women's movement in Britain and elsewhere following the Israeli invasion of the Lebanon in August 1982. The focus was provided by *Spare Rib* which published two articles (August and November 1982) on the 'atrocious' treatment of Palestinian women by Israel. Both displayed an ignorance of history and lack of understanding of Arab-Jewish relations to which Jewish women wanted to reply, but were refused. Letters from Jewish women to *Spare Rib* and *Outwrite* were only published if explicitly 'anti-Zionist'. Protest erupted which divided the feminist movement in Britain. In the acrimonious debate that followed, which was concerned with the broader issues of racism and cultural imperialism, Jewish, black and 'Third world' women came under attack. This was particularly traumatic in terms of feminist politics as it was these women who were attempting to challenge their oppression within the women's movement. These were the circumstances in which the Women's Liberation Movement became involved with 'anti-Zionist' politics.

For many Jewish feminists the recollection is fraught with pain. The AWP (All Women's Place) in London has not been a safe place for Jewish women. Faced with antisemitism in an anti-Zionist guise, Jewish feminists are being forced to explore the parameters of their relationship with Israel for themselves. The Jewish feminist magazine, *Shifra,* grew out of this need for a safe, autonomous space. *Shifra* is a celebration of growing critical awareness, and not simply reactive; it responds to both religious and secular identities, and represents different positions within feminism.

There is also widespread ignorance about the relationship of diaspora Jews with Israel. There are a host of assumptions. First, Jews are confused with Israelis. The Middle East question is often invoked in terms of Arabs and Jews. At times, this may be simply ignorance. At others, it is clearly disingenuous. It is also assumed that all Jews have an intimate knowledge of Israel and of Jewish and Israeli history, whereas many of us have been cut off from Jewish history and learning through the force of assimilation. Jews everywhere are also thought to be directly responsible for Israeli policy, although citizens of another state. Lastly, it is assumed that all Jews have a clear and unchanging position on Zionism and the Jewish state, and that the issues involved are simple and easily defined. Such perceptions would be laughable if they were not threatening. For *Spare Rib* and *Outwrite,* and the pro-Palestinian left generally, there are 'good' and 'bad' Jews who pass or fail the 'anti-Zionist' litmus test of political purity.

On the right, antisemitic discourse presents basic similarities in that it seeks to pinpoint Jews within the national community, but there are also differences. Some sections of the antisemitic right support pro-Zionist policies because further Jewish diaspora immigration to Israel would reduce the number of indigenous Jews; at the same time, it would thwart Arab nationalism. In both cases, they share a common belief that 'bad' Jew (for the left) and Jews as a whole (for the right) have a dubious loyalty, and cannot be trusted. Despite the intervening history, it is as if we have gone full circle since the Dreyfus Affair. At the same time, in various parts of the world Jews and Jewish institutions are still being selected as targets by hit squads — the singling out and subsequent murder of Dora Bloch at Entebbe, the bomb attack at the Parisian synagogue at Rue Copernic, the cold-blooded murder of the American Jew, Leon Klinghoffer, on the Italian liner, the Achille Lauro... These victims bore no responsibility for the formulation or implementation of any anti-Arab policy. They are targeted as *Jews.* Jewish community centres in most of western Europe are under a permanent security alert. British or French Christians are not accustomed to celebrating Christmas or Easter under constant fear of attack. For Jewish communities this has become a common experience during the High Holy Days. And as *Searchlight* spokesman, Gerry Gable, pointed out at a GLC meeting in London in December 1985 on racist attacks, in areas of Asian and Jewish population racist attacks against both communities have increased. Gable is seen as largely responsible for *Searchlight's* revelations about links between the Conservative Party and the extreme right. As reported in April 1986, *Searchlight* discovered a plot to abduct and murder Gable involving British intelligence and an as yet unnamed right-wing Conservative MP. It was investigated by Special Branch, and a report given to Mrs. Thatcher, but no charges have been brought so far. This plan suggests the lengths a member of the government is prepared to go in order to control anti-racist activity. Over the last few years the obstensibly liberal slogan of 'free speech' has come to mean 'free speech for racists'; and on certain university campuses, free speech for antisemites.

The growing acceptability of antisemitism under the guise of anti-Zionism poses a particular problem for Jews in the broader anti-racist and feminist movement. Its existence is increasingly denied on the left. Jews are consequently marginalised and silenced. This issue of the hierarchy of oppressions is frequently raised; and it is obviously true that the majority of British Jews are white and enjoy white skin privilege. It is important to understand, and to remember, why this privilege exists, and how it operates. There are other crucial differences: for most British Jews, Britain was a place of refuge from the pogroms of Eastern Europe. Despite the Aliens Act and the presence of the Mosley's British Union of Fascists, and its predecessor, the British Brothers' League, Britain was still a place of refuge. For blacks, on the other hand, Britain and the British state is the site of repression and of anti-black racism. However, simply to dwell on differences can be divisive. Already different interests in the States, Britain and elsewhere are seeking to polarise Jewish and black communities. In Britain the invitation extended to the American Louis Farrakhan, leader of the Black Muslim group, Nation of Islam, calls for closer analysis.

Farrakhan is alleged to have said that 'Hitler was a very great man', to have referred to the 'dirty practices' of Judaism; and to enjoy the support of the Ku Klux Klan in the States.[47] Tapes of his speeches circulating in Britain refer to Jewish merchants and Jewish money-power in a language reminiscent of Chesterton's *The Unhappy Lords,* a text advertised and sold by the British National Party.

The invitation to Farrakhan came from the Hackney Black People's Association in East London. In January 1986 the Home Secretary, Douglas Hurd, banned him from entering Britain.[48] This provoked outrage in some sections of the black community claiming that it interfered with black people's right to free speech. The Jewish Cultural and Anti-Racist Project, JCARP, a Greater London Council funded project of the Jewish Socialist Group, which has been working to bring about alliances between Jews and black people, was profoundly embarrassed. Its spokesperson, David Rosenberg, commented that Farrakhan's speeches could cause severe damage to these alliances, and he did not regret the banning. He noted, however, that there was a sharp contrast between the state's willingness to ban Farrakhan and its unwillingness to use its power to expel Italian fascists in Britain.[49] Linda Bellos, a former member of the *Spare Rib* collective, who is black and Jewish, now leader of the London Borough of Lambeth, and vice-chairperson of the Labour Party black sections' campaign, said that it was hypocritical of the government to allow the South African leader, P.W. Botha, and the Klan leader, Bill Wilkinson, into the country, but to ban Farrakhan. And added that if Farrakhan had made antisemitic statements, they do not support them, but that black people had the right to be heard and a right to dissent.[50]

Clearly an authoritarian, racist state will not behave equally towards visiting black and white leaders; or be equally sympathetic to the two extremes of the political spectrum that they may represent. The banning order is yet another example of state interference in the lives of black people in Britain. There is a limit to patience. Resistance to the ban is resistance to the state.

For Jews involved in building alliances, and critical of growing authoritarianism, Farrakhan's banning and his potential presence are both problematic. We need to sharpen our understanding of the role of the state in institutional racism; and how certain stands could assist the law and order merchants at a time when the 1985 White Paper has defined 'disorderly conduct' as a new penal category to be enforced by the police, but has done nothing to tighten legislation concerning racist attacks. For black people this knowledge of institutional racism comes from the experience of being black in Britain. The mere fact of being black provokes everyday racism. Contemporary white Jewish experience is palpably different. Yet in the case of Hackney, formerly an area of Jewish settlement, there are striking analogies. London's East End, including Cable Street, was the theatre of violent anti-fascist struggles in the 30's. Jews confronted fascists selling literature in the streets, and were arrested. Today, in the same streets, blacks confront fascists selling literature, and are arrested. It is these experiences that must unite, not separate, stigmatised minority communities. Feminist political ethics may provide a framework. We need to develop ways of listening, learning and organising which takes account of the racist and class dimensions as well as our struggles against women's oppression. And feminists, as distinct from traditional left-wing parties, are committed to fighting *all* oppressions.

The impact of the Holocaust denial myth depends to a significant extent on the political context in which it has been launched and the sets of meanings in circulation. Antisemitism and racism take different historical forms in different societies at different times in history. At the present moment antisemitic discourse in which Jews are portrayed as wielding extraordinary economic power and political influence both nationally and internationally is by no means limited to a few ultra-right publications; and this discourse has historical resonances. References to the class structure of the Jewish population, which frequently denies the existence of working class members, and of a radical element, are part of an older antisemitic stereotype. More subtle is the assumption that the middle class Jew is a 'rich Jew', not simply a rich person. These assumptions are also being made of Asians in the business community.

Antisemitism posing as 'anti-Zionism' is perhaps the newest dimension; and there are variations. While conflating Jews with Israelis, it presents a negative picture of both. Some left-wing forms advocate assimilation, arguing that socialist and Jewish identities are incompatible, despite evidence to the contrary — such as the East European history of the Jewish Bund; the Jewish international involvement in the Spanish Civil War on the Republican side, and the anti-fascist Jewish Brigades in world war two. Jews have a very long and very fine radical tradition. This too is being denied. Left-wing groups are constantly surprised to encounter radical self-identifying Jews. Whereas for black cultures resistance to assimilation may be welcomed by some sections on the left, although this may be slow,[51] Jews are perceived differently. The 'good Jew' is the assimilated Jew. The self-identifying Jew is perceived as a bizarre anachronism and a source of embarrassment. This perception is also shared by fellow Jews who may have internalised these more subtle forms of antisemitism. Whenever Judaism, Jewish culture, Jews as a people, or, indeed, the idea of Israel is represented in totally negative terms, we are dealing with antisemitism; This is an everyday experience.

There have been other pressures to assimilate[52] — at the expense of a language and a previously thriving Yiddish culture. This is the price of assimilation. Many Jews do not wish to 'pass'. Blacks cannot 'pass'. These are as yet unresolved dilemmas within the left. Such gross oversimplifications stem in part from the equating of Judaism solely with religion, not with cultural identity as a plural and dynamic phenomenon. This ignorance derives from an ethnocentric vision. The need to claim our identities is still necessary in a society that denies any cultural heritage other than the ruling one, even though that identity can only validate part of our lives.[53]

The antisemitic, 'anti-Zionist' attack on the legitimacy of the Israeli state, as distinct from a critique of its policies, constitutes the mainstay of antisemitic discourse on an international level. This has a number of implications for Jewish diaspora identity. While Jewish institutions and their representative bodies channel the bulk of Jewish energies, political and cultural, towards Israel, diaspora life is devalued; and Jewish activities that are not primarily Israeli-focussed or religious, face enormous problems of funding.[54]

Just as 'Jewish Bolchevism' was seen by the Nazis as part of the international Jewish conspiracy theory whereby Wall Street financed the Russian revolution, in the Israeli debate 'Zionist racism' and 'Zionist Nazism' invite similar 'solutions', transporting the trauma of extermination to the Middle East and to the diaspora communities.

Throughout European history in periods of exceptional strain, antisemitism has been accompanied by a belief in some form of Jewish conspiracy promoted by organised killers. Racism has never been at a loss for 'proofs' to make its stereotypes convincing. The Holocaust transformed racial theory into practice. The Holocaust has passed. But antisemitism and racism are not relics. They have survived, and are claiming new victims. The Holocaust denial has renewed the obsessive myth of Jewish conspiracy. Such an ideology retains at its core the image of genocide.

Notes

1. The Holocaust: interpretations

1. The etymology is Greek. HOLO whole (**kauston** burnt).
 The Supplement to the *Oxford English Dictionary* (1976) has recorded that the word **Holocaust** is frequently applied to the mass murder of Jews in the war of 1939-45.
 The Hebrew term is **Shoah.** This means the Catastrophe/Ruin. There is no implication of sacrifice. 'Shoah' was the title given to Claude Lanzmann's much acclaimed documentary film.
2. From the Greek **genos** race + CIDE, a suffix meaning a person or substance that kills.
 The Sunday Times, 21 October 1945, noted that 'The United Nations indictment of the 24 Nazi leaders has brought a new word into the language — genocide'. (Supplement to the *Oxford English Dictionary,* Vol. II, 1976).
3. L. Dawidowicz, **The War against the Jews, 1933-45,** (Harmondsworth, Middx: Penguin Books, 1977)
4. Quoted by Y.M. Rabkin, 'Drawing lessons from racist propaganda', *Jerusalem Post,* 10 May 1985
5. See *Shifra,* vol 1, no 1, (Kislev 5745/December 1984), 18-20.
6. S. Davidson, 'A Painful Reminder, An Incomprehensible Time', *Times,* 29 April 1985.
7. *Guardian,* 6 August 1985.
8. See M. Gilbert, *Auschwitz and the Allies* (London: Michael Joseph, 1981).
9. *Daily Mail,* 9 May 1985.
10. See G. Seidel and R. Günther, 'Family, Nation, History in the media reporting of the Falklands war' in G. Seidel, ed., *The Nature of the Right*, (Amsterdam: Benjamins, 1987).
11. 'Despite all the killing and destruction that accompanied it, the Second World War was a good war', A.J.P. Taylor (1961) *The Origins of the Second World War* quoted by A. Barnett, 'World War II: Myths and Realities', *New Statesman,* 3 May 1985. Dawidowicz has argued in 'Lies about the Holocaust', *Commentary,* December 1980 that this 'mischievous book' became the banner under which a swarm of Nazi apologists, cranks and anti-semites rallied' (p.31). Taylor argued that Hitler did not plan a general war but that this was 'a mistake, the result on both sides of diplomatic blunders'. The book was

roundly attacked by historians, but remains a standard reference text.

12. The major work of reference is M.R. Marrus and R.O. Paxton, *Vichy, France and the Jews,* (New York: Basic Books, 1981). It was published in French in 1981 by Calmann-Lévy. See also R. Laloum, *La France antisémite de Darquier de Pellepoix,* (Paris: Editions Syros, 1979) and M. Abitbol, *Les Juifs d'Afrique du Nord sous Vichy,* (Paris: G.P. Maisonneuve et Larose, 1983).
13. See, for example, A. Tomforde, 'New Row as Bitburg ghosts refuse to lie down', *Guardian,* 3 May 1985.
14. The phrase describing the President's visit to the Bitburg cemetery is that of Rabbi Albert Friedlander in *The Times,* 4 May 1985.
15. Statement made by Itzhak Rabin, Israeli Defence Minister, to a meeting of Holocaust survivors at Yad Vashem (the Holocaust Memorial Museum in Jerusalem), reported in the *Jewish Chronicle,* 10 May 1985.
16. *New York Times,* 18 April 1985.
17. *Jewish Chronicle,* 3 May 1985.
18. Quoted in the *Daily Telegraph,* 20 April 1983.
19. Ibid. W. Blitzer, 'Elie Wiesel's appeal fails—Reagan will visit SS graves', *Jewish Chronicle,* 26 April 1985.
20. *Jewish Chronicle,* 10 May 1985.
21. *Daily Express,* 1 May 1985.
22. *Daily Telegraph,* 30 April 1985.
23. *Sunday Telegraph,* 5 May 1985.
24. *New York Times,* 10 May 1985.
25. Quoted by C.C. Aronsfeld, 'The German Far Right Press and the 40th Anniversary of VE Day', Research Report of the Institute of Jewish Affairs, no 4, (May 1985).
26. N. Cohn, *Warrant for Genocide: The Myth of the Jewish World Conspiracy and the Protocols of the Elders of Zion,* (London: Eyre and Spottiswoode, 1967).
27. *Spotlight,* 13 May 1985.
28. See chapter 7.
29. Quoted from the official text of President Reagan's remarks at Bitburg (United States Information Services, US Embassy, London).
30. *Jewish Chronicle,* 10 May 1985. The Egyptian source has no particular significance. Rather, it suggests the extent of the

geo-political circulation of the Holocaust denial literature, and the fact that it is not limited to Christian cultures.

31. Quoted by C.C. Aronsfeld, 1985, op.cit.
32. Y. Bauer, 'Whose Holocaust?' *Midstream,* (November 1980).
33. L. Dawidowicz, *The Holocaust and the Historians,* (Cambridge, Mass.: Harvard University Press, 1981), 16.
34. Y. Bauer, 1980, op.cit.
35. *Guardian,* 7 April 1985. The most hushed-up acts of genocide include that of Australian Aborigines by white settlers and the genocide of the Armenian people by the Turks in 1915.
36. Dawidowicz, op.cit., 1981, 17.
37. *Morning Freiheit,* Sunday English Section, 4 August 1985.
38. See W. Korey, 'Babi Yar — without Jews', *Jewish Chronicle,* 1 October 1982. Yevtushenko's poem about Babi Yar which dared to make specific reference to Jews massacred in 1941 met with an enthusiastic reception in the west, but was frowned upon at home.
39. R. Aronson, *The Dialectics of Disaster, A Preface to Hope,* (London: Verso Editions, 1982), 13.
40. See *Jewish Chronicle,* 16 August 1985 and 22 November 1985. See also O. Sholat, 'The Flip-Sides of Meir Kahane', *New Outlook* (July 1985), 28, 7.
41. See, for example, T. Sommer, 'Begin strikes a low blow', *Newsweek,* 18 May 1981.
42. The symposium took place on 16 May 1985 under the auspices of the Institute of Jewish Affairs, London.
43. D. Cesarani, 'The Alternative Jewish Community', Lecture given at Leo Baeck College, London, 5 March 1985.
44. E. Sarah, 'Knowing No Bounds… or… what's a nice Jewish Lesbian doing holding up the Sefer-Torah?' *Shifra* vol 1, no 1, (Kislev 5745/December 1984), 9-12.
45. G. Amipaz-Silber, *Revolt in Auschwitz,* World Zionist Press Service, 4 November 1980, Martyrs and Heroes Remembrance Day. See also R. Ainsztein, *Jewish Resistance in Nazi-Occupied Europe,* (London: Paul Elek, 1974). Titles of other Jewish resistance studies are listed in the bibliography of M. Gilbert, *Atlas of the Holocaust,* (London: Michael Joseph, 1982).
46. H. Arendt, *Eichmann in Jerusalem. A Report on the Banality of Evil,* (Harmondsworth, Middx.: Penguin Books, 1979, 3rd edn.), 257-269.

2. *The Holocaust: the facts*

1. F. Galton, *Eugenics, its definition, scope and aim.* In Sociological Society *Sociological Papers,* (London: MacMillan, 1905), 150. See M. Billig, *Ideology and Social Psychology,* (Oxford: Blackwell, 1982), chapter 4. For the full implications of a eugenics policy, see S. Chorover, *From Genesis to Genocide,* (Cambridge, Mass.: MIT Press, 1979).
2. Quoted by L. Dawidowicz, *The Holocaust and Historians,* (Cambridge, Mass.: University Press, 1981), 65-7.
3. A. Hitler, *Mein Kampf* (trans. R. Mannheim), (London: Hutchinson, 1974).
4. Hitler, op.cit.
5. A. Jacquard, *Moi et les autres,* (Paris: Seuil, 1983), 61 (trans. GS)
6. M. Billig, *L'Internationale raciste: de la psychologie à la 'science des races',* (Paris: Maspero, 1981). This is an expanded version of M. Billig, *Psychology, Racism and Fascism,* (Birmingham: Searchlight pamphlet, 1979); and M. Billig, 'The Origins of Racial Psychology', *Patterns of Prejudice,* vol 16, no 3, (1982a), 2-16. See also Billig, 1979, op.cit., 5-7. The most detailed account of Günther and the Nordicist school is contained in H-J Lutzhöft, *Der Nordische Gedanke in Deutschland,* (Stuttgart: Ernst Klett, 1971).
7. G.G. Field, 'Nordic Racism, *Journal of the History of Ideas,* vol. 30, no. 3, (July 1977), 523-40.
8. H.F.K. Günther, *The Racial Elements of European History,* (London: Methuen, 1927), 78. Günther was formally honoured by Alfred Rosenberg, head of Hitler's Foreign Political Office and later Reich Minister for the Occupied Territories. In February 1941 Rosenberg presented Günther with the 'Goethe Medal'. He was the guest of honour at the inaugural conference of the Frankfurt Institute for Research into the Jewish Question in March 1941. Günther's colleague at the University of Berlin, Walter Gross, set the tone and intimated the 'solution':

   > 'We look upon Jewry as quite a realistic phenomenon which was exceptionally clever in matters of earthly life, but which likewise is subject to historical death. And as far as the historical phenomenon of the Jew is concerned, we believe that this hour of death has come irrevocably'.

(quoted in M. Weinreich, *Hitler's Professors: The part of scholarship in Germany's crimes against the Jewish people,* (New York: Yiddish Scientific Institute, 1946), 112; quoted by Billig, 1979 op.cit.). Günther died in 1967.

9. Quoted by L. Poliakov, *The Aryan Myth, A History of Racist and Nationalist Ideas in Europe* (trans. E. Howard), (New York: Meridian Press, 1974).
10. R. Hilberg, *The Destruction of the European Jews,* (Chicago: Quadrangle Books, 1961), 656.
11. G. Guillaumin, 'Pratique du pouvoir et idée de Nature', (1): 'L'Appropriation des femmes', *Questions Féministes,* no 2, 5-30, (février 1978); (2): 'Pratique et idée de Nature: le discours de la Nature', *Questions Féministes,* no 3, 5-30, (mai 1978). For English translation, see 'The Practice of Power and Belief in Nature', Part 1: 'The Appropriation of Women': Part 11, 'The Naturalist Discourse', *Feminist Issues,* 1. no 3, Winter 1981, 3-28 and 1, no 3, Spring 1982, 87-107. See also S. Rose, L.J. Kamin and R.C. Lewontin, *Not in Our Genes. Biology, Ideology and Human Nature,* (Harmondsworth, Middx.: Penguin Books, 1984); and G. Seidel, ed., *The Nature of the Right,* (Amsterdam: Benjamins, 1987).
12. The ghetto was a feature of Jewish life in many western cities from the sixteenth to the eighteenth century. See A. Eban, *Heritage* (London; Weidenfeld and Nicolson, 1985), 177.
13. See, for example, Y. Gutman, 'The Genesis of Resistance in the Warsaw Ghetto', in *Yad Vashem Studies,* ix, Jerusalem, (1973), 29-70.
14. Gilbert, 1978, op.cit.
15. W.L. Shirer, *The Rise and Fall of the Third Reich,* (London: Secker and Warburg, 1974, 10th edn.), 958-9.
16. Quoted by Dawidowicz, 1977 op.cit.
17. G. Hausner, *Justice in Jerusalem,* (London: Nelson, 1967).
18. L. Poliakov, *Harvest of Hate,* (London: Elek Books, 1956),
19. G. Reitlinger, *The Final Solution,* (London: Valentine and Mitchell, 1961), 102.
20. H. Friedlander, 'The Language of Nazi Totalitarianism', *Shoah,* vol. 1, Part 2, Fall, 1978, pp. 16-19. This has a short but valuable bibliography. See also E.K. Bramsted, *Goebbels and National Socialist Propaganda 1925-1945,* (Michigan State University: Cresset Press, 1965).
21. Poliakov, 1956, op.cit., 146.

22. Gilbert, 1981, op.cit. See also W. Laqueur, *The Terrible Secret,* (London: Weidenfeld and Nicolson, 1981).
23. Poliakov, 1956, op.cit., 200.
24. See G. Sereny, *Into that Darkness, from Mercy Killing to Mass Murder,* (London: Deutsch, 1974).
25. Document 3868 P-s quoted in A. Suzman and D. Diamond, *Six Million Did Die: The Truth Shall Prevail,* (Johannesburg: South African Board of Deputies, 1980), 93-4.
25. M. Gilbert, *Final Journey,* (London: Allen and Unwin, 1979).
27. Reitlinger, op.cit, 122.
28. See also M. Gilbert, *The Holocaust, The Jewish Tragedy,* (London: Collins, 1986).
29. L. Dawidowicz, *A Holocaust Reader,* (New York: Behrman, 1976).
30. See, for example, Hilberg, op.cit.
31. See the bibliographic essay in M.G. Kren and L.H. Rappoport, *The Holocaust and the Crisis of Human Behaviour,* (New York: Holmes and Meier, 1980); and in L. Dawidowicz, 1976, op.cit.
32. The two principal published sources concerned with German policy and practice are the *Trial of the Major War Criminals before the International Military Tribunal: Official Text,* 42 volumes, Nuremberg 1947-1949 and the *Trial of War Criminals Before the Nuremberg Military Tribunals under Control Council Law,* no 10, 15 volumes, Washington, D.C., 1949-1953. There is also a comprehensive guide to more than 3,000 documents submitted at the Nuremberg Trials in J. Robinson and H. Sachs, eds., *The Holocaust, The Nuremberg Evidence,* (Jerusalem: Yivo Institute, New York and Yad Vachem, 1976) listed in the important bibliography in M. Gilbert, *Atlas of the Holocaust,* (London: Michael Joseph, 1982).
33. R. Ringelblum, *Notes from the Warsaw ghetto,* trans. J. Sloan, (New York: McGraw-Hill, 1958).
34. L. Poliakov, 'Le Dossier de Kurt Gerstein', *Le Monde Juif,* no. 36, (1964), 4-20; L. Poliakov, 'Nouveaux Documents sur Kurt Gerstein', *Le Monde Juif,* no. 37, (1964), 4-16.
35. Dawidowicz, 1976, op.cit., 105-9.
36. Ibid.
37. H. Arendt, *The Trial of Adolf Eichmann or the Banality of Evil,* (Harmondsworth, Middx.: Penguin Books, 1979).

38. See Dawidowicz, 1981, op.cit., 13.
39. L.Y. Steinitz and D.M. Szonyi, eds., *Living After the Holocaust, Reflections by the Post-War Generations in America,* (New York: Bloch, 1976).

3. International Neo-Nazi Network: the French, German and American New Right, and the discourses of inequality

1. I. R. Barnes and V.R.P. Barnes, 'A "Revisionist Historian" manipulates Anne Frank's Diary', *Patterns of Prejudice,* vol 15, no 1, (1981), 27-32.
2. The extraordinary pre-war photographs of Roman Vishniac in *A Vanished World* (London: Allen Lane, 1984) illustrate the grinding poverty of Jewish life in Nazi-dominated Berlin, Warsaw, Vilna, Lodz, Mukachevo, Uzhgorod and Trava between 1933 and Kristallnacht in November 1938.
3. L. Dawidowicz, 'The Holocaust as Historical Record', *Dimensions of the Holocaust* (Lectures at Northwestern University, Evanston, Illinois) (New York: Center for Studies on the Holocaust and Anti-Defamation League of B'nai Brith, 1977).
4. N. Cohn, *Warrant for Genocide: The Myth of the Jewish World Conspiracy and the Protocols of the Elders of Zion,* (London: Eyre and Spottiswoode, 1967).
5. Along with Hitler's *Mein Kampf, The Myth of the Twentieth Century* was one of the official texts of Nazism, although the national socialist movement was more orientated towards liturgy and symbols than towards the written word. See J.P. Stern, *Hitler, The Führer and the People,* (Glasgow: Fontana Collins, 1975) and G.L. Mosse, *Nazism: A Historical and Comparative Analysis of National Socialism* (Oxford: Blackwell, 1978). See also C.C. Aronsfeld, 'The First Anti-Semitic International', *Critical Social Policy,* vol 2, no 3, (Spring 1983), 66-73.
6. M. Billig, *L'Internationale raciste: de la psychologie à la 'sciences des races'*, (Paris: Maspero, 1981). (This is an expanded version of M. Billig, *Psychology, Racism and Fascism, Searchlight* pamphlet, 1979). See also M. Billig, 'The Origins of Racial Psychology', *Patterns of Prejudice,* vol 16, no 3, (1982a), 2-16.

7. This is exemplified in C. Lombrosco, *L'homme criminel* (Paris: Alcan, 1887). Lombroso argued that one could tell a murderer by the shape of their head, and that inherited characteristics determined mental and moral traits. For a scholarly and compelling study of the progression and political significance of these kind of determinist claims, see S.L. Chorover, *From Genesis to Genocide* (Cambridge: Mass: MIT Press, 1980) (paperback edition).
8. *Washington Post,* 28 May 1978. See also F. Laurent, *L'Orchestre noir* (Paris: Stock, 1978).
9. See chapter 4 for the role played by the Liberty Lobby in the Holocaust denial.
10. L.Cheles, 'Le "new-look" du néo-fascisme italien', *MOTS,* no 12, (mars 1986).
11. According to *Searchlight,* January 1986, 9-11, Saudi Arabia has not made a direct contribution to operating costs for a number of years, and 85% of WACL's total income in 1984 came from South Korea. It is channelled through the Korean Central Intelligence Agency.
12. Reproduced in *Searchlight,* January 1986, 10.

    The Christian rhetoric in the States has a very particular function as an integrative force of the Moral Majority, a vehicle of traditional morality. Apart from its mobilising force in white, Christian societies, there is clearly a campaign against the World Council of Churches in their opposition to apartheid and to racism in general. This campaign (which is also echoed by the British New Right) emphasises a return to 'traditional Christianity', that is, one which is primarily pietistic and seemingly above politics, and hence has no voice in combatting oppression (See D. Edgar, K. Leech and P. Weller, *The New Right and the Church* (London: Jubilee Group, 1985). The implications for women's equality are enormous, as exemplified in the campaign against the Equal Rights Amendment in the States. The connections between right-wing Christian groups, extreme right-wing political movements and South African backing are the subject of an important study by D. Knight, *Beyond the Pale: The Christian Political Fringe* (Leigh, Lancs: CARAF publications, 1982).
13. The current WACL President, retired General John Singlaub, publicly admitted to buying arms on behalf of the CIA for the contras in their illegal war against Nicaragua ('President

Reagan's Private War', *World in Action* programme, ITV, 24 March 1986, produced by Mike Jordan).

14. These links have been traced by Billig, 1981, op.cit. (See n6)
15. M. Walker, *The National Front* (London: Fontana, 1977), 103 seq.
16. G. Thayer, *The British Political Fringe* (London: A. Blond, 1965) cited by Billig, 1979, op.cit.
17. P.A. Taguieff, 'La stratégie culturelle de la nouvelle droite en France, 1968-1983' in A. Spire ed., *Vous avez dit fascismes?* (Paris: Editions Arthaud/Montalba, 1984), 13-152.
18. Concerning Don Martin's political activities and affiliations, see *Patterns of Prejudice,* vol 17, no 2, 1983, 39-40.
19. See P. Spoonley, 'New Zealand First! The Extreme Right and Politics in New Zealand, 1961-1981', *Political Science,* vol 33, no 2, (December 1981), 99-125.
20. See *Searchlight,* April 1982. See also chapter 4.
21. P.A. Taguieff, 'L'héritage nazi, des Nouvelles Droites européennes à la littérature niant le génocide', *Les Nouveaux Cahiers,* no 64, spring 1981, 3-22; On the French New Right, and its precursors, see GARAH, *Morituri: ceux qui doivent mourir,* (Paris, Editions GARAH, 1974), the earliest and invaluable study of the origins of GRECE: see also J. Brunn (ed), *La Nouvelle Droite* (Paris: Nouvelles Editions Oswald, 1979); P.A. Taguieff, 1984, op.cit; B. Brigouleix, *L'extrême droite en France* (Paris: Editions Fayolle, 1977), J.P. Fargier, *Les Bons à Rien* (Paris: Presses d'aujourd'hui, 1980).

    La Fédération des Etudiants Nationalistes (FEN) was a successor to *Jeune Nation,* an ultra-nationalist semi-clandestine group set up in 1954 around Pierre Sidos, a Vichy supporter. The FEN was an extreme right-wing student group set up in 1960 to combat the marxists in the National Union of Students and to support action in favour of *'Algérie française'* (in opposition to Algerian independence). They published a monthly journal, *Cahiers Universitaires* (University Notebooks). Another political tendency in FEN produced the journal *Europe Action* and helped set up *Occident* (The West), a group of violent, extreme right-wing activists which provided the stewardship for right-wing meetings and used force to break up left-wing demonstrations and meetings. There was a political split in April 1964 when Sidos regained ascendancy. *Occident* was dissolved in November 1968, and reemerged as *Ordre Nouveau* (New Order) in 1969 when it regrouped with some dissidents from the earlier split, notably François Duprat. In 1966 the FEN takes on party status as the MNP *(Mouvement Nationaliste du Progrès* — National Progress Movement), an ostensibly republican party to field Tixier Vignancour, a principal OAS barrister, in the 1967 presidential elections. Most of the founders of GRECE were active in the MNP. In 1967 other MNP members launched the magazine, *Militant,* a focal point for the setting up of Jean-Marie Le Pen's *Front National* (FN) in November 1972. The *Parti des Forces Nouvelles* (Party of New Forces) was formed in 1974 as a break-away group from the FN (see n 45). The *Rassemblement Européen de la Liberté* (European Assembly of Freedom) came into being in November 1966 to field candidates in the March 1967 elections and hence gain access to the media. It was singularly unsuccessful. The organ of the REL was *Europe Action hebdomadaire* (Europe Action Weekly) for which most of the former contributors to *Europe Action* continued to write. A political and financial scandal led to the break-up of the MNP-REL from which three small autonomous groups emerged. One of these was the future GRECE, closely linked to *Europe Action.* (See P.A. Taguieff, 1984, op.cit.), 25-7.

22. A. Schnapp and J. Svenbro, 'Du Nazisme à Nouvelle Ecole: repères sur la prétendue Nouvelle Droite', *Quaderni di Storia,* 11, (1980), 107-19.
23. See, for example, A. de Benoist, *Les idées à l'endroit* (Paris: Editions Libres Hallier, 1979, 57-76), 250-9; P. Vial, *Pour une renaissance culturelle, Le GRECE prend la parole* (Paris; Copernic 1979); and GRECE, *Pour un gramscisme de droite, Actes du 15e colloque national* (29 November 1981), (Paris: GRECE, 1982).

    Ferraresi has noted that the Italian New Right, patterned on the French New Right, which campaigns *'per una rinascita culturale'* (for a cultural renaissance) is also concerned with metapolitics and cultural hegemony. *'Gramscismo di destra'* (right-wing gramscism) defines this strategy. See F. Ferraresi, ed., *La Destra radicale* (Milan: Feltrinelli, 1984); and F. Ferraresi, 'Les références théorico-doctrinales de la droite radicale en Italie', *MOTS,* no 12, mars 1986. *Elementi* of the Italian New Right is one of the periodicals advertised in the

Salisbury Review, a journal of the British New Right, (see chapter 7).

See G. Seidel, 'The concept of culture, "race" and nation in the British and French New Right', in R. Levitas, ed., *The Ideology of the New Right* (Oxford: Polity Press/Blackwell, 1986).

See also V. Carofiglio and C. Fernandes, 'Les aventures de la droite française et les avatars de Gramsci', 3e colloque international de Lexicologie politique, Ecole Normale Sup érieure de Saint-Cloud, septembre 1984 (to appear in *MOTS*, no 12, mars 1986).

24. On Gramsci, see, for example, C. Mouffe, ed., *Gramsci and Marxist theory* (London: Routledge and Kegan Paul, 1979).
25. Via the *Club de l'Horloge* (Clock Club) and its other largely publishing networks, including *Figaro Magazine*. See Taguieff, 1984, op.cit., 114-7; and the subsection 'The French New Right's entryism' in this chapter.
26. See, for example, the special issue devoted to eugenics in *Nouvelle Ecole*, no 14, January-February 1971. It includes a historical article on pre-war German eugenics which avoids making any connections between eugenic theories and genocide. The issue as a whole was enthusiastically received by the American racist, Revilo P. Oliver, who in 1966 was expelled from the right wing John Birch society for having publicly suggested that the world's troubles would end if all the Jews were gassed tomorrow at dawn. See B.R. Epstein and A. Foster, *The Radical Right: Report on the John Birch Society and its Allies*, New York: Random House 1966, 110 seq., cited by Billig, op.cit., 1981, 137-8. From the GRECE stable, see Y. Christen, *Le Dossier Darwin, la sélection naturelle, la sociobiologie, le darwinisme social* (Paris: Copernic, 1983); and, for a critical and diachronic perspective, see Billig, 1979 and 1981, op.cit.
27. Quoted by M. de Guibert, 'Recherche d'une respectabilité': thèmes neo-Nazis dans Nouvelle Ecole et le GRECE', *(Droit et Liberté*, no 379, supplement).
28. R. de Herte (pseudonym for Alain de Benoist), editorialist of *Eléments* acting as spokesperson for GRECE, rejected Christianity (and the Judaeo-Christian heritage) in these somewhat abstract terms, well within any Race Relations legislation:

> firstly [Christianity] is not our religion... Christianity was born outside Europe... Judaism is certainly perfect for Jews and Islam is for Arabs... There is no reason why Europeans perpetually let their thought be moulded by a religious ideology which does not belong to them. ('La Question Religieuse', Entretien avec R. de Herte, *Eléments,* no 17-18, September-November 1976. Trans: GS).

Judaeo-Christianity (which derives from Judaism, hence from Jews) is therefore constructed as alien. When read in conjunction with earlier texts, the meaning is quite clear.

29. See C. Guillaumin, 'Caractères spécifiques de l'idéologie raciste', *Cahiers internationaux de sociologie,* vol LIII, 1972, *247-274;* and P.A. Taguieff, *'Les présuppositions définitionnelles d'un indéfinissable: 'le racisme''', MOTS,* no 8, (mars 1984), 71-107; and P.A. Taguieff, 'L'identité nationale saisie par les logiques de racisation', *MOTS,* no 12, (mars 1986).
30. See, for example, R. de Herte (Alain de Benoist) 'La révolution conservatrice', *Eléments,* no 20, (April-May 1977). This remarkable phrase was coined by Moeller van den Bruck in 1906. It is used to refer to the anti-democratic ideology common to numerous movements of the German extreme right under the Weimar Republic. Apart from van den Bruck, exponents include Jünger, Schmitt, Spengler and Evola. Evola in particular has undergone a revival on the continental racist right. Julius Evola is characterised by the historian Ernst Nolte as one of the most extreme fascist antisemites in Italy (E. Nolte, Three Faces of Fascism, London: Weidenfeld and Nicolson, 1965). After the war Evola had links with *Nation Europa* which coordinated European fascist movements. The Spanish fascist group, CEDADE, (which has contributed to the Holocaust denial movement) and GRECE's publishing house, Copernic, have both republished his work. Weinreich, 1946, op.cit., has drawn attention to Evola's article 'Western Civilisation and the Jewish spirit' in a pamphlet entitled *The Jews wanted the war* published in 1942 by the Centre of studies on the Jewish problem in Florence. This Centre was the Italian counterpart of the Reich Institute for history of the New German opened by Alfred Rosenberg and Rudolf Hess in 1935 (see Billig, 1981, op.cit., 147, n 23); see also Ferraresi,

ed., 1986, op.cit.

On the conservative revolution, see also L. Dupeux, 'La Révolution Conservatrice et l'anticapitalisme nationaliste sous la république de Weimar', *Revue d'Allemagne et des pays de langue allemande,* tome VI, no 2, (April-June 1974); D. Goeldel, *Moeller van den Bruck (1876-1925), un nationaliste contre la révolution* (Frankfurt: Peter Lang, 1984); P. Vaydat, 'L'antisémitisme de la révolution conservatrice', *Annales du CESERE,* Université de Paris XIII, 3, 1980, 47-86. For a discussion of the conservative revolution in relation to political discourse, see J.P. Faye, *Langages Totalitaires* (Paris: Hermann, 1972).

31. Brunn, op.cit., 1979, 380.
32. J. Mabire, *Thule - Le Soleil Retrouvé des Hyperboréens* (Paris: Laffont, 1977) 71 and 81, quoted in *Droit de vivre,* (May 1980), 26, n 63.
33. P.A. Taguieff, 1984, op.cit., 59-61. See also P.A. Taguieff, 'De la race indo-européenne à la biopolitique', *Politique Hebdo,* no 1, (30 March-5 April 1981).
34. *Nouvelle Ecole,* no 6, December-January (Winter 1968-9), 89 (Trans: GS). For other ways in which GRECE glosses over fascism, see G. Seidel, 'Le fascisme dans les textes de la Nouvelle Droite', *MOTS,* no 3, (October 1981), 47-62.
35. Billig 1979, op.cit., Billig 1981, op.cit; and 1982a, op.cit. For more derivative sources, see P.A. Taguieff, 'Présence de l'héritage nazi', *Droit et Liberté,* no 397, January 1980, 15-16; I.R. Barnes: Pedigree of GRECE, I and II. *Patterns of Prejudice,* (July and September 1980).
36. Konrad Lorenz lends *Nouvelle Ecole* a 'biological' justification for its racist, elitist and eugenic theories, while the psychological justification is provided by the flawed work of Jensen and Eysenck. (In English, see K. Lorenz, *Civilised Man's Eight Deadly Sins* (London: Methuen, 1973), and K. Lorenz, *Beyond the Mirror* (London: Methuen, 1978). It was the same Lorenz who in 1943 argued that the 'folk community' must defend itself against genetic decay, and this called for 'racial politics based on science', and the separation of cultures. See K. Lorenz, 'Die angeborenen Formen moglicher Erfahrung', *Zeitschrift für Tierpsychologie,* 1943 cited by K. Leech in 'The New Radical Right and the Church in Britain', in D. Edgar, K. Leech, P. Weller, *The New Right and the Church* (London: Jubilee Group, 1985), 16-30.

See also S. Rose, L.J. Kamin and R.C. Lewontin, *Not in Our Genes* (Harmondsworth, Middx: Penguin Books, 1984), particularly 239-264; and S. and H. Rose, 'Less than human nature, Biology and the new right', *Race and Class* XXVII, 3, (winter 1986), 47-66.

37. Gayre was former editor of *Mankind Quarterly* to be succeeded by Pearson. Gayre's writing leant heavily on Günther's work.
38. On Jürgen Rieger, see *Patterns of Prejudice,* vol 17, no 2, (1983), 40-44.
39. See. Hirsch, 'To "unfrock and charlatans"', *Race Relations Abstracts,* vol 6, no 2, 1981, 1-651. See H. and S. Rose, 'The IQ Myth', *Race and Class,* vol 20, no 1, 1978, 63-74. K. Richardson and J. Spears, ed., *Race, Culture and Intelligence* (Harmondsworth, Middx: Penguin Books, 1972. S. Rose, L.J. Kamin and R.C. Lewontin, 1984, op.cit., 83-129; P.B. Medewar, 'Unnatural Science', *New York Review of Books,* 3, (February 1977), 13-18.
40. See, in particular, M. Billig, 'Professor Eysenck's political psychology', *Patterns of Prejudice,* 13, 1979, 9-16; and M. Billig, *Ideology and Social Psychology* (Oxford: Blackwell, 1982b), 120-6; and Billig, 1982a, op.cit.
41. See Billig, 1979, op.cit.
42. The Club de l'Horloge has organised debating forums with the now defunct *Magazine Hebdo.* Its publications include *Les Racines du Futur* (1977, 1984); *La Politique de Vivant* (1979); *Le Défi Démographique* (1979); *Le Péril bureaucratique* (1980); *Le Grand Tabou* (1981); *Un nouveau printemps pour l'éducation* (1982); *Echecs et injustices du socialisme* (1982); *Le Socialisme contre le Tiers Monde* (1983); *L'école en accusation* (1984): and *Socialisme et Fascisme: une même famille?* (1984).
43. Although this regroups the current right-wing opposition as a whole, the influence of the *Front National* is clearly discernible working though satellite 'cultural' organisations. Former members of *Occident* and *Ordre Nouveau* are also involved. See E. Plenel and A. Rollat, *L'effet Le Pen* (Paris: Editions de la Découverte and *Le Monde,* 1984), 87-91; and E. Plenel and Rollat, 'The revival of the Far Right in France', *Patterns of Prejudice,* vol 18, no 2, (April 1984), 20-27.
44. See *Le Matin,* 14 May 1984; and for the extent of his current

press empire, see *Le Monde,* 5-6 January 1986.

45. In 1974 Pauwels helped set up the extreme right wing PFN *(Parti des Forces Nouvelles* — Party of New Forces) a breakaway part from Le Pen's *Front National* and a regrouping of the former *Occident* in the PFN's favour. In November 1976, following its Congress, the PFN decided to have talks with Jacques Chirac's party. For Le Pen, the PFN divided 'the national opposition', and the two parties entertain intense rivalry. There appears to have been a regrouping, however, notably at a meeting at the *Mutualité* on 16 October 1983 and around the daily fascist paper, *Présent,* launched in January 1982, of which François Brigneau (originally one of the triumvirate of PFN's political bureau) of the virulently racist and scandalmongering *Minute*, is co-director, and to which Bernard Romain Marie Antony of the *Front National,* now Euro MP with Le Pen, also contributes and wrote the first editorial *(Présent,* 5 January 1982).

Bernard Romain-Marie Antony was brought to public attention as a result of a number of articles in *Le Monde* reporting the extraordinary *Mutualité* meeting in which the anti-Dreyfus tradition was very much alive. (See in particular E. Plenel, *Le Monde,* 19 October 1983; A. Rollat,*Le Monde,* 27-28 November 1983). For Romain-Marie, 'murder international and the communist international are comprised essentially of Jews'; and 'communism is Jewish'. Statements of this kind were in keeping with the rest of the proceedings in which 'marxism, freemasonry, Jews and Protestants' — and emphatically Judaism — were seen to be the inspiration of the socialist government's policies. This all has a very familiar ring and a long history. Opponents of the French Revolution of 1789 also saw the invisible enemy initally as Protestants, then from 1807 it was a Jewish and masonic plot that occupied centre stage (see L. Poliakov, *Histoire de l'antisémitisme. L'Europe suicidaire,* 1870-1933, (Paris: Calmann-Lévy, 1977), 46.

Romain-Marie organised the meeting in which the discourse of antisemitism and racism was unbridled. It was also attended by Le Pen who kept a relatively low profile. Roman-Marie is an integrist Catholic, founder of the *Chrétienté Solidarité* **(Christian Solidarity Committees) and President** of the CNIP *(Centre National des Paysans Indépendants* —

National Centre of Independent Farmers). In 1981 the CNIP regrouped a number of familiar PFN members with the complicity of Philippe Malaud, CNIP Chairman, following the defection of Alain Robert one of the PFN founders, now a CNIP Central Committee member. Malaud is currently a Euro MP. A number of former PFN leaders stood in the 1983 local elections under CNIP auspices. (See Plenel and Rollat, 1984, op.cit., 21-31; 60-67).

Media reporting and political analyses which focus largely or exclusively on Le Pen (who is increasingly careful to mediate his discourse) tend to ignore or underestimate parallel ultra-right regroupings which ostensibly keep within the legal, democratic framework.

46. See N. Krikorian, 'Européanisme, nationalisme et libéralisme dans les éditoriaux du *Figaro Magazine,* 1977-1984', *MOTS,* no 12, (mars 1986).
47. A de Benoist, *Vu de droite* (Paris: Editions Copernic, 1977).
48. 'Qui a déclenché la guerre?', *Europe Action,* (November 1964), 13-16.
49. See chapter 5.
50. See chapter 5.
51. A de Benoist, 'Contre tous les racismes', *Eléments,* no 8-9, (1974).
52. M. Barker, *The New Racism* (London: Junction Books, 1981); see also G. Seidel, 'The white discursive order' in M. Díaz-Diocaretz, I. Zavala and T. van Dijk, eds. *Proceedings of the Utrecht Symposium on Critical Theory,* 1985 (Amsterdam: Benjamins, 1986).
53. It was also Hitler's view that the lower social strata everywhere consist of racially mixed and therefore inferior beings.
54. P. Krebs, *Deutschland in Geschichte und Gegenwart,* Germany Past and Present, no 1, (1981), 31-2.
55. Our humanism is **vertical** it places individuals into a **hierarchical** structure which accounts for differences. Egalitarian humanism is horizontal, all individuals have the same place in the collective and are interchangeable.

    Ibid. For a comparable statement from the British New Right's journal, *Salisbury Review*, in a Christian context, see Seidel in Levitas, ed., 1986a.

Dietrich Eckart (1868-1923) was a journalist and author who enjoyed the confidence of Hitler. He edited the *Völkischer Beobachter,* the official Nazi newspaper.

56. The Thüle reference is striking. The Thüle Society was an offshoot of the Teutonic Order, and a predecessor of the NSDAP. These German links suggest an extension of GRECE's sphere of influence, and a strengthening of the ideological forces in western Europe involved directly and indirectly in the Holocaust denial.
57. P. Moreau, 'Révolution conservatrice et nouvelles droites allemandes', *Les Temps Modernes,* 1982, 893-959.
58. Ibid.
59. *Criticón,* no 56, November-December 1979 quoted in *Patterns of Prejudice,* vol 14, no 1, (January 1980); see also 'Radical Round Up', *Patterns of Prejudice,* vol 16, no 1, (1982), 35 seq.
60. See my comments on Robert Faurisson's trial in chapter 5.
61. See 'Legal Review' *Patterns of Prejudice,* vol 14, no 7, January 1980, 32-5, concerning legislation relating to the Holocaust denial, which has a long history, see S.J. Roth, 'Making the denial of the Holocaust a crime in law', IJA *Research Reports,* no 1, March 1982; and S.J. Roth, 'West Germany water down "denial of the Holocaust" Bill', *Patterns of Prejudice,* vol 19, no 2, (1985), 41-3.
62. *The Times,* 19 January 1982.
63. See *Patterns of Prejudice,* vol 18, no 2, (1984), 42.
64. See chapter 6.
65. See *Patterns of Prejudice,* vol 16, no 2, (April 1982), 35-9.
66. In WISE (Wales, Ireland, Scotland, England) a racist organisation was set up by Joan Mason in 1974 following an advertisement in the *Daily Telegraph* in the mid-1970s. It brings together anti-immigration campaigners in and around the Conservative Party with members of the Monday Club, like Harvey Proctor, the late Ronald Bell, and the late George Kennedy Young, former deputy head of Britain's espionage servies, members of the extremist Tory Action, and other known activists on the racist, fascist right, and now acts as a coordinating committee. Prominent figures seen at WISE meetings include Dowager Lady Jane Birdwood, formerly of the Anti-Immigration Standing Committee, now of Self Help (whose magazine *Choice,* typically talks of 'multi-racial madness plaguing Britain') and the World Anti-Communist League; Mary

Stanton from the National Alliance and Bee Carthew of 'Powellite', an extreme right-wing anti-immigration pressure group to which Victoria Gillick, the Roman Catholic anti-abortionist lobbyist, is also alleged to have supported (See 'The racist past of a morality campaigner', *Searchlight,* February 1984). WISE meetings have also been attended by Kenneth McKilliam, formerly of John Tyndall's National Front (now the British National Party), Paul Kavanagh and Andrew Fountaine, present and past members of the National Front Constitutional Movement, and Tony Malski, formerly of the British Movement whose activities have frequently been reported in *Searchlight.*

67. Duplicated letter from David Irving dated 3 June 1982.
68. Reported in *The Standard,* 18 February 1982.
69. *Oxford Mail,* 23 April 1982.
70. *Nation Europa,* July and August 1973.
71. See chapter 4.
72. *Searchlight,* April 1982.
73. *Searchlight,* March 1982.
74. *Searchlight,* June 1982.
75. There was nothing subtle or ambiguous in Streicher's writings in the Nazi paper, *Der Stürmer,* or in its hateful cartoons. For example, he wrote in May 1939:

    There must be a punitive expedition against the Jews in Russia. A punitive expedition which will finish them off, as any murderer and criminal must expect. Sentence of death, execution! The Jews in Russia must be killed. They must be exterminated root and branch! (Quoted by J-P Stern, *Hitler, The Führer and the People* (London: Fontana/Collins, 1980), 109-10.

    It was Streicher who propagated the 'ritual murder' lie (of Jews killing Christian children to use their blood) in its May 1934 issue (though this antisemitic myth is very much older).
76. See C.C. Aronsfeld, 'Revisionist historians whitewash Julius Streicher', *Patterns of Prejudice,* vol 19, no 3, (1985), 38-9.
77. See also J. Sayers, *Biological Politics, Feminist and antifeminist perspectives* (London: Tavistock, 1982); R. Bleier, *Myths of the Biological Inferiority of Women: An Exploration of the Sociology of Biological Research,* University of Michigan, *Papers in Women's Studies,* 2, 1976, 39-63. For a discussion on the domination of nature in marxist

and radical thought, see, for example, A Schmidt, *The Concept of Nature in Marx* (London: New Left Books, 1971).

78. For Guillaumin's major theoretical contribution, see C. Guillaumin, 1978, op.cit (see chapter 2, 7-11).

For a radical feminist anthropological perspective, see N.C. Mathieu, 'Homme — culture et femme — nature?' *L'Homme*, vol XIII, 3, (1973); N.C. Mathieu, 'Masculinité — Féminité', *Questions Féministes*, no 1, Paris, Editions Tierce, (1977); 'Critiques épistémologiques de la problématique des sexes dans le discours ethno-anthropologique', paper presented to an international meeting of experts concerning 'The Reflection on the feminine problematic in research and higher education' organised by the United Nations, Lisbon, September 1985. Unesco report SHS-85/Conf 612/CCL6.

79. D. Edgar, 'Reagan's hidden political agenda', *Race and Class*, XXII, 3, (winter 1981), 221-238.

80. W.S. Rusher, *The Making of the New Majority Party* (Illinois: Green Hill, 1975).

81. The two key family issues pursued by the religious Right have been abortion and religious schools and religion or prayer in school. See M. David, 'Teaching and preaching sexual morality', *Journal of Education*, vol 166, no 1, (March 1984) 48-77.

82. See, for example, A. Kopkind, *New Times*, 30 September 1977, 21-23. A Hunter and L. Gordon, *Radical America*, November 1988-February 1978, 9-25; M. David, 'The New Right in the USA and Britain', a new anti-feminist moral economy', *Critical Social Policy*, vol 2, no 3, Spring 1983, 31-46; 'The Family in the New Right' in R. Levitas, ed., *The Ideology of the New Right* (Oxford: Polity Press/Blackwell, 1986), 136-168. M. David and R. Levitas, 'Antifeminism in the British and American New Right', in G. Seidel, ed., 1987a, op.cit.

See also Z. Ehrenreich, *The Hearts of Men* (London: Pluto, 1983) 161; see also A. Dworkin, *Right-Wing Women* (New York: Perigree Books, 1982); R. Petchesky, *Abortion and Woman's Choice: The State, sexuality and reproductive freedom* (New York and London: Longman, 1984); Z. Eisenstein, 'The sexual politics of the New Right: on understanding the crisis of liberalism', *Signs: Journal of Women and Culture*, vol 7, no 3, (1982), 567-88; M.

Abramovitz, 'The conservative program is a woman's issue', *Journal of Sociology and Social Welfare,* VIX, (September 1982), 399-442.

83. See Seidel, ed., 1987a, op.cit.
84. M. David and R. Levitas in Seidel, ed., 1987a, op.cit.
85. E.O. Wilson, 'Human Decency is Animal', *New York Times Magazine,* 12 October 1975, 38-50 quoted by S. Rose, L.J. Kamin and R.C. Lewontin, *Not in our Genes* (Harmondsworth, Middx: Penguin Books, 1984) 19-20.
86. N. Podhoretz, *Breaking Ranks* (New York: Harper and Row, 1978), 9 quoted by D. Edgar, 'The Free or the Good' in Levitas, ed., op.cit.
87. See N. Moreau-Bisseret, 'Le discours d'ordre de la démographie (France 1945-1985), ('The discourse of order and of demography'), Seidel, ed., 1987a, op.cit.
88. Similarly Le Pen exhorts **white** women to 'reproduce the family and the nation' (Meeting at l'Espace Balard, Paris, 13 May 1984); see G. Seidel 'L'enjeu du discours droitier: exclusions et résistances' in Seidel, ed., 1987a, op.cit. See also C. Lesselier, 'Les femmes et l'extension de l'espace droitier', in G. Seidel, ed, 1987a, op.cit; C. Guillaumin, 'Sexism, a right-wing constant in all discourse', in Seidel, ed., 1987a, op.cit.
89. The Nazi state was savagely repressive in its policy to women. See, for example, R. Thalmann, *Etre femme sous le 3e Reich* (Paris: Laffont, 1982); C. Koonz, 'Le séparatisme féminin et les nazis' in *Stratégie des Femmes* (Paris: Editions Tierce, 1984); G. Bock, 'Racism and sexism in Nazi Germany: Motherhood, compulsory sterilization, and the state', *Signs,* vol 8, no 3, 1983; M.H. Macchiochi, 'Les femmes et la traversée du fascisme' in *Eléments pour une analyse du fascisme* (Paris: UGE, 1976), tome 1; V. Ware, *The National Front and Women, Searchlight* pamphlet, 1978. G. Seidel 'Language, ideologies and the National Front: representations of "race" and nation in National Front and anti-National Front discourses', unpublished paper, SSRC Anthropology seminar, University of Sussex, April 1979.

    For the hitherto completely neglected focus of Vichy legislation on women, see M. Bordeaux (in preparation).

    In Nazi Germany, the role set out for women are generally summarised as 'Kuche, Kirche, Kinder' ('Cooking, church and children'). In Vichy France, Marshal Pétain's motto was 'travail, famille, patrie' ('work family, fatherland'). This has recently been echoed by Raymond Barre, former Prime Minister in the run-up for the French 1986 legislative elections. (see *Le Monde,* 17 December 1985, 13).

90. David in Levitas, ed., 1986a, op.cit., 139-40.
91. David, 1986a, op.cit.
92. David and Levitas in Seidel, ed., 1986a, op.cit.
93. Edgar, 1981, op.cit.
94. J.Q. Wilson, *Thinking about Crime* (New York: Basic Books, 1967).
95. Edgar, 1981, op.cit., 231.
96. Seidel, 1986a in R. Levitas, ed., op.cit.
97. Knight, op.cit. (see n 13).
98. S. Bruce, *One Nation Under God? Observations on the New Christian Right in America,* Queen's University, Belfast, Department of Social Studies, 1984.
99. For the use of 'Zionism' by the National Front, in the conspiracy tradition see M. Billig, *Fascists: a social psychological view of the National Front* (London: Academic Press, 1978), 164 seq. See also M. Billig, 'Antisemitic themes and the British Far Left', *Patterns of Prejudice,* I, vol 18, no 1, (1984), 3-15; II, vol 18, no 2, (April 1984), 28-34.

    For a historical perspective on this slippage, see L. Poliakov, *De l'anti-sionisme à l'antisémitisme,* (Paris: Calmann-Lévy, 1969).

    For an account of how this slippage has affected Jewish students in Britain, see, for example, N. Lucas, 'Jewish students, the Jewish Community, and the Campus War in Britain', *Patterns of Prejudice,* vol 19, no 4, (1985), 27-34. See also chapter 7.
100. Bruce, 1984, op.cit.
101. See Ferraresi, ed., 1984, op.cit.
102. See J.J. Linz, 'Political Space and Fascism as a Later-Comer: Conditions conductive to the success or failure of Fascism as a Mass Movement in Inter-War Europe' in S.U. Larsen, B. Hagtvet and J.P. Mykleburst, eds., *Who were the Fascists?* (Bergen: Universitetsforlaget, 1980), 153-189. This a further developed in J.J. Linz, 'Some Notes Towards a Comparative Study of Fascism in Sociological Historical Perspective' in W.

Laquer, ed., *Fascism: A Reader's Guide* (London: Wildwood House, 1976).

See also G. Seidel, 'The white discursive order: the British New Right's discourse on cultural racism with particular reference to the *Salisbury Review*' (Amsterdam: Benjamins, 1986), op.cit.

103. *K. Joseph and J. Sumption, Equality* (London: John Murray, 1979).
104. Quoted by Rose et al., 1984, op.cit., 6.
105. See P. Gordon and F. Klug, *New Right, New Racism,* 1986; R. Levitas, ed., 1986, op.cit., D. Edgar, 'Bitter Harvest', *New Socialist*, September-October 1980, 19-24, reprinted in J. Curran, ed., *The Future of the Left* (Oxford: Polity Press/ Blackwell, 1984), 39-57.
106. R. Levitas, 'Competition and Compliance — The Utopias of the New Right' in Levitas, ed., 1986, op.cit, 80-106.
107. See Seidel, in Levitas, ed., 1986, op.cit.
108. On Hayek, see A Belsey, 'The New Right, Social Order and Civil Liberties' in R. Levitas, er., 1986, op.cit., 167-197; and A Gamble, 'The free economy and the strong state' in R. Miliband and J. Saville, eds., *Socialist Register* 1979, London: Merlin, 1979. See A. Gamble, 'The Political Economy of Freedom', in Levitas, ed., 1986, op.cit., 25-54.
109. See D. Edgar in Levitas, ed., op.cit., 55-70; and F. Klug and Gordon, 'Boiling into fascism', *New Statesman,* 10 June 1983.
110. See *The Guardian,* 30 July 1985, 8.
111. See n 66.
112. G. Seidel, 'Political discourse analysis', T. van Dijk, ed. *Handbook of Discourse Analysis* (New York: Academic Press, 1985), chapter 4.

4. The American scene, the Institute for Historical Review, and left-wing antisemitic discourse

1. *L.C. Dawidowicz, 'Lies about the Holocaust', Commentary,* December 1980.
2. *Searchlight,* January 1982.

3. M. Walker, *The National Front,* (Glasgow: William Collins Fontana Paperbacks, 1977), 193-4; N. Fielding, *The National Front,* (London: Routledge and Kegan Paul, 1980).
4. The role of the British League of St. George in coordinating these links has been documented in different issues of *Searchlight.*
5. *New York Times,* 6 March 1981.
6. See chapter 5.
7. *New Nation,* no 1, summer 1980.
8. *Searchlight,* June 1981.
9. Personal communication, September 1985.
10. C.C. Aronsfeld, 'Hoax of the Century', *Patterns of Prejudice,* (November-December 1976), 13-16.
11. In the discussion that follows, page references are to the second British edition, 1977. A.R. Butz, *The Hoax of the Twentieth Century, (California: Noontide Press and Historical Review Press, 1977).*
12. *Ibid., 248.*
13. *J. Robinson and H. Sachs, The Holocaust — The Nuremberg Evidence,* (Jerusalem: Yivo Institute, New York and Yad Vashem, 1976).
14. Ibid., 30.
15. See chapter 5.
16. Butz, op. cit., 30.
17. Ibid.
18. Ibid., 105.
19. Ibid., 36.
20. Ibid.
21. Ibid., 37.
22. Ibid., 49.
23. Ibid., 58.
24. Hilberg, op. cit., 566.
25. Gilbert, op. cit.
26. Butz, op. cit., 59.

    A number of antisemitic statements and posters generated by the pro-Waldheim Austrian presidential campaign in spring 1986 following revelations of Waldheim's war record made by the World Jewish Congress, are in a similar vein.
27. Ibid., 69.
28. Ibid.
29. Ibid., 73.

30. See chapter 5.
31. Butz, op. cit., 131.
32. Ibid., 100.
33. Ibid., 105.
34. Ibid., 131.
35. Ibid.
36. Hilberg, op. cit.
37. Ibid., 247.
38. See Laqueur, op. cit.
39. Butz, op. cit., 150.
40. Ibid., 250.
41. Ibid., 173.
42. Ibid., 198.
43. Ibid., 203.
44. Ibid., 205.
45. Ibid.
46. Ibid., 246.
47. Quoted by L. Dawidowicz, 'The Holocaust as Historical Record', *Dimensions of the Holocaust,* Lectures at Northwestern University, Evanston, Illinois, (New York: Center for Studies on the Holocaust and Anti-Defamation League of B'nai Brith, 1977), 21.
48. *Searchlight,* October 1981.
49. *Patterns of Prejudice,* vol 9, no 4, (July-August 1975).
50. *Anti-Defamation League Bulletin,* vol 33, no 6, June 1978.
51. *Daily Mirror,* 28 June 1981.
52. M. Rodinson, 'Quelques idées simples sur l'antisémitisme', *Revue d'Etudes Palestiniennes,* no 1, (Autumn 1981), 5-21.
53. W. Grimstad, *The Six Million Reconsidered,* (Southam, Warks.: Historical Review Press, 1977; UK edition 1979), 12.
54. Ibid.
55. See chapter 3.
56. Grimstad, op. cit., 81.
57. Ibid., 18.
58. L. Brenner, *Zionism in the Age of the Dictators, A Reappraisal,* (Beckenham, Kent: Croom Helm; Westpoint, Connecticut: Lawrence Hill and Co., 1983).
59. See J. Gewirtz, 'The lie of Zionist-Nazi collaboration', *Jewish Chronicle,* 25 January 1980. See also Y. Bauer, 'How Zionists sought to save Jewish lives, "Working with the Nazis" — the lie is nailed', *Manna,* (Autumn 1984), 3-5.

60. B. Cheyette, *Patterns of Prejudice,* (July 1983), 62-5. See also G. Ben Noah, 'Rewriting the Holocaust', *Socialist Organiser,* (4 October 1984).
61. S. Avineri, *The Making of Modern Zionism, The Intellectual Origins of the Jewish State* (London: Weidenfeld and Nicolson, 1981).
62. E. Black, *The Transfer Agreement: the Untold Story of the Secret Agreement between the Third Reich and Jewish Palestine,* (London: MacMillan, 1981).
63. Quoted by L. Harap, ' "Zionist-Nazi Collaboration" Refuted — Lenni Brenner's Trickery Exposed', *Jewish Currents,* (May 1984), 5-40.
64. A. Schölch, 'The Third Reich, the Zionist Movement, and the Palestine Conflict', *Vierteljahrshefte für Zeit Geschichte,* 1985.
65. Y. Bauer, *From Diplomacy to Resistance, a History of Jewish Palestine, 1939-1945,* (New York: Atheneum, 1973).
66. W. Laqueur, *A History of Zionism,* (London: 1982), 556.
67. Y. Bauer, 'Jewish Policy during the Holocaust', *Mainstream,* December 1984, 22-5.
68. Bauer, 1973, op.cit.
69. Correspondence and editor's comments, *Jewish Currents,* February 1984, 42-3.
70. 1974, director Louis Malle.
71. 1970, director Marcel Ophuls.
72. Schölch, op.cit.
73. B. Wasserstein, *Britain and the Jews of Europe, 1939-1945,* (Oxford: Oxford University Press, 1979).
74. Billig, 1984, op.cit.
75. K. Polkehn, 'The secret contacts: Zionism and Nazi Germany, 1933-41', *Journal of Palestine Studies,* 19/21, (1976). This refers to an earlier version, K. Polkehn, 'The collaboration of the Zionists with the German empire and German fascism', *Resistentia-schriften,* no 12, (1971), Frankfurt (reprinted from the GDR weekly magazine, *Horizont).*
76. L.A. Korneev, *Klassovaya sushchnost Sionizma* (The Class Essence of Zionism), (Kiev: Politizdat Ukrainy, 1982), reviewed in H. Spier, *Soviet Jewish Affairs,* vol 14, no 2, (1984), 74-7. For a description of a more recent article by Korneev published in *Trud,* 17 August 1983, see T.H. Friedgut, 'Soviet anti-Zionism and antisemitism — another cycle', *Soviet Jewish Affairs,* vol 14, no 1, (1984), 21-2.

77. Korneev, op.cit., 7.
78. Ibid., 133.
79. Ibid., 135.
80. *Izvestiya,* 29 January 1983.
81. *Sovestskaya Kultura,* 28 April 1983.
82. 'The Soviet anti-Zionist Committee', *Soviet Jewish Affairs,* vol 13, no 3, (1983), 68.
83. See Martynov's open letter in 'Jews and Russian culture', *Soviet Jewish Affairs,* vol 14, no 2, (1984).

5. The French scene and the Faurisson affair

1. M.R. Marrus and R.O. Paxton, *Vichy et les Juifs* (Paris: Calmann-Lévy 1981), 337. English language edition: *Vichy France and the Jews* (New York: Basic Books, 1981).
2. Serge Klarsfeld in his *Memorial aux Juifs Déportés de France* (Paris: Editions Klarsfeld, 1978) has published the names of 75,721 French deportees in the succession of convoys.
3. Marrus and Paxton, 1981, op. cit., 313.
4. It inaugurated a spate of novels with Jewish and antisemitic themes. The title of the Drumont book was enthusiastically taken up and developed elsewhere — as *Jewish Russia, Jewish Algeria, Jewish Austria,* and *Jewish England.* Drumont also promised a novel devoted to *Jewish Europe* which would expose the international Jewish threat. However, the book did not materialise.

   Poliakov notes that at the end of the nineteenth century Jews accounted for 0.02% of the French population of whom more than half lived in Paris. See L. Poliakov, *Histoire de l'antisémitisme, L'Europe Suicidaire,* 1870-1933 (Paris: Calmann-Lévy, 1977), 56-7; 64.
5. Z. Sternhell, *La Droite révolutionnaire* (Paris: Seuil, 1978), 209.
6. C. Capitan-Peter, *Charles Maurras et l'idéologie d'Action Française* (Paris: Seuil, 1972).
7. E. Nolte, *Three Faces of Fascism,* New York: Holt, Rinehart and Winston, 1966; see also, R. Soucy, *Fascism in France. The case of Maurice Barrès* (Los Angeles: University of California Press, 1972); E. Weber, *Action Française* (Paris: Stock, 1964).

8. H.R. Kedward, *The Dreyfus Affair* (London: Longman, 1965); M.R. Marrus, *Les Juifs de France à l'époque de l'affaire Dreyfus*. Preface by P. Vidal-Naquet (Paris: Calmann-Lévy, 1972).
9. M. Barrès, *Scènes et doctrines du nationalisme*, Paris, 1902, 150-154 quoted by Poliakov, 1977, op. cit., 67.
10. M.R. Marrus and R.O. Paxton, op. cit. 1981.
11. M. Bardèche, *Qu'est ce que le fascisme?* (Paris: Les Sept Couleurs, 1961).
12. M. Bardèche, *Nuremberg ou la Terre Promise (Paris: Les Sept Couleurs, 1948).*
13. *P-A. Taguieff, 'L'Héritage nazi', Les Nouveaux Cahiers,* no 64, (spring 1981), 3-22. See also M. May, 'Denying the Holocaust', *Index on Censorship, 6, 1985, 29-33.*
14. *P. Rassinier, Debunking the Genocide Myth* (Torrance, California: Historical Review Press, 1978), 1288.
15. Rassinier, 1978, op. cit., 276.
16. Rassinier, 1978, op. cit., 289.
17. Rassinier, 1978, op. cit., 315-6.
18. See Bardèche, 1948, op. cit.
19. *'L'Express,* 28 October-4 November 1978. The *Express* interview quoted from the *Petit Parisien,* 1 February 1943.
20. Marrus and Paxton, op. cit., 261 seq. See also P. Kingston, *Anti-Semitism in France during the 1930s* (Hull: University of Hull, Occasional Papers in Modern Languages, no 14, 1983).
21. H. Arendt, *Eichmann in Jerusalem: A Report on the Banality of Evil,* (Harmondsworth, Middlesex: Penguin Books, 1979, 3rd edn.).
22. G.L. Mosse, *The Nationalization of the Masses: Political Symbolism* and *Mass Movements in Germany from the Napoleonic Wars through the Third Reich,* (New York, Fertig, 1978), 230.
23. In terms of their antisemitic vulgarity, there was not much to choose between them. In 1942 Vallat, addressing the students of the *Ecole des Cadres,* referred to Jews as 'worms which love gangrene sores'. Darquier referred to Bernard Lecache, president of the International Ligue against Antisemitism (LICA), as 'this circumcised swine' (quoted by Marrus and Paxton, op.cit.), 261.
24. Regarding Darquier, see *J. Billig, Le Commissariat général aux questions juives,* t. I, 1955, t. II, 1957 and t. III, 1960,

Paris, Institut d'études des questions juives; J. Laloum, *La France Antisémite de Darquier de Pellepoix* (Paris: Syros, 1979).

25. D. Wallef, 'The Composition of Christus Rex', in Larsen, Hagtvet and Myklebust, eds., *Who Were the Fascists?*, Oslo: Universitetsforlaget, 1980), 517-23.
26. *Le Monde,* 29 December 1978. For an accessible study of Faurisson's mode of argument, see N. Fresco, 'Les redresseurs des morts, ou comment on révise l'histoire', *Les Temps Modernes,* June 1980, 2150-2211. In English translation, 'The Denial of the Dead', *Dissent,* Fall 1981. For a linguistic study, see J. Authier-Revuz and L. Romeu, 'La place de l'autre dans un discours de falsification de l'histoire. A propos d'un texte niant le génocide juif sous le IIIe Reich', MOTS, no 8, mars 1984 (special number, G. Seidel, ed.), 53-70.
27. Barnes and Barnes, op. cit.
28. Quoted by S. Thion, *Vérité historique ou vérité politique?* (Paris: La Vieille Taupe, 1980), 93. (Trans: G.S.)
29. *Le Monde,* 16 December 1979, 29 December 1978, 16 January 1979.
30. Quoted by Thion, op. cit., 89. (Trans: G.S.)
31. N. Chomsky, *American Power and the New Mandarins,* (New York, Pantheon, 1969); S. Thion and J.C. Pomonti, *Des Courtisans aux Partisans: essai sur la crise cambodgienne (Paris: Gallimard, 1971.)*
32. *P. Vidal-Naquet, personal communication, 3 December 1982.*
33. *Le Monde,* 20 December 1980.
34. P. Vidal-Naquet's 'A Paper Eichmann' has been published in *Democracy (USA),* April 1981 in English. It was first published as 'Un Eichmann de papier' in *Esprit,* (September 1980), 8-56. Faurisson has since written a reply: *Réponse à Pierre Vidal-Naquet* (Paris: La Vieille Taupe, 1982). See also Vidal-Naquet's 'Thèses sur le révisionnisme', contribution to the International Colloquium on Nazi Germany and the Jews, Paris, 1982.
35. N. Chomsky's preface to R. Faurisson, *Mémoire en Défense, contre ceux qui m'accusent de falsifier l'histoire: La question des chambres à gaz* (Paris: La Vieille Taupe, 1980), XIV-XV. (Trans: G.S.)
36. Thion, op. cit., 16.

37. Ibid, 138.
38. H. Alleg, *La Question,* (Paris: Minuit, 1958), P. Vidal-Naquet, *La Torture dans la république* (Paris: Maspero, 1975).
39. Thion, op. cit., 136-7.
40. *La Guerre Sociale,* no. 3, (June 1979).
41. J. Shirley, 'A tale of horror on the Berlin Express', *Sunday Times,* 29 March 1981.
42. P. Rassinier, *Debunking the Genocide Myth* (Torrance, California: Institute for Historical Review, 1978), 214.
43. *Le Monde,* 31 May; 1, 3, 4 and 30 June 1981.
44. G. Sereny, 'The Nazi record on trial', *New Statesman,* 10 April 1981, 4.
45. *Le Droit de vivre,* September 1981.
46. *Patterns of Prejudice,* vol 15, no 4, (October 1981), 51-5. The 'Roques Affair' is the latest postscript. A doctoral thesis improperly awarded to Henri Roques in June 1985 at Nantes University in the presence of Faurisson was withdrawn after the intervention of the French Minister responsible for research. The thesis implicitly denied the existence of the gas chambers.
    (See 'M. Roques n'est pas docteur', *Le Monde,* 4 July 1986; and P. Webster, 'Minister cancels doctorate claiming innocence of Nazis', *Guardian,* 3 July 1986.
47. Billig, 1978, op. cit.
48. This is further discussed in chapter seven.
49. Faurisson, 1980, op. cit., 121.
50. Ibid., 14.
51. Billig, 1984, op. cit., chapter 9.
52. See G. Wellers' letter 'Un Roman inspiré', *Le Monde,* 21 February 1979; see also E. Kogon et al., *Les Chambres a Gaz, Secret d'Etat,* (Paris: Editions de Minuit, 1984).
53. E. Apfelbaum, 'Forgetting the Past', *Partisan Review,* 4, 1981, 608-7.
54. G. Seidel, 'Neo-Nazism Myth: Faurisson and History on Trial', paper presented to the Tenth World Congress of Sociology (Sociolinguistics section, subsection: Language and Power), Mexico, August 1982.
55. P. Vidal-Naquet, *Les Juifs, la mémoire et le présent* (Paris: Maspero, 1981).

6. The British exponents of the Holocaust denial myth

1. Billig, 1978, op. cit., 157-9.
2. A. Suzman and D. Diamond, *Six Million Did Die: The Truth Shall Prevail,* (Johannesburg: South African Jewish Board of Deputies, 1977, 2nd edn 1978).
3. See chapter 5.
4. This altogether reminiscent of articles and photographs in *Europe-Action,* the forerunner of the French New Right. See chapter 3.
5. See chapter 4 for examples from the *Club de l'Horloge.*
6. *See chapter 4. The UK edition was published in 1979 by the Historical Review Press.*
7. *R. Harwood, Nuremberg and other war crimes,* (Brighton: History Review Press, 1978). Quoted by N. Cohn, op. cit., 159.
8. Harwood, 1978, op. cit., 9.
9. G. Seidel, 'Sur le discours du Front National, *Langage et Société,* (June 1979), 55-70.
10. Harwood, 1978, op. cit., 9.
11. R. Cecil, *The Myth of the Master Race: Alfred Rosenberg and Nazi Ideology,* (Birkenhead, Cheshire: Willmer Bros, 1967).
12. Harwood, 1978, op.cit., 26.
13. Ibid., 27.
14. Ibid. See H. Friedlander, op. cit., chapter 2.
15. Arendt, op. cit.
16. Hilberg, op. cit.
17. Harwood, 1978, op. cit., 111.
18. Ibid., 53.
19. C. Mueller, *The Politics of Communication. A Study in the Political Sociology of Language, Socialisation and Legitimation,* (Oxford University Press, 1973); H. Friedlander, op.cit; Hilberg, op.cit., 266.
20. Ibid., 61.
21. See chapter 3.
22. Quoted in A. Suzman. *The Holocaust, The Falsehoods and the Facts,* (Johannesburg: South African Jewish Board of Deputies, 1980), 42.
23. M. McLaughlin, *For Those Who Cannot Speak,* (Brighton: History of Review Press, 1979), 3.

24. Ibid., 15.
25. Ibid., 4.
26. Ibid., 3.
27. Ibid., 32.
28. Ibid., 7, 17.
29. Ibid., 16.
30. Ibid., 19.
31. Ibid., 15.
32. Ibid., 19.
33. Ibid., 20.
34. Ibid.
35. Ibid., 20.
36. Ibid.
37. Ibid.
38. Ibid.
39. Ibid., 30.
40. Ibid., 31.
41. G. Seidel, 'Representations of "**Race**" and "**Nation**" in National Front and anti-National Front Discourses', unpublished paper presented to the SSRC Anthropology Seminar, Anthropological research in industrial societies with special reference to Western Europe (Convenor: R. Grillo), University of York, April 1979.
42. McLaughlin, 1970, op. cit., 32.
43. D. Edgar, 'Racism, Fascism and the Politics of the National Front', *Race and Class*. (1977), 111-31.
44. Ibid., 33.
45. *Searchlight*, May 1982.
46. J. Raspail, *Le Camp des Saints*, (Paris: Laffont, 1978).
47. 'The most pervasive and harmful myth today, of course, is that of the so-called 'Holocaust' and all its attendant fables… … we Revisionists are doing far more than setting the past aright… We are literally building a foundation of fact for the future — a future which will be based on constructive, not destructive myths; *or a body of morality and social mores* and constraints based on what is good for the people of the West rather that what is good for minority pressure groups, bankers, distorting ideologies or alien interests, Willis A. Carto, 'On the Uses of History', *Journal of Historical Review*, vol 3, no 1, (Spring 1982) (reprinted from the 1981 Convention) (my emphasis, G.S.).

48. D. Irving, *Hitler's War,* (London: Hodder and Stoughton, 1977).
49. See H. Trevor-Roper, 'Hitler: Does History Offer a Defence?', *Sunday Times,* 12 June 1977.
50. J. Herf, "The Holocaust" Reception in West Germany', *New German Critique,* no 19, (winter 1980), 30-52. 'Heimat', the widely acclaimed eleven-part West German film of Edgar Reitz, screened on BBC TV in 1986, is full of such ambiguities and silences.
51. K. Bird in 'The Secret Policemans's Historian', *New Statesman,* (3 April 1981).
52. Irving, 1977, op. cit., XV.
53. B. Smith, 'Two Alibis for the Inhumanities: A.R. Butz, *The Hoax of the Twentieth Century,* and David Irving, *Hitler's War', German Studies Review,* (October 1978), 327-35.
54. Irving, 1977, op. cit., 12.
55. C.W. Sydnor, Jr, 'The Selling of Adolf Hitler: David Irving's *Hitler's War', Central European History,* vol xii, no 2, (June 1979), 169-99.
56. Irving, 1977, op. cit., 391.
57. Ibid., 186-7. The copy of the Wannsee Protocol cited by Sydnor is in the Foreign Ministry's microfilmed records, NA/T-120/Reel 780.
58. Irving, 1977, op. cit., XXI.
59. H. Trevor-Roper, *Hitler's Table Talk, 1941-44: his private conversations,* (London: Weidenfeld & Nicolson, 1973, 2nd edn.).
60. Ibid., XI.
61. D. Irving, *The Destruction of Dresden,* London: Kimber, 1963).
62. Irving, 1963, op. cit., 106-7.
63. Ibid., 42.
64. D. Irving, *Uprising! One Nation's Nightmare: Hungary 1956,* (London: Hodder and Stoughton, 1981).
65. Ibid., 13-16.
66. Ibid., 184-5.
67. Ibid., 48.
68. Ibid., 49.
69. Ibid., 75.
70. Ibid., 49.
71. Ibid., 131.

72. See Kingston, op. cit.
73. See chapter 3.

7. Conclusions: Contemporary Antisemitism and Racism

1. Cohn, 1967, op.cit.
2. S. Hall, 'Drifting into a law and order society', The Cobden Trust Human Rights Day Lecture, 1979 (London: The Cobden Trust, 1979); and S. Hall, 'The great moving Right show', *Marxism Today,* (January 1979).
3. Y. Harkabi, *Antisemitism,* Jerusalem: Israel Pocket Library, 1974. See also Y. Harkabi, *Arab Attitudes to Israel,* Jerusalem: Israel Universities Press, 1971; and *Patterns of Prejudice,* vol 9. no 4, (July-August 1975). See also D. Piper, 'The Politics of Muslim Anti-Semitism', *Commentary* (August 1981), 39-45.
4. *Sunday Times,* 12 July 1981; see also Centre for Contemporary Studies, *Rock and the Right,* (London, 1981).
5. E. le Garrec, 'Anti-racisme et féminisme', *Touche pas à mon pote,* mai-juin, no 2, (1985), 14. The language has already been manipulated commercially.
6. 'Anti-Semitic play again raises furor in West Germany', *Jerusalem Post,* 29 July 1985.
7. A. Tomforde, 'Nazi game inventor cleared', *Guardian,* 22 September 1984.
8. J. Herf, 'The "Holocaust" Reception in West Germany', *New German Critique,* no 19, (winter 1980), 30-52; P. Marthesheimer and I. Frenzel, *In Kreuzfeuer: Der Fernsehfilm Holocaust. Eine Nation ist betroffen,* (Frankfurt, Fischer Taschenbuch Verlag, 1979).
   See also L. Inowlocki, 'Denying the Past: Right-Wing Extremist Youth in West Germany', *Life Stories/Récits de Vie,* vol 1, 6-15 (Colchester: Biography and Society Research Committee of the International Sociological Association in conjunction with the Oral History Society, 1985).
9. *Pflasterstrand* 47, 1-15 February 1979, 23; 25. Quoted by Herf, op.cit.
10. S. White, 'French opposition to "Holocaust" ', *Spectator,* 3 March 1979.

11. For a recent, poignant assessment, see M. Syrkin, 'The Teaching of the Holocaust', *Midstream*, February 1985, 47-56. Recent and impressive British initiatives include ILEA teaching packs from the Learning Resources Branch based on the Auschwitz exhibition.
12. For studies on the role of women in Nazi Germany, see: T. Mason, 'Women in Germany, 1925-40: Family, Welfare and Work', *History Workshop*, part 1, no 1, (spring 1976), 74-113 and part 2, no 2, (autumn 1976), 5-32; J. Stephenson, *Women in Nazi Germany*, London: Croom Helm, 1975; and R. Thalmann, 1982, op.cit. On the role and representations in contemporary Nazi organisations and texts, see V. Ware, *Women and the National Front*, Birmingham: Searchlight Pamphlet, 1978, and C. Lesselier in Seidel, ed., 1987, op.cit.
13. R. Scruton, 'The case against feminism', *Observer*, 22 May 1983, 27.
14. David, 1984, op.cit.
15. S. Griffin, *Pornography and Silence* (London: Women's Press, 1981).
16. A. Dummett and I. Martin, *British Nationality — The AGIN Guide of the New Law* (London: Action Group on Immigration and Nationality (AGIN) and National Council for Civil Liberties, 1982); and S. Cohen, *The Thin White Wedge, Guide to the New Nationality Act* (Manchester: Manchester Law Centre. 1981); P. Gordon and F. Klug, *British Immigration Control. A brief guide* (London: Runnymede Trust, 1985); P. Gordon, *Policing Immigration. Britain's Internal Controls* (London: Pluto Press, 1985).
17. S. Cohen, *That's funny: you don't look antisemitic. A left-wing analysis of anti-semitism* (Leeds: Beyond the Pale Collective, 1984).
18. Barker, op.cit.
19. Reported in the *Times*, 31 January 1978.
20. See M. Billig, 'Antisemitism in the 1980's', Cardinal Bea Memorial Lecture, *The Month*, 15, 4 (April 1982), 125-30.
21. G. Seidel, 'Culture, nation and "race" in the British and French New Right' in R. Levitas, ed., *The Ideology of the New Right* (Oxford: Polity Press/Blackwell, 1986), chapter 4.
22. See Gordon and Klug, 1986, op.cit.
23. J. Casey, 'One Nation — the Politics of Race', *Salisbury Review*, 1 (Autumn 1982), 23-8.

24. Ibid.
25. See the *Times Higher Educational Supplement,* 17 January 1988, 17.
26. Casey, op.cit.
27. Ibid.
28. Ibid.
29. Ibid.
30. Casey, op.cit.
31. See, for example, R. Scruton, 'Who are the real racists?', *Times,* 30 October 1984.
32. N. Murray, 'Anti-racists and other demons: the press and ideology in Thatcher Britain', *Race and Class,* XXVII, 3, (January 1986), 1-19. Murray argues that it is the *Mail,* addressing itself to the key Thatcherite constituency, the lower middle-class, that has led the assault on anti-racism and the other 'enemies within'. It has interpreted its news in terms of the linked components of New Right ideology: 'the loony left', law and order, 'indoctrination' in schools, and the anti-racist threat. See Seidel. The British New Right's enemy within: the anti-racist', in T. van Dijk and G. Smitherman, eds., *Discourse and Discrimination* (Beverly Hills, California: Sage, 1987).
33. A. Brown, *The Trials of Honeyford. Problems in multicultural education,* (London: Centre for Policy Studies, 1985).
34. D. Dale, 'The New Ideology of Race', *Salisbury Review* (October 1985), 17-22. See G. Seidel, 1987, op.cit.
35. Casey, op.cit.
36. Dale, op.cit.
37. Their journal, the *Liberator,* is a combination of eclectic views interspersing anti-state 'libertarianism' with articles defending apartheid. (See 'Might of Student Right', *New Statesman,* 1 February 1985).

    At Nottingham University, the Vice-Chancellor of the Conservative Association and a fellow member were caught red-handed as they painted swastikas and NF phrases like 'Jews out' and 'Death to Jews' in German on some halls of residence. They have since been suspended and banned from the campus *(Searchlight,* April 1986, 8).
38. Reported in the *Guardian,* 20 July 1984.
39. For a succinct critique on amendments to the public order law, see G. Bindman, 'Out of Court', *Guardian,* 2 August 1985.

40. *Searchlight,* May 1982; see also G. Pierce, *Guardian,* 15 March 1983.
41. G. Seidel, 'The white discursive order' in T. van Dijk, M. Díaz-Diocaretz and I. Zavala, eds., *Proceedings of the Utrecht Summer School of Critical Theory* (Amsterdam: Benjamins, 1986).
42. S. Hall et al., *Policing the Crisis* (London: Macmillan, 1978). See also Greater London Council, *Racial Harassment in London. Report of a Panel of Inquiry set up by the GLC Police Committee* (London: GLC, 1984); P. Gordon, *White Law* (London: Pluto Press, 1983).
43. Given the presence in the Thatcher government of prominent Jews, any question of antisemitism tends to be not only invisible, but an illegitimate concern. It is nevertheless scandalous that these members tend to be named and identified first and foremost as *Jews* (though few are actually self-identifying) rather than as Conservatives. (These include Nigel Lawson, Keith Joseph, and, until early 1986, Leon Brittain). *It is their capacity as Tories that they serve in the government, not as Jews.* In Britain, there is no identifiable Jewish vote. Yet it is in terms of their visibility as Jews that they continue to invite comment. The question of 'Jew ministers' was also raised by a member of the parents' action committee during the press conference given at the Honeyford strike school. Fortunately, the press did not take it up. For non-Jewish anti-racists present, the comment went unheeded, and 'unheard'.

    It was in the aftermath of the Westlands affair concerning the purchase of military helicopters, the European or the US option, which resulted in the dramatic resignation of Defence Minister Michael Heseltine in January 1986, and the subsequent resignation of the Home Secretary, Leon Brittan, that muffled antisemitism in the back benches was given a public voice. In a television interview, John Stokes, Conservative MP for Halesowen and Stourbridge, Worcestershire, expressed the desire to see as Brittan's successor 'a full-blooded, red-faced Englishman'. Interviewed by the *Jewish Chronicle,* he denied the charge of antisemitism *(Jewish Chronicle,* 3 January 1986 and 14 February 1986). It was later revealed that Stokes addressed a meeting of WISE, an ultra-right group which, according to *Searchlight,* has been chaired and frequented by known neo-Nazis, and has links with the Monday Club, the main anti-immigration lobby. In Dod's Parliamentary Companion of 1985, Stokes' interests are noted as the monarchy, Church of England, and law and order.

The right constantly seeks to name and identify Jews, whether or not they consider themselves to be of Jewish descent. In the case of ultra-orthodox male Jews, their visibility is also at issue; and for observant Jews generally, particularly for those moving in Christian circles, public celebration of their Judaism takes considerable courage and integrity in a nationalist and Christian society.

Since the enlightenment, the growth of nation states, and the progressive phase of nationalism in the 1840s, Jews have always been perceived as a 'problem': they remained a largely religious and certainly universal people, and did not 'fit in' to the scheme. The increased secularisation, which of course has affected both Jewish and Christian communities, has not changed this nationalist perception. As Avineri's study on the intellectual origins of Zionism has shown, it was the historically specific European Jewish response to these developments that led to Zionism in the nineteenth century (Avineri, op.cit.). It cannot be explained simply by anti-semitism which is a much older phenomenon, predating the emergence of nation states.

44. Seidel, in Levitas, ed., op.cit., 1986a.
45. See chapter 3, n 32.
46. R. Scruton, *The Meaning of Conservatism,* (Harmondsworth, Middx: Penguin, 1980).
47. See B. Guetta, 'L'inquiétante ascension d'un tribun noir antisémite', *Le Monde,* 11 October 1985, 6.
48. See *Jewish Chronicle,* 7 February 1986 (leader); 14 February 1986.
49. See J. Jenkins, '3941 miles away, Farrakhan can still make waves', *New Statesman,* 24 January 1986.
50. *Guardian,* 20 January 1986. See also the letter from M. Rubenstein, Editor, *Equal Opportunities Review,* 'Too expensive free speech' in the same issue.
51. Admittedly, there is ambiguity and division on the left. The Trotskyist Militant, for example, subsumes everything to the class struggle, and sees black culture as a deviation. Struggles in Liverpool illustrate this kind of reductionist thinking on the

left which continutes to straightjacket minority identities.

52. B. Williams, 'The Antisemitism of Tolerance: Middle Class Manchester and the Jews, 1870-1900' in A.J. Kidd and K.W. Roberts, eds., *City, Class and Culture: Studies of Cultural Production and Social Policy in Victorian Manchester* (Manchester: Manchester University Press, 1985).
53. L. Bellos, 'Black Jew?', *Shifra,* 1, (Kislev, 5745/December 1984), 22-3.
54. For a critical discussion of these far-reaching issues, seldom voiced within the official Jewish community, see D. Cesarani, 'Israel and the Diaspora: negation of the negation', of which a shortened version was published in *Manna,* September 1985.

SUBJECT INDEX

INDEX